D1351661

PHOTOGRAPHIC GUIDE TO THE

WADERS
OF THE WORLD

PHOTOGRAPHIC GUIDE TO THE
WADERS
OF THE WORLD

DAVID ROSAIR • DAVID COTTRIDGE

Bounty
Books

First published in 1995 by Hamlyn

This edition published 2004 by Bounty Books,
a division of Octopus Publishing Group Ltd,
2-4 Heron Quays, London E14 4JP

Copyright © Octopus Publishing Group Limited 1995
Text copyright © David Rosair 1995

ISBN 0 7537 0960 0

A CIP catalogue record for this book is available from
the British Library

Edited by Cathy Lowne
Designed by Vivienne Brar
Page layout Louise Griffiths
Wader topography by Mike Langman

Printed and bound in China

Contents

Introduction and Acknowledgements

The *Hamlyn Photographic Guide to the Waders of the World* endeavours to bring together for the first time photographs of the vast majority of all the world's 212 species of wader in conjunction with concise text for this most enigmatic group of birds.

Advances in photographic technology, coupled with easier access to remote regions often supporting the rarer or more localized species, have now made this book possible – something unthinkable just ten years ago. Inevitably photographs of some species are not present, either the species in question has never been photographed or we have been unsuccessful in obtaining a satisfactory image. The number missing is minimal and the coverage is the results of many, many hours of searching worldwide to trace different pictures of various species – some published for the very first time here. Our priority has been initially to obtain a satisfactory image in any plumage and then to get further photographs in alternative plumages and ages.

The result is the collation of nearly 720 photographs of waders, in various plumages, both on the ground and in flight, depicting racial variation as and where available. We believe that good photographs now firmly rank alongside the best of coloured plates, complementing the latter and even at times bettering the best drawings available. Hopefully you will gain double enjoyment from seeing not only many hundreds of diagnostic identification features clearly depicted, but also rarely observed waders from distant lands for the very first time.

The text, simply laid out opposite each set of photographs has largely followed the order of species in the excellent *Shorebirds* by Hayman, Marchant and Prater. Names have been updated in accordance with the British Birds List of English Names of the Western Palearctic Birds (*British Birds* 86 1 January 1993 pp. 1–9). The text consists of an introduction on breeding range, followed by detailed identification, including plumage characteristics in various ages, flight pattern, call, racial variation where applicable, habitat and relevant behaviour, and finally movements including migration patterns and vagrancy. We have omitted Canarian Black Oystercatcher, White-winged Sandpiper and Obi Woodcock, which are presumed to be extinct, and Cox's Sandpiper, regarding which there are grave doubts as to its authenticity as a species, and which may yet prove to be a hybrid. In accordance with *Birds of the High Andes* (Fjeldsa and Krabbe, 1990) Cordilleran Snipe and Andean Snipe have been 'lumped' whilst the distinctive small yellow-legged race of Magellan Snipe has been split off as Puna Snipe. Current thinking on wader classification has necessitated including three more species

under the 'wader' umbrella – Plains Wanderer, the small partridge-sized bird from south-eastern Australia and both Snowy and Black-faced Sheathbills.

In preparation for this book we have endeavoured to observe as many of the world's waders as possible ourselves, with particular emphasis on identification, environmental habitat and movements. Major trips in recent years have taken us from the remote Chatham Islands east of New Zealand to the wilds of Tierra del Fuego, and from the excitement of Mai Po in Hong Kong to the beauty and serenity of the Seward Peninsula of Alaska. We have also experienced the open grasslands of Samburu, Kenya, the stony beds of the Rapti riverbed, Nepal, the grandeur of the Negev Desert in Israel and the beautiful isolation of St Helena. Each time the quest has been the same – to photograph and study what to us are the most wonderful and mysterious of all groups of birds – waders.

There are many people who have assisted us greatly in preparing this book. In particular we wish to thank the following:

For compiling the trip, travelling and observing species:

New Zealand and the Chatham Islands John Brodie-Good (Wildwings), Brian and Sue Bell, Anthea Goodwin, Sheila Petch, Robyn Sewell, Val and Lois Croon, Greg and Karen Preece; Euan Kennedy, Steve Sawyer and Dave Murray (Department of Conservation); John Marchant and John Fennell.

Argentina including Tierra del Fuego Paul Dukes (Cygnus), Ricardo Clark and Domingo Gallucia.

Alaska and Colorado Adrian Rosair, David Sonneborn; Robert Gill and Lee Tibbetts (Alaska Science Centre); Brett Sandercock, Dennis Paulson, Caroline Reader; Richard Hill (US Forest, Department of Agriculture).

Chile Adrian Rosair, Richard Scofield, Michel Sallaberry, Peter Roberts and Don Taylor.

Nepal John Brodie-Good (Wildwings), David Mills (Naturetrek), and Duncan Coates.

Venezuela Adrian Rosair, Mary Goodwin and Edgar Soublette.

Zimbabwe, Namibia, South Africa, St Helena and Ascension John Brodie-Good (Wildwings), Curnow Shipping Company, The Governor, St Helena, The Administrator, Ascension, the Foreign and Commonwealth Office, Ian Sinclair, Jim Enticott, Dr Neil McCulloch, Bo Rolands,

Simon Cook, Nick Thorpe, Pat Musk, Keith and Gail Wearne and Chris and Brian Edwards.

Mai Po, Hong Kong, Lew Young and Simba Chan (Peter Scott Field Studies Centre).

In particular we would wish to thank Richard Chandler for his invaluable assistance in helping to age and race many of the photographs. For assistance with travel arrangements, advice and collating photographs we would also like to thank Alan Tate, Alan Greensmith, Roland Seitre, Tony Greenland, Mark Brazil, Per Alstrom, Brian Chudleigh, Pete Morris and Chris Kightley.

Special thanks also to Anwar in Park Lane Post Office, Tottenham, London.

Finally we would especially like to thank Christopher Abrams for many hours spent assisting with rearranging and transferring text onto disk and also Sylvia Wallace for ably helping with the preparation, design and layout of the text onto computer.

Wader topography

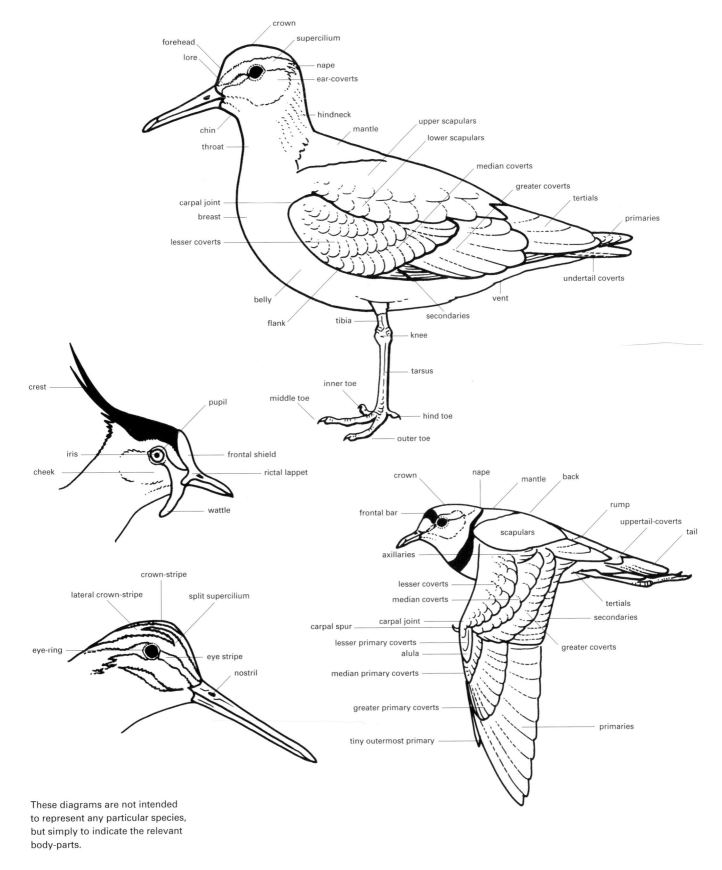

These diagrams are not intended
to represent any particular species,
but simply to indicate the relevant
body-parts.

Jacanidae

Lesser Jacana
Microparra capensis L 16.50 cm
Tiny size invites confusion with downy
African Jacana, patchily and locally
distributed throughout permanent
wetlands up to 3000 m across sub-Saharan
Africa.
PLUMAGE Adult Narrow rufous eye-stripe,
chestnut-red crown and nape and orangey-
red forehead enclose conspicuous white
supercilium. Hindneck and mantle glossy
violet-black, sometimes extending onto
brownish back and rump. Scapulars,
tertials and coverts brown, greater coverts
paler brown tipped white. Rest of face and
entire underparts white, sides of neck and
breast washed pale yellow, flanks rich
chestnut-brown. Bill olive-brown, pinkish
on lower mandible. Legs long, olive-grey.
Juvenile Extremely similar to adult.
Mantle, back and scapulars fringed buff. **In
flight** Blackish flight feathers with broad
white trailing edge to secondaries and
inner primaries contrast with paler brown
greater covert panel. Uppertail coverts and
tail rich chestnut-brown. Long trailing legs.
Underwing black bordered white with
chestnut axillaries.
CALL Quiet 'puup'; also soft 'tchur'.
HABITAT AND BEHAVIOUR Frequents variety of
wetlands including swampy edges of
lakes, rivers, dams, coastal lagoons and
small ponds, with low emergent
vegetation. Feeds walking across
vegetation especially water lilies. Shy,
often taking to flight strongly but low,
momentarily raising wings above head
upon alighting.
MOVEMENTS Sedentary, occasionally
deserting receding waters.

African Jacana
Actophilornis africana L 30.50 cm
The common jacana or 'Lily-trotter' of sub-
Saharan Africa, widespread on wetlands
from sea-level up to 1500 m.
PLUMAGE Adult Obvious vivid blue frontal
shield almost covering short, narrow
anterior supercilium. Thick black eye-stripe
joining glossy black crown, nape and
hindneck. Cheeks and foreneck white
shading to golden-yellow on upper breast.
Upperparts and rest of underparts rich
chestnut-brown with slight greenish tinge
to mantle, scapulars and coverts. Bill vivid
blue. Legs long, olive-grey with extremely
long toes. **Juvenile** Reduced frontal shield.
Dark hindneck, cap and eye-stripe
enclosing obvious white supercilium.
Upperparts bronze, heavily tinged green.
Underparts white with yellow sides to
breast and chestnut-red flanks. **In flight**
Uniform chestnut upperparts with blackish
flight feathers and long trailing feet.

CALL Both noisy and varied, including a
rattling screech upon taking flight and a
quieter, grating 'kyowrr, kyowrr'.
HABITAT AND BEHAVIOUR Found on all types of
open water with floating and low,
emergent vegetation including lakes,
dams, waterways, marshes and temporary
pools. Habitually walks across vegetation
using enormous long toes adapted for
support. Occasionally swims.
MOVEMENTS Sedentary, but can disperse
hundreds of kilometres to transient pools.

Madagascar Jacana
Actophilornis albinucha L 30.50 cm
Head and neck plumage 'reversed' with
African Jacana, restricted to wetlands of
Madagascar, mainly in the north.
PLUMAGE Adult Crown white heavily flecked
black extending to white nape and
hindneck, latter bordered below pale
golden-yellow. Rich blue frontal shield.
Lores black flecked white, ear coverts,
chin, throat and foreneck black. Rest of
upperparts and underparts chestnut except
for white lower vent and undertail coverts.
Bill bright blue. Legs and feet long, pearl-
grey tinged olive. **Juvenile** Extremely
similar to African Jacana differing in
broader black loral stripe and blacker
crown and hindneck. **In flight** Blackish
primaries and secondaries contrast with
remainder of chestnut upperwing, mantle
and scapulars. Long trailing legs and feet.
CALL Very similar to African mainland
species.
HABITAT AND BEHAVIOUR Occurs along
marshes, rivers and boggy perimeters of
lakes from sea-level to 750 m. Noisy,
feeding in typical jacana manner on highly
vegetated watercourses.
MOVEMENTS Sedentary, slowly spreading
south and west with habitat deforestation.

Comb-crested Jacana
Irediparra gallinacea L 22.85 cm
Commonly known as 'Lotusbird', breeding
across wetlands of S Philippines, E
Indonesia, New Guinea and N and E
coastal Australia.
PLUMAGE Adult Crown, hindneck and upper
mantle black faintly glossed purple,
extending across lower breast, upper belly
and upper flanks. Thin black line from eye
to base of lower mandible. Supercilium,
face and sides of neck pale golden-yellow
enclosing whitish-buff chin and throat.
Lower mantle, scapulars, coverts and
tertials olive-brown. Lower belly, rear
flanks and undertail coverts white. Bill
pinkish-red tipped black. Fleshy pink wattle
at base of forehead rising into conspicuous
reddish vertical wattle or 'comb', often
becoming yellowish when bird becomes

excited. Iris yellow. Long legs and
enormous long toes and claws greyish-
green. Females considerably larger than
males. **Juvenile** Chestnut cap. Upperparts
fringed warm buff. Underparts white
lacking black breast band. Reduced frontal
wattle and comb. **In flight** Greenish-brown
mantle, scapulars and wing coverts
contrast with blackish flight feathers, rump
and tail. Long trailing legs and toes.
CALL Various high-pitched chittering notes.
RACES Three are recognized: *gallinacea* (S
Philippines, S Borneo, Timor, Molluccas);
novaeginea (N and C New Guinea)
upperparts blacker glossed purple with
lower scapulars olive-brown;
novaehollandiae (S New Guinea, N and E
Australia).
HABITAT AND BEHAVIOUR Favours deep,
permanent freshwater swamps and
lagoons, even small ponds, with extensive
floating emergent vegetation. Delicately
wades across aquatic weeds picking food
from surface. Usually occurs singly or in
pairs during breeding season when
strongly territorial. Chicks carried by
parents under wings, whilst during danger
may dive remaining submerged for several
minutes with just bill above water. Flight
short, low and swift. May form large
concentrations outside breeding season.
MOVEMENTS Largely sedentary, although
distribution more extensive during rainy
season.

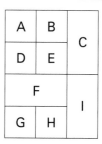

A Lesser Jacana adult
B Lesser Jacana
C African Jacana adult
D African Jacana juvenile
E African Jacana adult
F Madagascar Jacana adult
G Madagascar Jacana juvenile
H Comb-crested Jacana adult
I Comb-crested Jacana *novaehollandiea* adult

Jacanidae

Pheasant-tailed Jacana
Hydrophasianus chirurgus
L 31.00–58.00 cm

Unique amongst jacanas in being both migratory and possessing separate non-breeding plumage, nesting on freshwater wetlands in India, across SE Asia to S China, Philippines and S Borneo.

PLUMAGE Adult breeding Unmistakable. Head and neck white with black nape patch extending as narrow black line down sides of neck to upper breast. Bright yellow hind neck. Rest of body chocolate-brown except white area across complete closed wing. Outer primaries black and elongated with racket-shaped extension. Very long black-brown tail with central tail feathers further elongated. Bill slate-blue tipped yellow. Legs bluish-grey. **Adult non-breeding** Crown and hindneck black-brown. Warm buff supercilium joins golden-yellow neck sides. Black-brown 'necklace' from lores through eye and down sides of neck joining across upper breast. Upperparts green-brown, rest of underparts white. Much shorter tail. Bill dull yellow becoming brown towards tip. Legs dull greenish-grey. **Juvenile** Similar to non-breeding adult but cap rufous, sides of neck buff and upperparts brown extensively fringed buff. 'Necklace' less conspicuous. **In flight** White wings contrast with black primaries, brown body and elongated tail (breeding), and brownish innerwing coverts and short tail (non-breeding).

CALL In breeding season a loud, musical 'me-e-ou, me-e-ou', in winter a peculiar nasal 'tewn, tewn'.

HABITAT AND BEHAVIOUR Breeds on 'jheels' up to 1500 m with plenty of floating and emergent vegetation. Tame, readily swims, also strong flier. Gregarious in winter, forming flocks 50–100 birds.

MOVEMENTS Northern populations descend from the upper Himalayas during winter, birds regularly reaching Sumatra. Scarce visitor to Oman and Yemen (October–April). Vagrant Java and NW Australia.

Bronze-winged Jacana
Metopidius indicus **L 29.20 cm**

A thickish billed jacana, resident on fresh water throughout India and SE Asia.

PLUMAGE Adult Conspicuous long white rear supercilium. Red frontal shield. Rest of head, neck and underparts glossy black tinged green, with chestnut-red tail and undertail coverts. Base of hindneck glossed purple, with mantle, scapulars and tertials glossed bronze-green. Bill thickset, bright yellowish-green tinged red towards base. Legs and feet long, dark green. **Juvenile** Chestnut-brown cap with short fore-supercilium. Dusky lores and ear coverts. Hindneck black. Underparts whitish with

sides of neck pale rufous. Bill dull greenish-yellow. **In flight** Looks very dark with blackish flight feathers, bronze-green innerwing coverts, chestnut-red rump and tail, and long trailing legs.

CALL A short, harsh grunt. Also an aggressive, wheezy, piping 'seek-seek-seek'.

HABITAT AND BEHAVIOUR Breeds on lowland 'jheels' with emergent and floating vegetation. Able swimmer, partially submerging when alarmed.

MOVEMENTS Largely sedentary, with very little post-breeding dispersal movements.

Northern Jacana
Jacana spinosa **L 19.70 cm**

Resident throughout freshwater marshes of C America from Mexico south to Panama and the Greater Antilles, occasionally north to S Texas.

PLUMAGE Adult Head, neck and breast black glossed green, contrasting slightly with rest of chestnut-maroon underparts. Glossy chestnut-brown mantle, coverts, scapulars and tertials. Lime-green panel sometimes visible on edge of closed wing. Bill bright yellow tinged pale blue at base of upper mandible. Three-lobed yellow wattle. Long legs and toes greyish-green. Long pale carpal spur. Females appreciably larger. **Juvenile** Dark brownish cap and eye-line extending through ear coverts to join base of dark greyish-brown hindneck and upper parts. Buffish-white supercilium and under parts with chestnut-maroon flanks. Tiny dull, three-lobed frontal wattle. **In flight** Conspicuous lime-green flight feathers tipped blackish-brown especially on outer primaries, latter also showing prominent blackish shafts. Chocolate-brown primary and inner wing coverts, mantle, scapulars, rump and tail. Long trailing legs and toes.

CALL Noisy, clacking and rasping notes.

RACES Three recognized: gymnostoma (Mexico); spinosa (W Panama south to Guatemala and Belize); violacea (Cuba, Jamaica, Hispaniola): plumages similar.

HABITAT AND BEHAVIOUR Frequents fresh water marshes, swamps and lagoons with floating, emergent vegetation. Feeds in typical jacana manner picking insects from water surface or vegetation. Highly territorial and aggressive, performing aerial chases, frequently raising wings to expose brilliant lime-green coloration.

MOVEMENTS Largely sedentary, juveniles occasionally straggling north to S Texas to breed. Vagrant Florida.

Wattled Jacana
Jacana jacana **L 19.70 cm**

Southern counterpart to Northern Jacana, widespread throughout freshwater wetlands of S America east of the Andes

from W Panama south to La Pampa province, Argentina.

PLUMAGE Adult Head, neck and underparts black, flanks sometimes tinged dark maroon. Glossy chestnut-brown mantle, coverts, tertials and scapulars. Lime-green flight feathers often visible along edge of closed wing. Bill bright yellow. Two-lobed crimson-red wattles and rictal lappet hanging down from sides of bill-base. Females significantly larger with top of wattles tinged blue. Legs and long toes dull green tinged flesh. **Juvenile** Dark cap and blackish eye-line extending across ear coverts to join base of dark greyish-brown hindneck and upperparts. Supercilium and underparts buffish-white. Rictal lappet absent. Small dull frontal shield two-lobed providing safe distinction from Northern. **In flight** Conspicuous lime-green flight feathers tipped dark brown contrast strongly with dark brown primary coverts and chestnut-brown mantle, coverts, rump and tail. Long trailing legs and toes.

CALL High-pitched squawking notes.

RACES Six are recognized: nominate jacana (most of range); hypomelaena (W Panama to N Columbia); melanopygia (W Columbia and W Venezuela); intermedia (N Venezuela); scapularis (W Ecuador); peruviana (E Peru).

HABITAT AND BEHAVIOUR Frequents variety of lowland fresh waters with abundant floating and emergent vegetation. Aggressive, tending to fly when disturbed, often raising wings on alighting. Has interbred with Northern Jacana.

MOVEMENTS Sedentary. Vagrant record Chile

A	B	C
D	E	F
G	H	I
J	K	L

A   Pheasant-tailed Jacana adult breeding
B   Pheasant-tailed Jacana adult non-breeding
C   Pheasant-tailed Jacana first-winter
D   Pheasant-tailed Jacana adult breeding
E   Bronze-winged Jacana adult
F   Bronze-winged Jacana adult
G   Northern Jacana spinosa adult
H   Northern Jacana spinosa juvenile
I   Northern Jacana violacaea adult
J   Wattled Jacana jacana adult
K   Wattled Jacana jacana adult
L   Wattled Jacana intermedia juvenile

Rostratulidae and Pluvianellidae

Painted-snipe
Rostratula benghalensis L 24.10 cm
Highly skulking, sexually dimorphic wader, breeding in inland marshes in parts of Africa, Madagascar, and India east through Indo-China, Japan, SE Asia and E Australia.
PLUMAGE **Adult female** Brighter plumage. Greenish-black crown with golden-buff crown stripe, shading to vinous-brown neck and upper breast bordered below by broad blackish band extending around sides and back of neck. Distinctive elongated white eye-patch. Chin and throat whitish. Upperparts glossy greyish-green with scapulars and wing coverts finely barred black. Buffish lines forming 'V's along outer edges of mantle and inner scapulars. Rounded ashy-grey tail with large golden-buff spots, extending beyond tips of tertials. Conspicuous white 'harness' continuing from mantle 'V's to join white underparts, suffused creamy-buff on vent and undertail coverts, with blackish-brown patches to breast sides. Bill longish gently decurving towards tip, greyish-green tipped reddish-brown. Iris dark reddish-brown. Legs dull green tinged yellow. **Adult male** Smaller and duller. Head, neck and upper breast olive-brown streaked whitish on chin and throat. Golden-buff eye-patch and conspicuous golden-buff mantle 'V's. Wing coverts broadly spotted golden-buff. **Juvenile** Similar to adult male. Wing coverts greyer spotted paler buff. **In flight** Broad, rounded wings with legs often dangling. Flight feathers, rump and tail ashy-grey barred darker grey spotted golden-buff. Narrow black mid-wing panel. Coverts dark finely barred in female, spotted golden-buff in male.
CALL Usually silent when flushed, occasional loud 'kek'.
HABITAT AND BEHAVIOUR Breeds in heavily vegetated marshes and swamps with adjacent pools and muddy fringes. Mainly crepuscular, female displaying at night both on the ground and in flight, uttering series of notes resembling blowing across mouth of bottle. Both sexes perform 'head-forward' display, exposing wings and tail. Usually solitary or in pairs. Bobs rear end of body when feeding. Frequently freezes when disturbed, taking to flight short distance only.
MOVEMENTS Resident except NE China where summer visitor. Undertakes irregular local movements in response to fluctuating water levels. Vagrant Israel, Somalia, Zanzibar.

South American Painted-snipe
Nycticryphes semicollaris L 20.30 cm
Distinctly smaller with shorter, more decurved bill than its Old World congener,
inhabiting low-lying wetlands in Paraguay, Uruguay, SE Brazil, C Chile and N Argentina.
PLUMAGE **Adult** Sexes very similar. Head, neck and breast deep chocolate-brown with narrow buff crown-stripe from bill to nape and buff lores and supercilium continuing well behind eye. Mantle dark brown barred grey with conspicuous golden-buff lines forming contrasting 'V's along outer edge of mantle adjacent upper scapulars. Scapulars and coverts black and chocolate-brown variably boldly spotted white. Tertials barred dark chocolate and paler brown. Finely graduated tail dull brown finely barred black clearly extending beyond tips of tertials. Narrow white 'harness' on sides of breast joining mantle 'V' usually isolated from rest of dirty white underparts. Flanks and undertail coverts washed creamy-brown. Bill shortish, strongly decurved towards tip, base variable dull greenish-yellow with tip reddish-brown to black. Legs dull green. Webbing present between outer and middle toes. **Juvenile** Cheeks, throat, foreneck and breast buffish streaked dark brown. Scapulars and coverts broadly fringed creamy-buff. Creamy-buff 'harness'. **Flight** 'Batlike' and fluttery with legs dangling. Conspicuous mantle 'V's contrast with chocolate-brown mantle and upper wing spotted white. Rump, uppertail coverts and tail paler brown finely barred black.
CALL Invariably silent when flushed; plaintive whistle or hissing 'wee-oo' rarely heard.
HABITAT AND BEHAVIOUR Found in various low-lying wetlands, marshes, and wet pastures often in heavily grassed environment. Usually observed in pairs, but nests in small loose colonies frequently associating with Pectoral Sandpipers. When flushed flies only short distance, rarely rising more than 10 m above ground. Occasionally feeds in open, shallow water.
MOVEMENTS Largely sedentary, undergoing regular local movements in response to habitat conditions.

Magellanic Plover
Pluvianellus socialis L 20.30 cm
A rare turnstone-like plover, with breeding range restricted to the steppe region of S Patagonia in S Chile and S Argentina including Tierra del Fuego. Total population estimated maximum 1500 birds.
PLUMAGE **Adult** Whitish-grey forehead and dusky-grey loral line from bill to eye shading into dove-grey head, hindneck and upperparts. Chin and throat white.
Breast soft grey mottled brownish-grey on lower breast. Rest of underparts white. Bill markedly pointed, black with indistinct dull pinkish-red spot at base of culmen and base of lower mandible. Iris crimson. Legs short, crimson. **Juvenile** Upperparts distinctly fringed and spotted white. Breast streaked darker grey. Dull yellowish areas to base of culmen and lower mandible. Iris dull orange. Legs straw-yellow. **Flight** Fast and somewhat erratic. Dark grey primaries and secondaries alleviated by white bases to inner primaries, white shafts to outer primaries and tips to greater coverts. Rest of inner wing and mantle uniform grey. Broad white fringe to black centred rump, uppertail coverts and tail.
CALL Flight note high pitched whistled 'pieu', not unlike muted Eurasian Oystercatcher.
HABITAT AND BEHAVIOUR Nests adjacent lagoons and shallow lakes, alkaline, fresh or salt especially with broad pebbly or clayey fringed shores. Territorial display includes various upright and bowing movements. Unique amongst waders in regurgitating food to young. Highly camouflaged, slowly shuffling along grey stone beaches feeding amongst pebbles in typical turnstone-like manner. Usually in pairs or small family parties. Reasonably tame and approachable. Forms small flocks during winter when feeds by pecking at fly larvae.
MOVEMENTS Mainly sedentary, with local post-breeding movements to coastal localities, especially sheltered bays and river mouths. Limited movement north to Valdez peninsula, Argentina.

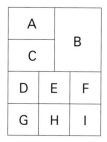

A Painted-snipe adult male
B Painted-snipe adult female
C Painted-snipe
D South American Painted-snipe adult male
E South American Painted-snipe adult male
F South American Painted-snipe adult female
G Magellanic Plover adult
H Magellanic Plover adult
I Magellanic Plover juvenile

Dromadidae and Ibidorhynchidae

Crab-plover
Dromas ardeola L 39.35 cm
A large and unmistakable black and white wader with a massive bill, breeding exclusively on the Indian coastline of the Persian Gulf and Arabian peninsula, and islets off N Somalia.
PLUMAGE **Adult** Head white with blackish masks in front of and behind eye, with varying amounts of blackish streaking on rear crown and nape. Some birds remaining completely white headed. Upperparts strikingly pied with black mantle and upper scapulars, white lower scapulars and lesser and median coverts. Greater coverts and flight feathers black. Tertials variable from white to silvery grey. Underparts pure white. Bill wholly black, and relatively short, massive and powerful looking, deep based with both mandibles curving to a point. Legs long, greyish-blue.
Juvenile Similar to adult, but black streaking on crown more extensive. Mantle and upper scapulars dark silvery-grey, with white of wing coverts, rump and tail washed grey. **In flight** Blackish flight feathers contrast with whitish inner wing. White back, rump and tail (adult). Feet project well beyond tail.
CALL Most characteristic sound a barking, far carrying 'crow-ow-ow' or 'ha-how'. On the breeding-grounds a constant 'tchuck-tchuck', often heard at night, audible at great distance.
HABITAT AND BEHAVIOUR Breeds in dense colonies on sandy coasts and marine islets, nesting in burrows dug out by the birds themselves. Feeding action very plover like, with diet almost exclusively crabs. Fairly approachable. Flies in large flocks in tight formation low and fast over the water.
MOVEMENTS Present extensively throughout the year, albeit non-breeding, around the W Indian Ocean coastline from E Africa and Madagascar north and east to Pakistan and W India. Bulk of the population moves south during August–November after breeding, also wintering on oceanic islands. Returns to breeding-grounds March–April. Regular visitor S Thailand peninsula. Vagrant Malaysia.

Ibisbill
Ibidorhyncha struthersii L 39.35 cm
An unmistakable wader restricted to the mountain river beds in the high plateaux of Central Asia.
PLUMAGE **Adult breeding** Crown, front of face, chin and throat black, narrowly bordered white, but not joining behind nape. Entire neck, breast and upperparts bluish-grey, with pale fringes to mantle, scapulars and wing coverts. Underparts white with black breast band narrowly bordered white above. Bill longish, strongly decurved and bright red. Legs bright red. Iris dark red. **Adult non-breeding** Similar to adult breeding but area around base of bill flecked white. Bill reddish-brown. Legs pinkish-grey. **Juvenile** Face brownish mottled white. Upperparts browner with extensive buffish-orange fringes giving 'scaly' effect. Breast band dark brown lacking white border. Bill dull pinkish-grey. Legs pinkish-grey. Iris dull reddish-yellow. **In flight** Dark grey upperwing with variable amount of white across bases of outer secondaries and inner primaries, with white subterminal spots on outer primaries. Rump and tail paler greyish-brown.
CALL A low, ringing repeated 'tee-tee-tee-tee', somewhat reminiscent of *tringa* sandpipers.
HABITAT AND BEHAVIOUR Inhabits shingle banks and islets on fast-flowing Himalayan streams between 1700–4400 m. Often wades belly-deep in water, probing under submerged stones for food. Excellently camouflaged amongst stony river banks, and very noisy when disturbed. Strongly territorial. Flies with flicking, rounded wings, reminiscent of Stone-curlew.
MOVEMENTS Largely sedentary, nesting end of March to early June. In winter some descend to lower altitudes, inhabiting foothills and plains as low as 100 m.

A	B	C
D	E	F
G		H
I		J

A Crab-plover adult and juvenile
B Crab-plover
C Crab-plover adults and juvenile
D Crab-plover juvenile
E Crab-plover adult and juvenile
F Crab-plover juvenile
G Ibisbill breeding adult
H Ibisbill adult non-breeding
I Ibisbill adult non-breeding
J Ibisbill adult non-breeding

Haematopodidae

Eurasian Oystercatcher
Haematopus ostralegus L 43.15 cm
The only oystercatcher with a neck collar in non-breeding plumage, with different racial populations nesting across Britain, Europe and Russia and also Kamchatka peninsula south to N China.
PLUMAGE Adult breeding Strikingly pied. Head, neck, breast and upperparts glossy black. Rest of underparts white. Bill chisel-shaped, orange, slightly paler towards tip. Legs pinkish-grey. Iris red. **Adult non-breeding** Similar to adult breeding with white collar around foreneck. Bill duller orange tinged grey towards tip. **Juvenile** Mantle, scapulars and wing coverts brownish-black fringed buff, lacking neck collar. Bill more pointed, with dull pink base, becoming brownish towards tip. **In flight** Bold white wing bar across inner secondaries, base of outer secondaries and base of most primaries. Back, rump and uppertail white with terminal tail band black.
CALL Usual call a piercing 'kleep' and when agitated a sharp, repeated 'kip'.
RACES Three are recognized: *ostralegus*(Europe and coastal Russia); *longipes* (C Russia) browner upperparts; *osculans* (Kamchatka south to N China) white lacking on outer primaries but more extensive on median coverts.
HABITAT AND BEHAVIOUR Breeds on shingle beaches, dunes and short grass clifftops. Also inland beside lakes, shingle river valleys and on grass and crops. Noisy 'piping display' includes familiar trilling call. Winters chiefly on the coast especially estuaries, sandy and rocky shores, often in huge, dense flocks. May also occur widely inland during migration. Diet largely bivalve molluscs, opened by using both 'hammering' and 'stabbing' techniques.
MOVEMENTS Migratory. *Ostralegus* being part sedentary, others undergoing post-breeding movements from late July to more southerly moulting and wintering grounds in W Africa. Vagrant to Azores, Greenland and Newfoundland, Canada. *Longipes* moves to Middle East, India and NE Africa with vagrancy to S Africa, Kenya and, more recently, Canada (in May 1994). *Osculans* winters in SE China, vagrant to Japan. Many immatures remain on wintering grounds. Commences returning to breeding-grounds from late January in W Europe but early May in Russia.

American Oystercatcher
Haematopus palliatus L 41.90 cm
Differing from its Eurasian counterpart in possessing a brown back, this Nearctic oystercatcher is restricted to the coasts of S USA and C and S America.

PLUMAGE Adult Head, neck and breast black. Mantle, scapulars, wing coverts and tertials dark brown indistinctly fringed whitish-buff. Underparts white. Bill orangey-red, yellowish towards tip. Legs dull pink. Iris yellow with orangey-red eye-ring. **Juvenile** Similar to adult but entire upperparts including head mottled and finely fringed buff. Bill pinkish-brown with darker tip. Legs dull grey. Iris brown with eye-ring dull red. **In flight** Bold white wing bar across inner secondaries and bases of outer secondaries, sometimes extending onto bases of inner primaries. Curved white patch restricted to uppertail coverts contrasting with dark brown back and rump and black tail.
CALL Extremely similar to Eurasian Oystercatcher.
RACES Five are known: nominate *palliatus* (E USA south to Uruguay, W Indies), with white wing bar extending onto bases of inner primaries; *pitanay* (west S America]; *frazari* (W Mexico); *galapagensis* (Galapagos Is), stouter billed and shorter legged, and *durnfordi* (Argentina), the last three darker above with mottled lower breast border. Minor differences may partly stem from hybridization with American Black Oystercatcher.
HABITAT AND BEHAVIOUR Entirely coastal at all seasons, nesting on rocky as well as sandy beaches.
MOVEMENTS Largely sedentary. Some *palliatus* move south to winter in C America. Vagrant north to Point Reyes and inland to Salton Sea, California; also Lake Ontario, Canada, New Brunswick and Nova Scotia.

Pied Oystercatcher
Haematopus longirostris
L 45.70–49.55 cm
Extremely similar to Eurasian Oystercatcher, with two well-differentiated races breeding throughout coastal Australia and inland South Island, New Zealand.
PLUMAGE Adult breeding At rest virtually identical to Eurasian Oystercatcher. Black extends somewhat farther down breast. **Adult non-breeding** Lacks white foreneck collar of Eurasian species. **Juvenile** Very similar to Eurasian, with blackish-brown upperparts, scapulars fringed buff. **In flight** Wing bar shorter than Eurasian and white rump patch not extending so far up back (*see* Races). Black leading edge to underwing.
CALL A ringing 'kleep-kleep' and a piercing 'peep-a-peep, peep-a-peep', very similar to Eurasian but somewhat harder and less plaintive than Sooty Oystercatcher.
RACES Two are recognized: nominate

longirostris (Australia, Tasmania, S New Guinea) with wing bar restricted to base of secondaries and tips of greater coverts, and white rump patch extending to lower back only; *finschi* (New Zealand), known as South Island Pied Oystercatcher or, colloquially, 'SIPO', being smaller with greater coverts all white forming broader wing bar, often extending onto inner primaries. White rump patch extending to a point farther up back. Often considered conspecific with Eurasian Oystercatcher.
HABITAT AND BEHAVIOUR Australian population breeds on sandy ocean beaches and sand dunes, whereas 'SIPO' nests inland on shingle river banks and lakeshores, but also on sub-alpine tundra up to 1800 m. Moves to the coast to winter on tidal mudflats and estuaries, forming quite large flocks. Strongly territorial with typical oystercatcher 'piping' display.
MOVEMENTS *Longirostris* is sedentary, dispersing after breeding to intertidal mudflats and estuaries. After nesting 'SIPO' moves directly to the N and E coasts of South Island, Stewart Is, and throughout coastal North Island, arriving at the last from late December, departing early July. Large numbers now winter around Aukland. Immatures summer in wintering area. Recently bred North Island.

A	B	C
D	E	F
H	I	G
	J	K

A Eurasian Oystercatcher *ostralegus* adult breeding
B Eurasian Oystercatcher *longipes* adult non-breeding
C Eurasian Oystercatcher *ostralegus* juvenile
D Eurasian Oystercatcher *ostralegus* adult
E Pied Oystercatcher *longirostrus*
F Pied Oystercatcher *finschii* adult
G Pied Oystercatcher *finschii* adult
H American Oystercatcher *galapagensis* adult
I American Oystercatcher *palliatus* adult
J American Oystercatcher *palliatus* adult non-breeding
K American Oystercatcher *palliatus* adult

Haematopodidae

Variable Oystercatcher
Haematopus unicolor L 48.25 cm
The only oystercatcher showing black, pied and intermediate forms, numbering about 2500, and confined to rocky and sandy coasts of New Zealand.
PLUMAGE **Adult** Slightly larger and bulkier than South Island Pied Oystercatcher ('SIPO'). Black phase *unicolor* entirely glossy black. At rest wing tips fall roughly level with tail tip. Bill red, somewhat shorter and deeper based than 'SIPO'. Legs also shorter and slightly duller pink. Pied phase *reischeki*: head, breast and upperparts glossy black. Rest of underparts white with broad mottled area across lower breast where black merges with white. White shoulder 'peak' absent. Bare part coloration similar to black phase. In flight short white wing bar confined to bases of secondaries and tips of greater coverts. Squarish white patch to uppertail coverts mottled black. Intermediate forms known as 'smudgies' are highly variable. **Juvenile** Black heavily mottled brown with buff tips to coverts and tertials. Bill dull reddish-grey, brighter towards base. Legs greyish-pink.
CALL Typical oystercatcher 'piping', somewhat less piercing than Eurasian.
HABITAT AND BEHAVIOUR Unlike 'SIPO' confined to the coast, favouring open sandy beaches and rocky foreshores, feeding largely on limpets and mussels. Performs typical 'piping' display. Breeds from December onwards, slightly later than 'SIPO'. *'Unicolor'* approximately 70 per cent of total population, increasing in frequency from North Island to South Island. During 1993 two pairs black phase interbred with 'SIPO', resultant chicks resembling 'SIPO'.
MOVEMENTS Sedentary. Occasionally gathers in small post-breeding flocks up to 150 birds, sometimes mixing with 'SIPO' in the larger harbours.

Chatham Islands Oystercatcher
Haematopus chathamensis
L 48.25 cm
Extremely rare with total population 75–100 birds, very closely related to the 'pied' form of Variable Oystercatcher, but totally restricted to the Chatham Is, 800 km east of New Zealand.
PLUMAGE **Adult** Appears very similar to pied form *reischeki* of Variable Oystercatcher. Overlapping black and white breast zone more clearly demarcated, with black blotching on lower breast extending up to shoulder, almost obscuring small white 'peak' between sides of breast and folded wing. Bare part coloration similar to Variable Oystercatcher but bill shorter and

deeper based, and legs shorter and stockier, both adapted to slightly different habitat and feeding technique. **Juvenile** Similar to 'pied' form of Variable Oystercatcher. **In flight** Differs from Variable Oystercatcher by wing bar extending inwards to reach tips of very innermost secondaries. White patch to uppertail coverts extends slightly onto lower rump, bordered at both base and tip with obscure black blotching.
CALL Virtually identical to Variable Oystercatcher.
HABITAT AND BEHAVIOUR Confined to coasts of Chatham Main Is, South East Is, Mangere Is and Pitt Is in the Chatham group. Bare parts adapted to feeding on rocky, platform foreshores. Highly territorial. Extremely vulnerable to predation from cats and wekas, hence recently more successful on predator-free island reserves. Full research and colour banding scheme currently in operation.
MOVEMENTS Sedentary, with only occasional local movements between islands.

Magellanic Oystercatcher
Haematopus leucopodus L 43.80 cm
Unique amongst oystercatchers in possessing a yellow eye-ring. Confined to the coast and inland grasslands of S Chile and S Argentina, Tierra del Fuego and the Falklands Is.
PLUMAGE **Adult** Head, neck, breast and upperparts black faintly glossed dark green. Rest of underparts white. Bill orangey-red lacking yellowish tip. Iris and eye-ring golden-yellow. Legs dull pink. **Juvenile** Upperparts admixed with brown narrowly fringed pale. Eye-ring and iris dull brownish-yellow. Legs grey. **In flight** Conspicuous elongated white patch across secondaries and tips of greater coverts contrasts with black mantle, rest of coverts and primaries. White uppertail coverts and base of tail. Rest of tail black. Leading edge of underwing and primaries black with rest of underwing white.
CALL Flight note plaintive whistle 'fee-uu, fee-uu', noticeably less piercing than Eurasian Oystercatcher.
HABITAT AND BEHAVIOUR Breeds coastally on gravelly beaches but also stony shores adjacent inland lagoons and grassy meadows and steppe, often considerable distance from water. Piping display involves bowing of head and bill along ground whilst characteristically raising and fanning tail. Gregarious outside breeding season, often forming large flocks.
MOVEMENTS Mostly sedentary, moving to coast in winter, with some birds from Tierra del Fuego migrating northwards.

A	B	
C	D	
E	F	G
H	I	J

A Variable Oystercatcher black phase adult
B Variable Oystercatcher (left to right) adult black phase, juvenile black phase, first-winter non-breeding pied phase, adult smudgie phase
C Variable Oystercatcher adult smudgie phase, first-winter non-breeding pied phase
D Variable Oystercatcher adult smudgie phase
E Chatham Islands Oystercatcher adult
F Chatham Islands Oystercatcher adult
G Chatham Islands Oystercatcher adult
H Magellanic Oystercatcher adult
I Magellanic Oystercatcher adult
J Magellanic Oystercatcher adult

Haematopodidae

American Black Oystercatcher
Haematopus bachmani L 43.80 cm
Almost identical to the Blackish Oystercatcher of S America, but restricted to the Pacific coast of N America from W Alaska including the Aleutians south to Baja California.
PLUMAGE **Adult breeding** Head, neck and underparts black, with slight brownish tinge from belly to undertail coverts. Mantle, scapulars, wing coverts and tertials distinctly brownish-black fringed pale. Bill longish, orange with yellowish tip. Legs pinkish-grey. Iris yellow with orange-red eye-ring. **Adult non-breeding** Very similar, sometimes showing pale feather edges to belly. Legs more dusky-grey. **Juvenile** Similar to adult, with mantle, scapulars and tertials fringed cinnamon-buff. Coverts brownish with black subterminal bars also fringed cinnamon-buff. Bill dull orange with blackish tip. Legs dull greyish-brown. Iris orange-brown with dull orange eye-ring. **In flight** Appears all black. Slight contrast between mantle and hindneck may be visible.
CALL A loud, penetrating 'whee-ep'. Also typical penetrating oystercatcher piping 'peep-peep-peep-peep'.
HABITAT AND BEHAVIOUR Breeds on rocky coasts, reefs and outlying islands. Alert and not shy, but often difficult to see against dark coloured rocks. Feeds on barnacle-covered rocks and high-lying mussel beds. Sluggish on the wing. Occasionally interbreeds with American Oystercatcher in southern part of range.
MOVEMENTS Largely sedentary, moving south from northern limit of breeding range in winter. Vagrant to Pribilof Is.

African Black Oystercatcher
Haematopus moquini L 42.50 cm
A rare oystercatcher with a total population of less than 5000, restricted to sandy beaches and rocky islets of S Africa.
PLUMAGE **Adult breeding** Entirely glossy black. Tail falls roughly level with wing tips. Bill orangey-red slightly paler at tip. Eye-ring scarlet, iris red. Legs fleshy pink. **Adult non-breeding** Virtually identical, worn feathers tinged brown post breeding. **Juvenile** Brownish-black, upperparts extensively fringed buff. Bill dull orange, becoming brownish towards tip. Eye-ring narrower almost lacking coloration, iris dull reddish-brown. Legs greyish-pink. **In flight** Uniform black, underwing showing white shaft to outer primary.
CALL Usual note loud, strident 'klee-eep'; when alarmed agitated 'pic, pic, pic'.
HABITAT AND BEHAVIOUR Found on exposed rocky offshore islands and mixed sandy/rocky beaches on mainland. Solitary nesting, performing typical oystercatcher 'butterfly' display flight. Feeds intertidally on mussels and limpets. Forms communal roosts during non-breeding season. Immatures occur on sandy and even muddy estuaries, lagoons and, rarely, saltpans. Mainland breeding sites threatened by tourist disturbance.
MOVEMENTS Largely sedentary, moving from rocky mainland shores to sandy beaches and rocky islands prior to breeding. Vagrant Angola, Natal.

Blackish Oystercatcher
Haematopus ater L 44.40 cm
Extremely similar to American Black Oystercatcher, this S American counterpart breeds on rocky coasts from Peru south to Chile and Argentina including the Falkland Is.
PLUMAGE **Adult** Head, neck and underparts entirely black. Upperparts dark brown. Wing tips fall roughly level or slightly short of tail tip. Bill shortish, stubby, bright orangey-red tipped yellow. Tip of lower mandible distinctly upturned. Iris yellow. Eye-ring red. Legs ivory-flesh. Extensive webbing between outer and middle toes. **Juvenile** Upperparts narrowly fringed buffish-brown. Bill dull red tipped yellowish-grey. Iris and eye-ring brown. **In flight** Appears wholly dark.
CALL Typical shrill piping 'kleep, kleep', virtually identical to American Black Oystercatcher.
HABITAT AND BEHAVIOUR Restricted to rocky, pebbly and occasionally sandy beaches and coastline. Occurs singly or in small parties. Typically feeds on limpets and other bivalves using well-adapted bill. Rarely hybridizes with Magellanic Oystercatcher.
MOVEMENTS Virtually sedentary. Occasional local movements north along coast during winter.

Sooty Oystercatcher
Haematopus fuliginosus L 47.00 cm
Scarcer than Pied Oystercatcher, this long-tailed species is confined to rocky beaches around the entire Australian coastline.
PLUMAGE **Adult breeding** Entirely sooty black. Tail clearly projecting beyond folded wing tips. Bill orange-red sometimes tipped yellow. Legs pinkish-red. Iris scarlet with orange-red eye-ring. **Adult non-breeding** Virtually identical, showing whitish tips to belly in fresh plumage only. **Juvenile** Duller brown with buffish fringes to mantle, wing coverts, belly and flanks. Bill dusky-brown. Legs grey. Iris brown with pale orange eye-ring. **In flight** All black and heavy looking.
CALL A ringing 'kleep-kleep' and also a piercing 'peepapeep, peepapeep'.
RACES Two are recognized: nominate *fuliginosus* (S Australia) and *opthalmicus* (Kimberley east to Cape York), the latter longer billed with more prominent fleshy eye-ring.
HABITAT AND BEHAVIOUR Found on rocky beaches, reefs and tidal pools, nesting between boulders on rocky islets and promontories. Wary, extremely well camouflaged against dark rocks. Rather solitary, but does mix and has interbred with Pied Oystercatcher.
MOVEMENTS Sedentary, with local post-breeding movements to rocky headlands on the mainland.

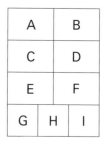

A	B
C	D
E	F
G	H	I

[A] American Black Oystercatcher adult
[B] American Black Oystercatcher adlt
[C] American Black Oystercatcher adult
[D] African Black Oystercatcher adult
[E] Blackish Oystercatcher adult
[F] Blackish Oystercatcher adult
[G] Blackish Oystercatcher adult
[H] Sooty Oystercatcher adult
[I] Sooty Oystercatcher first-winter non-breeding

Recurvirostridae

Black-winged Stilt
Himantopus himantopus L 37.45 cm
An unmistakable pied wader encompassing three 'subspecies' – Black-winged, Black-necked and Pied Stilts, with breeding range extending from temperate to tropical zones around the globe.
PLUMAGE **Adult breeding male** Crown, nape and hindneck variable white, greyish or black. Entire upperparts black glossed dark green. Underparts white. Bill thin, pointed, straight and black. Legs extremely long, carmine pink. Iris bright red. **Adult breeding female** Mantle, scapulars and tertials brownish or blackish-brown. Generally duller headed. **Adult non-breeding** On nominate race crown, nape and hindneck frequently washed greyish. **Juvenile** Upperparts brownish fringed buff. On nominate race crown and hindneck dusky brown. Base of lower mandible sometimes reddish. Legs dull fleshy-pink. Iris yellowish-brown. **In flight** Very long trailing legs. White patch from back to uppertail coverts contrasts with blackish upperparts and pale greyish tail. Juveniles show white tips to secondaries and inner primaries.
CALL Sharp 'kek'; also incessant, raucous 'kik-kik-kik-kik'.
RACES Five are recognized within the three 'subspecies': nominate *himantopus* – Black-winged Stilt (S Eurasia, Africa, India) variable white to dusky-grey crown, white hindneck and upper mantle; *mexicanus* – Black-necked Stilt (USA south to Peru and N Brazil) black crown, hindneck and upper mantle; *melanurus* (rest of S America) white crown, black hindneck and narrow white upper mantle; *knudseni* (Hawaii) uniform black crown, hindneck and upper mantle, face also mostly black; *leucocephalus* – Pied Stilt (Indonesia, Australasia) white crown and upper mantle, black hindneck.
HABITAT AND BEHAVIOUR Nests in loose colonies across variety of wetlands including shores of freshwater or brackish pools, coastal brackish lagoons, saltpans, swampy hayfields and rice paddies. Frequently feeds knee-deep in water. In New Zealand commonly hybridizes with Black Stilt.
MOVEMENTS Northern populations fron Eurasia and N America migratory, moving south from mid-July to winter in Africa north of equator and extreme S USA respectively. Return passage from March onwards. *Himantopus* vagrant Britain (recently bred), Sweden, Atlantic Is and Japan. *Mexicanus* vagrant Canada, Newfoundland. *Leucocephalus* also migratory reaching north to Philippines, vagrant Tasmania and Chatham Is. Southern populations sedentary.

A	B	C
D	E	F
G	H	I
J	K	L

A Black-winged Stilt *himantopus* adult
B Black-winged Stilt *himantopus* adult
C Black-winged Stilt *himantopus* adult
D Black-winged Stilt *himantopus* juvenile
E Black-winged Stilt *himantopus*
F Black-winged Stilt *himantopus*
G Black-winged Stilt *melanurus* adult
H Black-winged Stilt *melanurus*
I Black-winged Stilt *mexicanus* adult
J Black-winged Stilt *leucocephalus* adult
K Black-winged Stilt *leucocephalus* juvenile
L Black-winged Stilt *leucocephalus*

Recurvirostridae

Black Stilt
Himantopus novaezelandiae
L 38.10 cm
Probably the world's rarest wader with only 15 breeding pairs during 1993/94 season, actively hybridizing with Pied Stilt and totally confined to the river valleys of the McKenzie Basin, South Island, New Zealand.
PLUMAGE **Adult breeding** Sooty black with slight glossy greenish sheen to scapulars, coverts and tertials. Bill black, slightly longer than Pied Stilt with lower mandible slightly upturned towards tip. Legs bright pink, slightly shorter than Pied Stilt. Older birds, especially males may show white flecking on head and undertail coverts. **Adult non-breeding** During moult may show greyish-white mottling to forehead and chin. **Juvenile** Extremely similar to Pied Stilt, but upperparts lack pale fringes. Legs duller pink. Identification up to nine months assisted since usually in the company of adults. Immatures lack black hindneck and black breast band of Pied Stilt and show black markings on underparts, but plumage variation makes identification and separation from hybrid Black x Pied extremely difficult. **In flight** Clearly stilt-like with legs trailing less than Pied Stilt.
CALL Similar to Pied but higher pitched, less piercing and repetitive.
HABITAT AND BEHAVIOUR Breeding confined mostly to shallow, open 'braided' river beds, where adapted for foraging in shingle and stony waters, nesting somewhat earlier than Pied Stilt. Also feeds on adjacent marshes and tarns. Tends to move to river deltas during the winter when pair bonds established. Predation, habitat destruction and hybridization have led to catastrophic decline in numbers. Intensive management recovery plan including full on-site captive breeding programme currently being undertaken in effort to boost genetically pure Black Stilt numbers back into the wild. Possible long-term option to transfer birds to predator-free island.
MOVEMENTS Largely sedentary, remaining in close proximity to breeding-grounds all year. Approximately 10 per cent of populations move north with migratory hybrid Pied Stilts to Kawhia and Kaipara Harbours, North Island. Rare elsewhere.

Banded Stilt
Cladorhynchus leucocephalus
L 40.65 cm
A distinctive stilt with a remarkable opportunistic breeding biology, nesting on salt lakes in the very arid country of SW Western and South Australia.

PLUMAGE **Adult breeding** Appears pied at distance. Mostly white except for entirely black scapulars and folded wing and deep chestnut breast band, broadest in centre, trailing backwards and shading to black on belly. Bill black, slender and slightly upturned. Legs pinkish tinged orange. Toes partially webbed. **Adult non-breeding** Breast band and belly patch less well defined, partially obscured with brown and white tipped feathers. **Juvenile** Underparts entirely white lacking any breast band. **In flight** White mantle and trailing edge to secondaries contrasts with remainder of black upperwing. Tail white washed pale grey.
CALL A feeble, barking 'chuk-uk, chuk-uk'.
HABITAT AND BEHAVIOUR Breeds in huge, dense colonies on islands on salt lakes, lagoons and commercial saltworks. Nests not discovered until 1930. Highly opportunistic, exploiting temporary breeding habitats, continuing to raise broods while conditions remain suitable. Breeds all months of the year. White chick unique amongst waders, with young forming 'crèches' similar to flamingos. Feeds in deep water and swims, similar to avocet. Highly gregarious during non-breeding season, readily associating with Red-necked Avocet and Pied Stilt.
MOVEMENTS Highly nomadic, dispersing post breeding to other inland salt lakes, but also coastal lakes, lagoons and saltworks, dependent on conditions encountered. Vagrant Queensland, New South Wales and Tasmania.

Red-necked Avocet
Recurvirostra novaehollandiae
L 44.45 cm
With brightly coloured head at all seasons, this avocet is endemic to Australia, widely distributed across the large inland wetlands.
PLUMAGE **Adult** Head and neck dark chestnut with narrow white eye-ring and varying amounts of white at base of bill. Pair of broad black streaks along upperparts formed by blackish edges to outer mantle feathers and inner upper scapulars. Black wing coverts and tertials with black primaries projecting well beyond tail tip. Rest of plumage white. Bill slender, black and distinctly upcurved. Unlike other avocets bill length and shape similar in both sexes. Legs long, pale bluish-grey. **Juvenile** Similar to adult but head and neck paler chestnut, sometimes appearing quite washed out. Increased pale area around base of bill and eye. Scapulars and wing coverts paler brown fringed buff. **In flight** Similar to Pied Avocet with distinctive floppy flight, but

black of innerwing coverts extending across to base of greater coverts and tertials. Legs and feet project well beyond tail.
CALL Usual contact note a musical fluty 'toot-toot'.
HABITAT AND BEHAVIOUR Nests in loose colonies on edges of brackish and salt lagoons, largely inland. Breeding season very variable and highly dependent on availability of suitable habitat. Typical 'scything' feeding action, readily upending and swimming. Also feeds on intertidal mudflats. Readily associating with Pied and Banded Stilts.
MOVEMENTS Post-breeding dispersal occurs in small flocks, with many birds moving to tidal inlets and estuaries, but seasonal movements towards the coast highly affected by availability of water. Following end of drought during 1983, 95,000 birds present inland at Lake Eyre September 1984. Bred New Zealand during nineteenth century, but now extremely rare vagrant.

A	B	C
D	E	F
G	H	I
J	K	L

- A Black Stilt adult
- B Black Stilt adult
- C Black Stilt adult
- D Pied × Black Stilt
- E Pied × Black Stilt adult
- F Pied × Black Stilt adult
- G Banded Stilt adult breeding
- H Banded Stilt
- I Banded Stilt adult non-breeding
- J Banded Stilt
- K Red-necked Avocet adult
- L Red-necked Avocet

Recurvirostridae

Pied Avocet
Recurvirostra avosetta L 43.20 cm
The only black capped avocet, breeding widely on brackish and salt wetlands across temperate Eurasia east to Outer Mongolia, and south to NE and S Africa. PLUMAGE **Adult male** Black cap, nape and hindneck. Edge of mantle and upper scapulars black. Lesser and median coverts and primaries black. Lower scapulars and tertials mottled soft grey. Rest of plumage white. Bill black, slender, and strongly upcurved. Legs long, bluish-grey. **Adult female** Generally duller black with bill both shorter and more strongly upcurved. **Juvenile** Areas black on the adult are dull brownish-grey. White of upperparts strongly mottled grey-brown fringed buff. **In flight** Characteristically stiff-winged with black outer primaries, innerwing covert and scapular patches. Legs and feet project beyond tail.
CALL A clear liquid 'kluit', repeated more rapidly when alarmed.
HABITAT AND BEHAVIOUR Nests in large colonies around salt and brackish lagoons, with sandy flats and expanses of dried mud and short vegetation, both coastal and inland. Breeding habitat dependent on water level and salt concentration. Extremely noisy and aggressive. 'Scything' feeding action, often upending and swimming.
MOVEMENTS Mainly migratory, especially in northern part of range, but African and some W European populations mostly sedentary. Autumn passage commences from mid-July in south-westerly–south-south-westerly direction to moulting grounds, before migrating on during October to winter in Mediterranean basin and south to tropical and S Africa, Arabia and W India, Burma and E China. Large flocks recorded (45,000, Kenya). Spring passage commences early February, peaking during April. Non-breeders remain on wintering grounds. Vagrant E Atlantic Is and Japan.

American Avocet
Recurvirostra americana L 45.10 cm
The only avocet with a non-breeding plumage, nesting on the alkaline prairie Lakes of C Canada south to W and C USA and N Mexico.
PLUMAGE **Adult breeding male** Head and neck orangey-brown shading to paler orangey-buff on upper mantle and lower breast. White area surrounding eye and base of bill. Edges of mantle and upper scapulars black. Lower scapulars white forming band along upper closed wing contrasting with blackish wing coverts, with greater coverts tipped white. Blackish

primaries with tertials paler greyish-brown. Rest of underparts white. Bill black and strongly upcurved. Legs long, bluish-grey. **Adult breeding female** Bill shorter and more strongly upcurved. **Adult non-breeding** Orangey-brown coloration lost. Head and neck soft pearl-grey appearing very pale at distance. **Juvenile** Crown greyish shading to pinkish-chestnut on hindneck and upper mantle. Scapulars, coverts and tertials pale brown tipped pinkish-buff. **In flight** Appears darker winged than Pied Avocet owing to black on outer primaries extending across to outer secondaries and both primary and greater coverts.
CALL A sharp 'kleek' or 'klee-eek' rapidly repeated when agitated.
HABITAT AND BEHAVIOUR Breeds in loose colonies around shallow waters, especially alkaline lakes with exposed sparsely vegetated shorelines and mudflats. Often wades in deep water using typical avocet 'scything' action. Swims well. Outside the breeding season also frequents marine shorelines, often forming sizeable flocks up to 300 birds.
MOVEMENTS Partially migratory, wintering adjacent coasts in southern part of breeding range. Post-breeding dispersal movements to moulting grounds commence early August with onward migration continuing up to October. Return passage from mid-April. Vagrant Baffin Is, Greenland, Caribbean and Ecuador.

Andean Avocet
Recurvirostra andina L 45.70 cm
A scarce, stilt-like avocet, breeding exclusively within the Puna zone of the high Andes in N Chile, S Peru, NW Argentina and W Bolivia.
PLUMAGE **Adult** Appears rather stocky, short-legged. Head, neck, upper mantle and underparts pure white. Lower mantle and rest of upperparts glossy chocolate-brown. Bill black, strongly upturned. Iris orangey-red. Eye-ring orange tinged yellow. Legs shortish, slate-grey. **Juvenile** Upperparts indistinctly fringed rufous-brown. **In flight** Noticeably broad-winged. White lower back and rump contrast with uniform chocolate-brown mantle and upperwing. Tail chocolate-brown with obscure mottling to base of uppertail coverts.
CALL Loud, whistled 'kweek' or 'kwiuk', less shrill or piercing than Pied Avocet.
HABITAT AND BEHAVIOUR Found over 3600 m, breeding around alkaline and saline lakes with broad sandy fringes, open alkaline marshes and seasonally inundated meadows. Nests September–January

dependent on rainfall. Usually in parties up to 20 birds. Feeds in shallow water with typical sideways scything of bill. Often found associating with Chilean Flamingo.
MOVEMENTS Largely sedentary. Occasionally moves to lower altitudes outside breeding season. Casual visitor to Pacific coast, notably Peru.

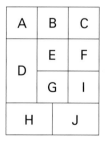

A	B	C
D	E	F
	G	I
H	J	

[A] Pied Avocet adult
[B] Pied Avocet juvenile
[C] Pied Avocet adult
[D] American Avocet adult breeding
[E] American Avocet first-winter non-breeding
[F] American Avocet
[G] American Avocet adult
[H] American Avocet adult non-breeding
[I] Andean Avocet adult
[J] Andean Avocet adult

Burhinidae

Stone-curlew
Burhinus oedicnemus L 41.90 cm

A widespread and partially migratory 'thick-knee', found in wide, open country across temperate Europe east to Lake Balkhash, south to Canary Is, N Africa and NW Arabia, and east to India and Burma.
PLUMAGE Adult male Whitish lores, cheeks and short curved supercilium above and around eye. Brown malar stripe from base of bill joining hindneck, with thin brown line below eye. Crown, ear coverts and upperparts greyish sandy-brown with broad dark brown feather centres. Diagnostic white lesser covert panel bordered by dark brown bar above and black bar below, both sharply defined. Greater covert panel with thin black shaft streaks, bordered black below. Chin and throat white. Neck, breast and flanks suffused brown strongly streaked dark brown. Rest of underparts whitish with yellowish-buff wash to undertail coverts. Bill shortish, black with yellow base including base of culmen. Legs dull yellowish-brown with swollen tibio-tarsal joints ('thick-knee'). Eye conspicuously large with bold yellow iris. **Adult female** Dark borders to lesser covert panel more diffuse. Upper part of grey greater covert panel somewhat obscured with buff feather edging. **Juvenile** Supercilium restricted to immediately above eye. Ear coverts mostly white. Coverts, lower scapulars and tertials fringed warm buff. Pattern of lesser coverts less well defined. **Flight** Often low with deliberate wingbeats. Pale mid-wing panel. White base to outer primaries and white base and tips to inner primaries.
CALL Series of clear, loud 'curl-ee' calls, mostly at night, often far carrying.
RACES Six are recognized: nominate *oedicnemus* (Europe east to Caspian Sea) and *harterti* (south and east of Caspian Sea), being the largest, the latter paler, greyer and less streaked; *distinctus* (W Canaries) and *insularum* (E Canaries), both smaller, the latter again paler and less streaked; *saharae* (Mediterranean Is, SE Europe, N Africa and N Arabia) smaller and sandier; *indicus* (India, Burma) smaller with less yellow on bill.
HABITAT AND BEHAVIOUR Favours extensive dry, open areas from farmland, heathland, short grassland to stony semi-deserts. Feeding action very plover-like. Mostly active at dusk and during the night. Fairly timid, frequently crouching for camouflage.
MOVEMENTS Northern races largely migratory moving south during September/October to winter in N and tropical Africa and east to Iraq and Arabia, returning to breeding-grounds from mid-March onwards. Southern races largely sedentary. Vagrant to Serengeti, Tanzania and Sierra Leone.

Senegal Thick-knee
Burhinus senegalensis L 34.90 cm

A wader of largely riverine habitat, patchily distributed in Africa from Senegal east to Nigeria and from Egypt south through Sudan to Ethiopia and NW Kenya.
PLUMAGE All plumages Extremely similar to Stone-curlew, differing mainly in slightly smaller size, bill structure and colour, pattern of wing covert panel, as well as habitat preference. White supercilium slightly broader extending farther around eye. Back and scapulars with thinner dark feather centres giving more finely streaked upperpart pattern. Distinct grey covert panel, upper part sometimes appearing paler, completely lacking white lesser covert bar. Bill longish, mostly black including culmen ridge, with narrow yellow base, less than Stone-curlew. Legs brighter yellow tinged brown. **In flight** Wings appear more rounded with more prominent white primary patches and bolder mid-wing panel.
RACES Two are recognized: nominate *senegalensis* (Senegal east to Nigeria) and *inornatus* (Egypt south to N Kenya) being darker in coloration.
CALL Less strident, more metallic than Stone-curlew. Song a repeated 'pi, pi, pi, pi, pi, pi', with accent on last few syllables.
HABITAT AND BEHAVIOUR prefers sandy areas adjacent water especially sandbanks and islands in rivers with vegetation for cover. Also cultivated areas adjacent towns and villages. Nests both singly and in loose colonies including roof tops of central Cairo. Forages along water's edge often standing motionless when disturbed. Fairly tame and approachable.
MOVEMENTS Sedentary in the Nile Valley, but in other parts makes short-distance movements corresponding to rains and subsequent water level changes. Regular wanderer to Lake Baringo, Kenya.

Water Dikkop
Burhinus vermiculatus L 39.35 cm

The southern counterpart to Senegal Thick-knee, present from Liberia east to Cameroon and most river systems in Africa south of the equator.
PLUMAGE Mainly differing from Senegal Thick-knee in upperpart coloration, covert pattern, bill structure and colour. Upperparts with dark brown barring in addition to dark feather centres giving distinct 'vermiculated' appearance, visible at close range. Grey covert panel bordered white above but lacking black lower border of Stone-curlew. Bill longish, fairly heavy, mainly black with greenish-yellow base. Legs dull yellow often tinged green or grey. **In flight** Broad rounded wings with feet projecting beyond tail. Pale mid-wing panel with conspicuous white patches to bases of outer and innermost primaries.
CALL A loud strident 'ti, ti, ti, ti, tee, tee, teee', fading away towards the end.
RACES Two are recognized: nominate *vermiculatus* (Zaire, S Uganda, Kenya to S Africa) and *büttikoferi* (Liberia east to Gabon and N Uganda) being darker brown in coloration.
HABITAT AND BEHAVIOUR Always found near water including river banks, mangrove swamps, and lake edges. Also coastal estuaries, creeks and occasionally beaches. More active and vocal by day than other thick-knees. Tame and approachable. Often reluctant to fly when disturbed, running away with head down. Gregarious, forming flocks up to 30 birds outside breeding season.
MOVEMENTS Mainly sedentary, only making local movements in response to fluctuating water levels.

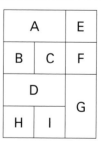

A Stone-curlew *saharae* adult
B Stone-curlew *oedicnemus* adult
C Stone-curlew *oedicnemus*
D Stone-curlew
E Senegal Thick-knee *inornatus* adult
F Senegal Thick-knee *inornatus*
G Water Dikkop *vermiculatus* adult
H Water Dikkop *vermiculatus* adult
I Water Dikkop *vermiculatus* adult

Burhinidae

Spotted Dikkop
Burhinus capensis L 43.20 cm
A large distinctly patterned African *burhinus* lacking a pale covert panel, breeding across a variety of arid country from Senegambia east to Somalia and S Arabia south to Namibia and S Africa.
PLUMAGE Adult Entire upperparts variable cinnamon-buff with bases of blackish-brown shaft streaks broadly barred and blackish subterminal spots fringed whitish, producing boldly patterned spotted and barred appearance. Head, neck and breast buffish-brown streaked blackish-brown. Narrow white areas above and below eye, chin and throat. Belly and flanks dirty white streaked dark brown. Undertail coverts warm buffish-cinnamon. Bill black with basal third dull yellow. Iris yellow. Legs bright yellow washed brownish on anterior surface. **Juvenile** Similar to adult but wing coverts with dark brown shafts and submarginal bars producing contrasting streaked not spotted pattern. **In flight** Blackish flight feathers with white subterminal flash across outermost primaries and white base to inner primaries. Wing coverts virtually concolorous with mantle and scapulars. Tail very graduated appearing strongly barred blackish-brown and white. Underwing with narrow blackish bar across greater primary and secondary coverts.
CALL Whistled 'ti-ti-ti-teeteetee-ti-ti-ti', rising to crescendo and then falling away, usually at night; when alarmed rapid 'pee-pee-pee'.
RACES Four are recognized: *capensis* (Keyna south to S Africa); *dodsoni* (coastal Somalia, SW Arabia) wamer coloured upperparts; *maculosus* (Senegal east to Somalia, N Kenya and Uganda) brightest tawny-buff upperparts; *damarensis* (Namibia, W Botswana, NW Cape Province) paler, greyer, markings less bold.
HABITAT AND BEHAVIOUR Frequents dry grassland, savannah, semi-arid deserts, rocky river beds, cultivated ground, even large suburban gardens, usually not associated with water. Mostly active at night and overcast days. When disturbed runs with head down before taking to rapid flight. Usually occurs singly or in pairs, forming loose groups up to 50 outside breeding season.
MOVEMENTS Sedentary, undergoing local movements in E Africa.

Double-striped Thick-knee
Burhinus bistriatus L 45.70 cm
A large, long-legged *burhinus*, inhabiting open grasslands of C America south to Venezuela and N Brazil and also Hispaniola.
PLUMAGE Adult Broad whitish supercilium curving downwards to sides of nape, bordered above by blackish lateral crown stripe. Pale brown forehead finely streaked dark brown shading to greyish-brown crown and nape finely edged pale brown. Upperparts dark greyish-brown broadly edged warm tawny-buff giving conspicuous boldly streaked appearance. Coverts slightly greyer edged tawny-buff. Chin white. Sides of face, neck and upper breast buffish-brown finely streaked dark brown shading to greyer-brown lower breast, sharply divided from rest of white underparts. Bill largish, heavy, black with dull yellowish base to cutting edge and lower mandible. Iris yellow. Legs long pale greenish-yellow. **Juvenile** Very similar to adult. Upperparts edged broader, brighter tawny-buff. Face, neck and breast washed warmer buff. **In flight** Black flight feathers with ill-defined greyish-white flash to outer primaries, bolder white flash to inner primaries. Uniform tawny-buff mantle, scapulars and inner wing coverts. Tail longish, graduated, central feathers tawny-buff, outer feathers paler brown with whitish subterminal band tipped black. Feet project beyond tail tip.
CALL Various strident chattering notes, mostly heard at night.
RACES Four are recognized: *bistriatus* (S Mexico south to Costa Rica) largest, dark with greyish breast; *pediacus* (N Columbia) pale with upperparts edged cinnamon-buff; *vocifer* (Venezuela east to N Brazil) dark with brownish breast; *dominicensis* (Hispaniola) small.
HABITAT AND BEHAVIOUR Favours open grassland, savannah and agricultural land. Largely crepuscular and nocturnal, when often seen along dirt roads. Occurs singly, in pairs and small scattered groups. Fairly tame. Expanding range with deforestation.
MOVEMENTS Largely sedentary. Vagrant Curacao, Texas.

Peruvian Thick-knee
Burhinus superciliaris L 40.65 cm
Smaller, greyer and shorter billed than Double-striped Thick-knee, with breeding range restricted to scrubby lowlands of W Peru south to N Chile.
PLUMAGE Adult Striking white supercilium from just anterior of eye curving downwards to side of nape, bordered above by blackish lateral crown stripe. Crown greyish finely streaked brown. Lores, cheeks and ear coverts whitish variably finely streaked grey. Upperparts pale greyish-brown, with median and greater coverts paler grey, bordered above by darker grey lesser coverts and lower scapulars. Chin white. Neck and upper breast mottled and finely streaked greyish-brown shading to greyish-white lower breast, flanks and upper belly. Lower belly white with undertail coverts mottled buffish-brown. Bill black, with yellowish base to cutting edge and lower mandible. Iris yellow. Legs longish, dull greenish-yellow. **Juvenile** Similar to adult. Upperparts with darker brown feather centres broadly fringed warm buff. Coverts with brownish submarginal lines fringed whitish-buff. Supercilia almost join across pale nape. Base of bill greenish-grey. Legs brownish-yellow. **In flight** Black flight feathers with white flashes across outer three primaries and bases of inner primaries contrasting with paler grey wing covert panel. Tail longish, graduated, central feathers greyish-brown, outer feathers with broad white subterminal band tipped black. Toes project slightly beyond tail tip.
CALL Chattering, scolding notes invariably heard at night.
HABITAT AND BEHAVIOUR Frequents arid grassland, wasteland and semi-desert in coastal lowlands extending to Andean foothills. Largely crepuscular and nocturnal.
MOVEMENTS Sedentary.

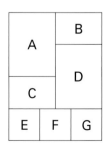

A Spotted Dikkop *capensis* adult
B Spotted Dikkop *capensis* adult
C Double-striped Thick-knee *vocifer* adult
D Double striped Thick-knee *vocifer* adult
E Peruvian Thick-knee adult
F Peruvian Thick-knee adult
G Peruvian Thick-knee

Burhinidae

Bush Thick-knee
Burhinus magnirostris **L 55.90 cm**
A large, conspicuous, long-legged *burhinus*, thinly distributed throughout dry, open woodland of Western, Northern and SE Australia.
PLUMAGE **Adult** Long whitish supercilium, forehead, lores, cheeks and throat. Small chestnut-brown patch at base of lower mandible. Chestnut-brown band in front of and beneath eye extending down sides of neck. Upperparts from crown to rump entirely grey with fine black shaft streaking. Underparts creamy-white heavily streaked blackish-brown across breast and flanks. Scapulars dark chestnut-brown forming obvious dark patches. Whitish median coverts streaked black bordered by brownish-grey greater coverts forming pale panel on closed wing. Tertials grey finely streaked black. Tail long, grey obscurely mottled and barred black, extending well beyond wing tips. Bill medium, tapering, black with slightly paler base to lower mandible. Eye large, yellow. Legs long, thin, greenish-yellow. **Juvenile** Extremely similar to adult. Generally paler above with brownish hindneck and back. Scapulars more mottled, with paler median covert panel. **In flight** Wingbeats noticeably stiff. Pale mid-wing covert panel and white patches across outer and innermost primaries contrast with blackish flight feathers. Legs trail noticeably beyond tail tip.
CALL Highly vocal at night. Variety of wailing sounds, commonest being mournful, drawn-out 'wer-loooo'.
HABITAT AND BEHAVIOUR Frequents open woodland especially eucalyptus, dry watercourses, coastal sandy scrub, and in the north orchards and plantations near human habitation. Performs dramatic courtship display. Inactive during the daytime. Reluctant to fly, using successful cryptic camouflage. Forms post-breeding flocks or 'clans' of up to 40 birds. Numbers declined significantly, especially in south-east of range due to urban development and farming.
MOVEMENTS Largely sedentary, although 'clans' outside the breeding season roam considerably in search of suitable feeding-grounds.

Great Thick-knee
Esacus recurvirostris **L 50.80 cm**
A large stone-curlew with a massive upturned bill, distributed in both riverine and coastal habitat across the Indian subcontinent east through Burma to Vietnam and Hainan Is.
PLUMAGE **Adult** Whitish forehead sometimes joining broad white patch through eye tapering towards hindneck, bordered by thin black line above and broad black patch below. White lores, cheeks and throat. Short black moustachial stripe at base of bill. Crown, mantle, scapulars and tertials dirty brownish-grey with fine dark feather centres. Lesser coverts blackish forming conspicuous narrow dark bar along closed wing, narrowly bordered white below. Rest of coverts pale grey. Neck and breast washed and mottled pale brownish-grey with rest of underparts dirty white. Bill massive, uptilted towards tip, largely black with sides of base of upper mandible and base of lower mandible bright yellow. Eye large with iris yellow. Legs dull yellowish tinged grey or green. **Juvenile** Very similar to adult with upperparts extensively fringed and spotted. **Flight** Strong and powerful with 'fingered' outer primaries, pattern rather bustard-like. Pale grey mid-wing panel. Blackish flight feathers contrasting with white flashes to outer primaries and double white patch to innermost primaries. Tail olive-brown. Toes project beyond tail tip.
CALL Given mostly at night, a series of wild, wailing notes 'kree-kree-kree-kre-kre-kre-kre'. Also a harsh alarm note.
HABITAT AND BEHAVIOUR Essentially riverain, especially rocky or shingly beds of larger rivers, but also coastal beaches, tidal estuaries and saltpans. Mainly crepuscular and nocturnal. Massive heavy bill adapted for feeding largely on crabs. Wary, often preferring to run away rather than fly. Usually in small groups, occasionally up to 20 birds.
MOVEMENTS Mainly resident, with some local seasonal movements, usually in response to feeding requirements.

Beach Thick-knee
Esacus magnirostris **L 55.90 cm**
Differing from Great Thick-knee in bill shape, head pattern and strictly coastal habitat, scarce but distributed throughout Malaysia, Philippines and Indonesia east to New Guinea, Solomon Is and N Australia.
IDENTIFICATION **Adult** Blackish forehead shading to olive-brown crown, nape, hindneck, mantle and back, with black mask from base of bill through eye curving down to sides of nape completely enclosing curving white supercilium. White chin and throat. Short black moustachial stripe at base of bill. Broad blackish lesser covert bar bordered white below. Rest of coverts soft pale grey. White carpal patch. Foreneck and upper breast warm buff finely streaked dark brown. Lower breast washed greyish shading to off-white belly. Vent and undertail coverts creamy-buff. Bill massive, straight, black, with yellow sides to base of upper mandible and yellow spot to extreme base of lower mandible. Large eye, iris yellow. Legs longish, dull yellowish-green. **Juvenile** Very similar to adult. Upperparts fringed buff. Lesser coverts duller brown fringed buff. Flight slow, heavy with outer primaries fingered. Brilliant white flash across black outer primaries. Inner primaries and primary coverts white. Pale greyish-white secondaries, greater and median coverts contrasting with dark olive-brown marginal and lesser coverts, latter bordered white. Tail olive-grey, outer feathers with alternating subterminal dull brown and whitish bars. Toes project beyond tail tip.
CALL Nuptial call harsh, mournful 'wee-loo'; alarm note subdued 'peet-peet'.
HABITAT Found on remote and undisturbed sandy beaches, tidal mudflats, coral reefs and mangroves. Both diurnal and nocturnal, foraging for small crabs with powerful bill, stalking prey in slow, deliberate heron-like manner. Occurs singly, in pairs and small groups.
MOVEMENTS Sedentary. Vagrant Victoria.

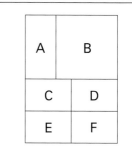

A	B
C	D
E	F

Ⓐ Bush Thick-knee adult
Ⓑ B Bush Thick-knee
Ⓒ C Great Thick-knee adult
Ⓓ D Great Thick-knee adult
Ⓔ E Beach Thick-knee adult
Ⓕ F Beach Thick-knee adult

Glareolidae

Egyptian Courser
Pluvianus aegyptius L 19.70 cm
Readily identifiable since unlike any other wader, with a unique incubation process and largely confined to sandy river beds across tropical Africa.
PLUMAGE Adult Clear white supercilium starting from base of bill and extending around and meeting at back of nape. Black mask through eye joining black hindneck, crown, mantle and back. Bluish-grey scapulars, coverts and tertials, with greater coverts broadly tipped white. Chin and throat white. Underparts rich peachy-buff, paler adjacent both sides of narrow black breast band. Bill black, slightly paler at base, sharply pointed. Legs shortish, bluish-grey. **Juvenile** Similar to adult, but body feathers of upperparts admixed with brown. Lesser and median coverts rusty-brown. **Flight** Fast and low on strikingly pied, broad-based wings. White flight feathers contrast with black diagonal bar towards base. Primaries tipped black. Tail bluish-grey broadly tipped white with black subterminal band on outer feathers.
CALL Commonest note a loud 'chersk' rapidly repeated.
HABITAT AND BEHAVIOUR Usually confined to middle stretches of large rivers, especially those with sand, silt or gravel bars. Method of incubation unique whereby eggs kept cool buried beneath the sand, the parent periodically wetting the sand with water carried in belly feathers. Chicks also buried in sand when danger threatens. Strongly territorial, flashing wings to intruders. Plover-like gait. Very tame and approachable. Ironically, has not bred in Egypt since early twentieth century. Outside the breeding season may occasionally frequent edges of lakes and ponds, when flocks of up to 60 birds recorded.
MOVEMENTS Largely sedentary, making irregular movements in response to water-level changes. Also undergoes longer seasonal movements. Vagrant to Jordan, Libya and Canary Is.

Cream-coloured Courser
Cursorius cursor L 22.85 cm
The most widespread and most migratory of coursers, breeding in arid regions of Cape Verde and Canary Is, N Africa east to Saudi Arabia, Iran, Afghanistan and S Russia.
PLUMAGE Adult Brilliant white supercilium and black eye-stripe starting above eye curving down and meeting at back of nape. Fore-crown dark sandy-brown shading to bluish-grey rear crown bordered by black triangular patch. Hindneck and entire upperparts sandy-

buff. Lores, cheeks and chin sandy-cream shading to pale sandy breast and flanks. Belly and vent pale cream. Bill longish, decurved, black with pale horn base. Legs ivory. **Juvenile** Indistinct creamy supercilium and brownish eye-line. Crown and upperparts buffish-brown with irregular darker brown subterminal lines. Underparts pale creamy-buff with obscure brownish spotting to breast. Base of bill more yellowish-brown. **In flight** Long pointed wings and jerky wingbeats. Black primaries contrast with sandy mantle and innerwing. Narrow white trailing edge to secondaries. Rump and tail sandy, latter edged white. Feet project beyond tail tip. Underwing black except for narrow white trailing edge to secondaries and brown leading lesser coverts.
CALL Rather silent. Occasionally a sharp, repeated 'wit-krit' or croaking 'praak'.
RACES Three are recognized: *cursor* (Morocco east to SW Iran, Socotra); *exsul* (Cape Verde Is) smaller, sandier; *bogolubovi* (N Iran to S Russia) more pinkish.
HABITAT AND BEHAVIOUR Frequents sandy or stony plains, arid scrub, semi-desert and desert, but also edges of cultivation. Typical courser gait running fast and stopping to peck, often bobbing head or tail. Quite approachable. When disturbed prefers to run short distances before taking flight. Occurs in loose flocks up to 30 birds.
MOVEMENTS Partial migrant. *Cursor* mostly migratory, moving south from mid-September across Sahara to winter in Sahel zone south to Senegambia, Mali, Chad and Sudan. Return passage from mid-March. *Bogolubovi* partially migratory wintering in S Iran and NW India. *Exsul* is resident. Post-breeding flocks sometimes wander north to Mediterranean coasts, giving rise to vagrant records in most European countries including Britain, Norway and Finland.

Burchell's Courser
Cursorius rufus L 20.95 cm
Intermediate in size, with racial variations similar to both Temminck's and Cream-coloured Coursers, found in semi-arid country in S and SW Africa, Kenya and Somalia.
PLUMAGE Adult White supercilium and black eye-stripe both curving backwards from above eye meeting at back of nape. Upperpart coloration variable. Underparts show clear colour separation from white rear belly, vent and undertail coverts. Bill longish, decurved, blackish with paler horn base. Legs ivory. **Juvenile** Crown and upperparts boldly notched and barred dark brown and buff. Wing coverts fringed buff.

Breast mottled darker brown.
CALL Flight note a grunting 'chuk, chuk'.
RACES Three are recognized. Nominate *rufus* (S and SW Africa) resembles Temminck's Courser but larger. Chestnut forecrown and sides of face. Dark sandy-brown upperparts. Underparts greyish-brown shading to deep chestnut-brown bar on lower breast. Shorter bill and legs. **In flight** broad white secondary panel contrasts with black outer wing. Tail darkish grey fringed white. Underwing shows broad white secondaries and brownish underwing coverts and axillaries contrasting with black outer wing; *littoralis* (Kenya, S Somalia) resembles Cream-coloured Courser but smaller. Paler sandy-brown above and below lacking dark lower belly. **In flight** thin white trailing edge to greyish-brown secondaries. Tail greyish-brown fringed white. Underwing shows secondaries tipped white and greyish underwing coverts and axillaries contrasting with black outer wing; *somalensis* (N Somalia) is palest of all, lacking dark belly patch. Underwing coverts and axillaries pale sandy-brown.
HABITAT AND BEHAVIOUR Favours open ground including short grassland, sandy or gravelly plains, saltpan, semi- and true desert. Forages similar to other coursers, using nasal salt gland to excrete sodium so helping water retention. When alarmed bobs head and tail and stands erect, often running away as opposed to flying.
MOVEMENTS Although resident, highly nomadic undergoing local movements.

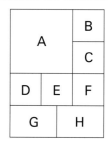

A	B
	C
D	E	F
G	H

A Egyptian Courser adult
B Egyptian Courser adult
C Egyptian Courser
D Cream-coloured Courser *cursor* adult
E Cream-coloured Courser *cursor* juvenile
F Cream-coloured Courser *cursor* adult
G Burchell's Courser *littoralis* adult
H Burchell's Courser *littoralis* adult

Glareolidae

Indian Courser
Cursorius coromandelicus L 22.85 cm

The only *cursorius* species with a white uppertail, common but patchily distributed across the entire Indian subcontinent, W Pakistan and Sri Lanka.

PLUMAGE Adult Crown rich chestnut with small black patch at rear. Brilliant white supercilium starting in front of eye curving down and meeting on nape. Black loral line continuing as bold black eyestripe also joining on nape. Upperparts uniform greyish-brown. Sides of face and chin creamy-white. Underparts rich cinnamon, gradually shading to chestnut on lower breast. Black belly patch. White vent and undertail coverts. Legs long, ivory. Bill black and clearly decurved. **Juvenile** Similar to adult but black lores and eyestripe lacking. Upperparts dull buff irregularly barred and blotched brown and cream. Wing coverts greyish-brown fringed buff. Underparts dull rufous blotched brown with white belly. **Flight** Silhouette reminiscent of pratincole. Black primaries and outer secondaries contrast with uniform grey-brown mantle and innerwing. Thin white trailing edge to secondaries. Upperparts coverts white. Tail greyish-brown with blackish subterminal bar broadly tipped and edged white. Underwing dark with conspicuous white trailing edge.

CALL Generally silent. Occasional alarm or contact note a low, clucking 'gwut'.

HABITAT AND BEHAVIOUR Found in low open country, dry stony areas, waste land with scattered shrubs, ploughed fields and village grazing grounds. Whilst feeding runs swiftly in short spurts. Occurs in pairs or scattered parties, often well camouflaged when remaining still.

MOVEMENTS Largely resident, but partly nomadic and local migrations undertaken. Not recorded outside Indian subcontinent.

Temminck's Courser
Cursorius temminckii L 20.30 cm

The smallest courser, resident and endemic to the short grasslands of mainly sub-Saharan Africa.

PLUMAGE Adult Differs from Indian Courser mainly in smaller size, pale lores and lack of white uppertail coverts. Forehead pale cinnamon shading into rich chestnut crown with small black patch at rear. Brilliant white supercilium and black eye-stripe starting above eye curving down and meeting on nape. Upperparts uniform greyish-brown. Chin and throat whitish shading into brownish upper breast and deep chestnut lower breast. Small black belly patch. Vent and undertail coverts white. Bill clearly decurved, greyish-black with pale horn base to lower mandible. Legs long, white tinged pale grey. **Juvenile** Similar to adult with buffish supercilium and dark brown eye-stripe. Crown streaked blackish. Upperparts irregularly notched and barred dark brown and buff, tipped white. Wing coverts fringed pale buff. Underparts paler with smaller poorly defined belly patch. **In flight** Black primaries and secondaries generally lacking white trailing edge readily distinguishable from Burchell's Courser, contrasting with uniform mantle and inner wing.

CALL Normally quiet. Flight note a sharp metallic 'err-err-err'.

RACES Two are recognized: nominate *temminckii* (most of range) and *damarensis* (Namibia) being paler. Rump and central tail greyish-brown, outertail white, with dark subterminal spots to rest of tail.

HABITAT AND BEHAVIOUR Frequents short grassland, semi-arid bush savannah, burnt grassland, ploughed fields and airfields. Feeds in typical courser manner alternately running and pecking at ground. Often stands very upright. Runs and flies fast. Occurs in pairs or flocks up to 20 birds.

MOVEMENTS Largely resident but migratory in extreme south of S Africa where present February to August. Highly nomadic in searching for suitable habitat.

Two-banded Courser
Rhinoptilus africanus L 21.60 cm

A small courser of dry, open habitat with three disjunct breeding populations across Ethiopia and N Somalia, S Kenya and C Tanzania, and S Africa.

PLUMAGE Adult Long curving buffish supercilium separates thin black loral line extending behind eye and greyish-brown crown fringed buff. Upperparts variable sandy to earth-brown dependent on local soil coloration, with dark subterminal bands broadly fringed pale, producing distinct scaly appearance. Buffish face, throat, neck, upper breast and whitish chin finely streaked blackish-brown. Underparts variable sandy-buff with two complete broad black breast bands continuing around base of hindneck. Bill short, slightly decurved, black. Legs pale greyish-white. **Juvenile** Similar to adult, initially lacking breast bands. Upperparts sandy-buff with thin dark subterminal bands narrowly fringed white. **In flight** Pale chestnut trailing edge to secondaries and inner primaries contrast with blackish primaries and primary coverts and narrow white band across uppertail coverts. Centre tail blackish broadly edged white, tipped sandy-buff.

CALL contact note plaintive 'peeu-weee'; alarm note sharp 'kikikikik'. Seldom calls in flight.

RACES Eight are recognized: *raffertyi* (Ethiopia); *hartingi* (Somalia); *gracilis* (C Keyna, N Tanzania); *illustris* (C Tanzania); *bisignatus* (Angola); *sharpei* (Namibia); *africanus* (S Namibia, W Cape Province); *granti* (C Cape Province, Transvaal). Northern populations medium sized, sandy above, pale buff beneath; central populations smallest, grey above, whitish below; southern populations largest, darker earth-brown above, deep buffish-brown beneath.

HABITAT AND BEHAVIOUR Frequents variety of flat, arid, stony and sandy regions with sparse scattering of vegetation. Usually occurs singly or up to three, largely nocturnal, feeding at night not by digging but running and jabbing at insects with bill. Feather coloration forms effective camouflage with local soil substrate. When alarmed bobs head and depresses tail, often preferring to run away rather than fly when approached.

MOVEMENTS Resident, occasionally undertaking local nomadic movements when undergrowth becomes too dense following rains.

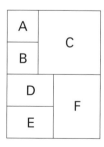

A Indian Courser adult
B Temminck's Courser *temmincki* adult
C Temminck's Courser *temmincki* adult
D Temminck's Courser *temmincki* adult
E Two-banded Courser adult
F Two-banded Courser adult

Glareolidae

Heuglin's Courser
Rhinoptilus cinctus L 26.65 cm
A large courser of open woodlands, breeding across a narrow strip of E Africa from N Somalia and S Ethiopia south to S Zambia and west to S Angola, N Namibia and northern S Africa.
PLUMAGE **Adult** Long supercilia, tawny-buff in front of eye becoming whitish behind eye meeting at nape enclosing dark greyish-brown crown with tawny-buff stripe through central forehead and forecrown. Indistinct thin dark line through lores and upper edge of ear coverts, latter warm buff faintly streaked dark brown. Thin brown streaked moustachial stripe. Upperparts including scapulars, coverts and tertials earth-brown broadly fringed warm buff giving scaly appearance. Sides of neck and underparts largely white with three breast bands. Narrow chestnut 'V' across throat and second narrow chestnut band across lower breast. Upper breast band buffish-brown coarsely streaked blackish-brown, partially bordered above at sides and completely bordered below by narrow blackish bands. Bill decurved, distal half black, basal half dull yellow. Legs dull greyish-yellow. **Juvenile** Similar to adult, initially breast bands duller buffish-brown, lower band faint or absent. Upperparts with broad submarginal lines fringed whitish-buff. **In flight** Primaries and secondaries brownish-black, latter fringed buff contrasting with paler mantle, scapulars and inner wing coverts. White band across uppertail coverts. Centre of tail greyish-brown tipped whitish, outer tail banded black and white. Toes project beyond tail tip.
CALL Mainly at night. Contact note 'chuik', alarm note 'kuee'. Song accelerated 'wikka-wikka wikka wikka' fading away towards end.
RACES Two are recognized: *cinctus* (most of range) smaller, upperparts fringed duller olive-buff; *seebohmi* (W Zimbabwe, S Angola, N Namibia and northern S Africa) chestnut bands washed pinkish-cinnamon.
HABITAT AND BEHAVIOUR Inhabits dry, open woodlands, thorn scrub and thorn savannah. Occurs singly, pairs or small groups up to six. Mostly nocturnal when frequently seen on dirt roads, resting in shade during daytime. When disturbed often freezes using excellent camouflage, usually preferring to run away rather than fly.
MOVEMENTS Largely sedentary, migratory in southern part of range. Local movements undertaken in C and E Africa.

Violet-tipped Courser
Rhinoptilus chalcopterus L 27.30 cm
The largest courser, with distinctive face pattern, but unique primary iridescence not visible in the field, found in scrub and open woodland across tropical and southern Africa.
PLUMAGE **Adult** Creamy-buff forehead and supercilium, narrowing behind eye. Dark brown crown mottled creamy-buff with short creamy central crown stripe to mid-crown. Lores, cheeks and ear coverts blackish-brown, the last with white patch narrowly bordered by chestnut-brown stripe above. Hindneck and entire upperparts earth brown. Chin and throat whitish with broad brown malar stripe sometimes joining in centre. Whitish area across breast separates black lower breast band and paler brown upper breast. Rest of underparts creamy-white, flanks washed warm buff. Bill black, dull red base to lower mandible. Narrow purplish-red eye-ring. Legs dull purplish-red. **Juvenile** Similarly patterned. Upperparts fringed buffish-brown. Malar stripe less extensive, black breast band narrower. **In flight** Primaries and secondaries black with all but outermost primaries tipped metallic violet narrowly bordered green proximally, contrasting with brown mantle and inner wing. Outer greater coverts narrowly tipped white. White uppertail covert patch to darker brown tail fringed white. Juvenile shows more pointed primaries, broader white tips to greater coverts forming wing bar and lacks white fringe to tail.
CALL Piping thick-knee type jee-kuu-ee; flight note plaintive gror-raang.
HABITAT AND BEHAVIOUR Frequents thorn scrub, savannah, open woodland and recently burnt areas. Occurs singly or small groups. Nocturnal, resting by standing up in shade during daytime. Mostly seen on roads at night. When flushed tends to fly short distance only.
MOVEMENTS Both resident and partial migrant. Non-breeding visitor to extreme south part of range, breeding visitor to north of region, movements sometimes correlated with rains.

Jerdon's Courser
Rhinoptilus bitorquatus L 26.65 cm
A large distinctive courser formerly restricted to hillsides in Andhra Pradesh, SE India, thought to be extinct since 1900, but rediscovered in 1986.
PLUMAGE **Adult** Long creamy supercilia from bill to nape, becoming whitish behind eye, enclosing dark brown crown with indistinct thin creamy central crown stripe. Sides of face and ear coverts brown flecked whitish. Hindneck and entire upperparts greyish-brown with narrow whitish-buff fringes to mantle, scapulars, coverts and tertials. Creamy-white chin and foreneck enclose pale chestnut-red throat. Brown upper breast narrowly bordered darker brown below separated from dark brown lower breast line by narrow white band. Lower breast suffused pale greyish-brown shading to creamy-white belly, vent and undertail coverts. Bill decurved, black with pale yellow base. Legs fleshy-white. **Juvenile** Undescribed. **In flight** Appears rounded winged. Black flight feathers with diagnostic white subterminal flashes across outer primaries contrast with white bases to secondaries, white outer greater coverts and uniform greyish-brown mantle and inner wing. White uppertail coverts to blackish tail narrowly tipped white. Underwing coverts and axillaries creamy-white.
CALL Described as plaintive cry.
HABITAT AND BEHAVIOUR Rediscovered in January 1986 in Penner Valley. Inhabits rocky undulating ground interspersed with thin scrub. Used to occur in small parties, occasionally calling.
MOVEMENTS Presumed to be sedentary.

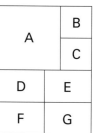

Glareolidae

Collared Pratincole
Glareola pratincola **L 24.75 cm**

Highly aerial, graceful and tern-like, breeding patchily on bare open sites across S Europe, east to Central Asia, NW India, SW Arabia and Africa.

PLUMAGE Adult breeding Black ring encircles creamy chin, throat and upper foreneck. Blackish lores with buffy lower eye-ring. Crown and entire upperparts uniform greyish-brown. Secondaries and primaries darker brown, the latter falling roughly level with tail tip. Breast olive-brown, with rest of underparts white. Bill short, decurved, black with red base extending across to nostrils. Legs brownish-black. **Adult non-breeding** Thin blackish streaks encircle throat and neck. Upperparts extensively fringed buff. Breast mottled grey-brown. **Juvenile** Crown and hindneck streaked darker. Upperparts with dark subterminal bars broadly fringed buff giving 'scaly' appearance. Wing tips project beyond shallow forked tail. Lack of distinct neck ring. Underparts whiter with breast streaked and mottled black. Red base to bill paler, less extensive. **In flight** Extremely buoyant. Uniform grey-brown mantle and innerwing contrast with darker outerwing. White shaft to outermost primary. Thin white trailing edge to secondaries subject to wear, so not always apparent. Deep chestnut underwing coverts and axillaries, often appearing darker. Lower rump and uppertail coverts white. Deeply forked blackish tail edged white.

CALL Variety of shrill, chattering, tern-like calls including 'kikki-kirrik' or 'trrrt'.

RACES Three are recognized: *pratincola* (Palearctic, NW India) largest; *erlangeri* (N Kenya, S Somalia) smallest; *fuelleborni* (rest of Africa) intermediate in size. African races darker with duller underwing coverts.

HABITAT AND BEHAVIOUR Frequents flat bare open areas, especially sun-baked mud bordering lagoons, river deltas and wetlands. Noisy, highly gregarious, sometimes hawking for insects in flocks of several thousands. During migration may appear at reservoirs or on the coast.

MOVEMENTS Nominate race highly migratory. May form large flocks prior to departure from late August to winter along south edge of Sahara from Senegal east to Ethiopia. Breeding-grounds reoccupied from late April. Vagrant Sri Lanka. African races largely resident, undergoing erratic seasonal movements associated with fluctuating water levels.

Oriental Pratincole
Glareola maldivarum **L 23.50 cm**

The eastern counterpart to Common Pratincole, found in similar habitat in NE Mongolia and S Manchuria south to India, Burma, Thailand and S China.

PLUMAGE Adult breeding Very similar to Common Pratincole. Upperparts uniform dark greyish-brown. Tail short, falling roughly halfway between tips of tertials and tail tip. Lower breast washed warmer orangey-buff. Smaller red area at base of bill not extending across to nostrils. **Adult non-breeding** Dirty creamy throat and neck patch encircled by bold blackish streaking. Underparts generally duller. Red at base of bill duller and more restricted. **Juvenile** Upperparts with dark subterminal lines fringed buff giving 'scaly' effect. **In flight** Uniform dark greyish-brown mantle, coverts and flight feathers, lacking white trailing edge to secondaries, except for very narrow buffish tips in juvenile, very difficult to see. Outer primary shaft dusky-grey. Tail fork very shallow with narrow black terminal band. Underwing coverts and axillaries chestnut, often appearing darker.

CALL Commonest calls include an abrupt 'chik' or 'kyik' similar to Common Pratincole, and a mellow 'to-wheet'.

HABITAT AND BEHAVIOUR Breeds on sun-baked plains adjacent large rivers, mudflats and marshes, rice stubble, ploughed fields and open grazing land. Gregarious at all seasons, often forming large flocks. Largely crepuscular, with feeding behaviour similar to Collared Pratincole.

MOVEMENTS Partial migrant. Resident, summer visitor and nomadic in India. In SE Asia mostly migratory, wintering in Indonesia, New Guinea and NW Australia, where large numbers occur November–April. Highly nomadic especially after heavy rains causing huge increase in insect population. Irregular S Australia. Vagrant New Zealand, Seychelles, Mauritius and north to Aleutian Is and England (three records to date).

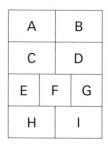

A Collared Pratincole *pratincola* adult breeding
B Collared Pratincole adult non-breeding
C Collared Pratincole *pratincola* first-winter non-breeding
D Collared Pratincole *pratincola* adult
E Collared Pratincole *pratincola* juvenile
F Oriental Pratincole adult breeding
G Oriental pratincole adult non-breeding
H Oriental Pratincole adult
I Oriental Pratincole adult

Glareolidae

Black-winged Pratincole
Glareola nordmanni. **L 23.50 cm**
Differing from Collared Pratincole largely in flight pattern, with a breeding range restricted to the steppes of SE Europe and S Russia.
PLUMAGE Adult breeding At rest extremely similar to Collared Pratincole, with tail tip falling short of wing tips. Larger black loral area extending from eye to over base of bill. Red area at base of bill not extending onto nostrils. **Adult non-breeding** Upperparts somewhat darker than Common Pratincole. **Juvenile** Very similar to Collared Pratincole, appearing very 'scaly' with overall darker upperparts. **In flight** Slightly broader winged with darker uniform greyish-brown mantle and innerwing showing little contrast with outer wing. Indistinct white shaft to outer primary. Secondaries lack white trailing edge, except for narrow buffish tips in juvenile, but difficult to see in the field. Tail less deeply forked with narrower black terminal band. Wholly black underwing.
CALL Variety of calls, lower pitched than Collared Pratincole. Flight call and at colonies 'kirlik-kirlik'; alarm call 'pwik-kik-kik'.
HABITAT AND BEHAVIOUR Confined to open steppes, often with tall vegetation including grassy meadows and cultivated fields, but always near water. Highly gregarious at all seasons. Active dawn and dusk, hawking after insects especially locust swarms. Readily flocks with Collared Pratincole and has interbred.
MOVEMENTS Highly migratory. Large post-breeding flocks form towards end of June, departing south during August and September. Most enter Africa from Cyprus and Saudi Arabia following Nile in high continuous flight, with massive flocks recorded, e.g., 10,000 Zambia. Winters NE Namibia, Botswana and south to Cape Province, S Africa. Occasionally winters in Chad, Sudan and Ethiopia. Vagrant through Europe west to Norway, Britain and Iceland.

Australian Pratincole
Stiltia isabella **L 22.85 cm**
A distinctive long-legged and long-winged pratincole, breeding on the blacksoil plains of the Australian interior, notably in SW Queensland and NW New South Wales.
PLUMAGE Adult breeding Head and upperparts warm sandy-brown. Long black primaries extending far beyond tail tip. Tip of tail falling roughly level with tertial tips. Indistinct blackish lores. Whitish chin and throat shading to sandy-buff upper breast and deep chestnut patches to lower breast and belly, often appearing black at

distance. Vent and undertail coverts white. Bill red with sharply defined black tip. Legs long, brownish-grey. **Adult non-breeding** Upperparts dark brown lacking sandy tones. Lores paler, with indistinct blackish streaking surrounding throat and sides of neck. Brown lower breast patches smaller, barely meeting in centre. Bill blackish with base dull red. **Juvenile** Underparts fringed sandy-buff. Bill virtually all black. **In flight** Appears very long winged, due to elongated outer primary, lacking in juvenile. Sandy-brown mantle, innerwing and inner primaries contrasting with blackish outer primaries. White shaft to outer primary. Squarish white tail with broad black subterminal bar to all but outer feathers. Legs project beyond tail tip. Black underwing coverts, axillaries and outer primaries contrast with pale grey inner primaries and secondaries.
CALL Flight note a sweet whistle 'weeteet' and a plaintive 'tuwhee', often far carrying.
HABITAT AND BEHAVIOUR Nests on dry, arid blacksoil plains in small loose colonies, usually near water. Readily feeds on the ground, the long legs adapted for swiftly running to catch insects. Frequently bobs head in plover-like manner. Post-breeding flocks readily mix with Oriental Pratincoles. Winters on grassy and flooded plains, mudflats and open beaches in N Australia.
MOVEMENTS Migratory, especially in southern part of breeding range. Unusually for a wader, moves north after breeding to winter across N Australia, Java, Borneo, Sulawesi and New Guinea. Movements within Australia related to level of rainfall.

A	B
C	D
E	F
G	H

A Black-winged Pratincole adult breeding
B Black-winged Pratincole adult breeding
C Black-winged Pratincole adult non-breeding
D Black-winged Pratincole juvenile
E Black-winged Pratincole
F Australian Pratincole adult breeding
G Australian Pratincole adult breeding
H Australian Pratincole juvenile

Glareolidae

Madagascar Pratincole
Glareola ocularis L 24.10 cm
A largish migratory pratincole with breeding confined to river beds of N Madagascar.
PLUMAGE **Adult** Forehead and crown very dark chocolate-brown shading to olive-brown nape, hindneck and entire upperparts. Wings extending well beyond tail tip. Lores and ear coverts blackish contrasting with narrow white facial stripe below and behind eye. Chin, throat, foreneck and breast earth-brown. Upper belly rich chestnut-red. Lower belly, vent and undertail coverts white. Bill sturdy, black with bright red base. Legs short, dark grey. **Juvenile** Mantle edged rufous. Paler chin with warm buff facial stripe. Breast streaked rufous-buff. **In flight** Uniform dark upperparts contrast with white uppertail coverts and shallow forked tail narrowly edged white. Underwing coverts and axillaries chestnut-red.
CALL Harsh tern-like 'wick-wick-wick' or 'kitt-kitt'.
HABITAT AND BEHAVIOUR Nests on fast-flowing rocky rivers. Highly gregarious, hawking at night for insects with tern-like flight, and on overcast days. Outside breeding season inhabits sand dunes, mud flats and edges of lakes and rivers near coast, sometimes in huge flocks, also feeds over woodland.
MOVEMENTS Migratory, moving to E African coast March–September from S Somalia south to Mozambique and also Comoro Is. Occasionally inland to Lake Victoria. Vagrant Ethiopia, Mauritius and Réunion.

Rock Pratincole
Glareola nuchalis L 18.40 cm
A small pratincole favouring fast-flowing rocky rivers. Breeds patchily across WC and S Africa from Sierra Leone east to W Kenya, south to Gabon, Tanzania and Mozambique.
PLUMAGE **Adult** Forehead, crown and hindneck dark sooty-brown. Lores and chin blackish. Narrow white collar from below eye extending backwards onto nape. Upperparts sooty-brown. Foreneck, breast and upper belly sooty-brown shading paler on lower belly. Vent and undertail coverts white. Bill bright red with tip and culmen black. Legs bright coral-red. **Juvenile** Dark greyish-brown lacking white collar. Upperparts and breast spotted warm buff. Duller red bill. Legs orangey-red. **In flight** Dark upperparts contrast with white uppertail coverts and white base and sides to shallow forked tail.
CALL Alarm note faint 'kip, kip, kip'; during breeding season also long musical trill.
RACES Two: *nuchalis* (Gabon east to W Kenya and Mozambique); *liberiae* (Sierra Leone to W Cameroon) hindneck chestnut, slightly shorter, more rounded wings.
HABITAT AND BEHAVIOUR Characteristically found on rivers and lakes with exposed

rocks, sometimes on muddy lagoon-edges or sandy beaches. At low water sits on rocks, during high water perches on branches. Highly gregarious. Largely crepuscular, hawks for insects, and active before or after rain on cloudy days. Also chases insects around streetlamps in towns. During courtship displays nuchal collar.
MOVEMENTS Both sedentary and migrant to parts of range. Undergoes seasonal movements in relation to changes in water levels. W African populations undertake more extensive north-south migrations.

Grey Pratincole
Glareola cinerea L 19.05 cm
A small, strikingly patterned pratincole preferring sandy rivers, breeding discontinuously across W and C Africa from Mali and Niger east to Central African Republic south to NW Angola and NE Zaire.
PLUMAGE **Adult** Forehead and crown pale grey. Long narrow white supercilium from bill behind eye bordered below by black loral line continuing around ear coverts and down sides of neck. Broad pale chestnut hindneck extending onto sides of neck. Mantle and rest of upperparts pale grey. Black folded wings project well beyond tail. Face, chin, throat and rest of underparts white with breast washed pale chestnut-buff. Iris brown. Base of bill deep red, distal half black. Legs orange-red. **Juvenile** Black loral line absent and supercilium pale sandy-buff. Upperparts fringed buff. Breast washed pale cinnamon-buff. **In flight** Striking wing pattern. Greater coverts and secondaries white, latter broadly edged black, contrasting with black primary coverts and primaries and white panel across central primaries. Rump, uppertail coverts and tail white, latter short, shallowly forked with black subterminal band.
CALL Contact note liquid 'prruup'; alarm note harsh 'tic-tic-tic'; also trilling song during breeding season.
RACES Two are recognized: *cinerea* (most of range); *colorata* (Niger River) latter with broader, paler hindneck and deeper chestnut breast coloration.
HABITAT AND BEHAVIOUR Favours larger, slow-flowing rivers and lakes edged by sand bars, where sits and is difficult to see. Gregarious. Feeds mostly during evening hawking for insects low over rivers, and near woodland and open country.
MOVEMENTS Post-breeding movements largely dictated by rains when tends to move towards estuaries and Lake Chad.

Little Pratincole
Glareola lactea L 17.80 cm
A very small pratincole, favouring large waterways up to 1500 m across the sub-continent and Myanmar south to Thailand.

PLUMAGE **Adult breeding** Forecrown dark brownish-grey shading to paler grey hindcrown and greyish-brown nape. Black lores from gape to eye. Ear coverts pale buffish-grey. Upperparts uniform warm brownish-grey. Black primary tips extending well beyond white-tipped tail. Throat warm pinkish-buff, breast buffish-grey. Rest of underparts white. Bill black with reddish patch to base. Legs short, greyish-black. **Adult non-breeding** Pale lores. Forecrown pale brownish-grey. Throat variably streaked pale brown. **Juvenile** Similar to non-breeding adult. Crown spotted buff. Upperparts with brownish subterminal band fringed buff. Whitish chin. Pale brownish spots encircle throat and upper breast. **In flight** Blackish primaries and trailing edge to secondaries contrast with broad white panel across bases of secondaries and grey mantle and inner wing. Rump, uppertail coverts and tail white, latter slightly forked with triangular black subterminal band.
CALL Short 'tuk, tuk,tuk'; when disturbed, agitated 'tiririt, tiririt'.
HABITAT AND BEHAVIOUR Breeds on larger placid rivers and streams with exposed sand or shingle bars, also large 'jheels' and coastal swamps. Largely crepuscular, hawking with angular flight after insects, often in large flocks or 'swarms'. On the ground chases insects in characteristic plover-like manner. Outside breeding season also found on coastal lagoons and estuaries.
MOVEMENTS Locally migratory, moving downstream August–April. Local movements also dictated by changing water levels. Vagrant Arabian Gulf, Oman.

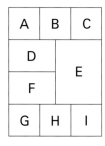

A	B	C
D		E
F		
G	H	I

A Madagascar Pratincole adult
B Madagascar Pratincole adult
C Madagascar Pratincole adult
D Rock Pratincole
E Rock Pratincole *nuchalis* adult
F Grey Pratincole *cinerea* adult
G Grey Pratincole *cinerea* adult
H Little Pratincole adult
I Little Pratincole adult

Charadriidae

Northern Lapwing
Vanellus vanellus L 29.20 cm
A widespread *vanellus*, breeding on grassland across a broad climatic range from British Isles east through Eurasia to S Ussuriland, and south to NW Morocco and east to Iran and Mongolia.
PLUMAGE Adult breeding male Forehead, crown and long wispy crest black. Sides of face white with blackish mask anterior to eye and through cheeks, shading to pale grey hindneck. Upperparts glossy green with purplish sheen to scapulars. Underparts white except for black chin and throat merging into black breast band. Orangey-brown undertail coverts. Bill short, black. Legs shortish, dull red. **Adult breeding female** Shorter crest. Mottled black and white face, chin and throat. **Adult non-breeding** Head mottled black and warm buff with clear white chin and throat. Scapulars, median and greater coverts fringed buff. Black breast band admixed with white. **Juvenile** Distinctly shorter crest with mantle, scapulars and coverts neatly fringed buff. **In flight** Distinctive sluggish, jerky wingbeats with bulging wing tips to adults, especially males. Uniform greenish-black mantle and upperwing with white tips to outer primaries, more evident in females. Shows white bases to secondaries during moult. Broad black tail band to white tail finely tipped orange. White underwing coverts contrasting strongly with black flight feathers.
CALL Commonest flight note a clear 'wee-up' (locally 'pee-wit'); also alarmed 'cheew-ep'.
HABITAT AND BEHAVIOUR Favours open grasslands and arable fields, including meadows, bogs and swampy heathland, from boreal to steppe and desert climates. Performs elaborate song display flight twisting, tumbling and rolling. During winter often forms huge flocks on grassland, also intertidal mudflats and saltings, especially during cold spells.
MOVEMENTS Largely migratory Post-breeding flocks move W across Europe from late June to moulting grounds in the Low Countries and British Isles. Onward diurnal migration continues during September Mediterranean Basin, NW India and E China. Undergoes strong diurnal cold-weather movements. Spring passage commences January peaking during March. Vagrant N American Atlantic seaboard, also S Africa.

Sociable Lapwing
Vanellus gregarius L 29.20 cm
A strongly migratory *vanellus*, with breeding range restricted to the steppes of C Russia and Kazakstan south towards Caspian and Aral Seas and Lake Balkhash.

PLUMAGE Adult breeding Black crown encircled by prominent white forehead and supercilium extending behind eye and meeting on nape. Black lores and narrow posterior eye-stripe. Ear coverts, cheeks and sides of neck warm buffish-brown. Upperparts uniform greyish-brown narrowly fringed pale. Primaries black. Chin and throat pale buff. Breast brownish-grey tinged lilac shading to blackish belly, becoming chestnut on lower belly and vent. Undertail coverts white. Bill slender, black. Legs black. **Adult non-breeding** Crown browner with buffish supercilium and indistinct loral line. Upperparts olive-brown. Breast mottled paler brown. Belly whitish lacking both black and chestnut coloration. **Juvenile** Blackish crown streaked buff with prominent buffish lores and supercilium. Upperparts brown with dark subterminal bars narrowly fringed buff giving 'scaly' effect. Face, neck and breast buff heavily streaked dark brown. **In flight** Completely white secondaries contrast with black primaries and brown mantle and inner wing. Lower rump, uppertail coverts and tail white, with broad black subterminal band to all but outer tail feathers. Toes project slightly beyond tail tip.
CALL Noisy on breeding-grounds; most common note harsh 'etch-etch-etch' or 'reck'.
HABITAT AND BEHAVIOUR Breeds on dry inland terrain often near water, favouring transitional zone between grassland and wormwood or sagebrush. Nests in small loose colonies, males engaging in 'spring gatherings'. During autumn moult forms large post-breeding flocks, up to 1000, wintering on dry wasteland, ploughed fields and stubble.
MOVEMENTS Highly migratory. Protracted autumn passage from early August to mid-November, with most birds wintering NW India and Pakistan. W Kazakstan birds move west of Caspian Sea to winter in small numbers in Iraq, Arabia and NE Africa. Spring passage commences early March. Vagrant most European countries, Morocco, Somalia, S India and Sri Lanka.

White-tailed Lapwing
Vanellus leucurus L 27.30 cm
An elegant, long-legged *vanellus*, breeding predominantly in wetland habitat in S Russia from the Caspian Sea east to Lake Balkhash, and south-west to Iran, Iraq and recently Syria and Turkey.
PLUMAGE Adult Creamy forehead with crown and nape brownish-grey. Rest of head and face greyish-cream. Hindneck and upperparts greyish-brown glossed lilac. White panel along greater coverts of closed wing. Primaries black. Chin and throat whitish. Foreneck pale brown. Breast grey. Belly pinkish-buff shading into whitish vent

and undertail coverts. Bill slender, black. Large eye with narrow reddish eye-ring. Iris reddish-brown. Legs very long, bright yellow. **Juvenile** Crown mottled dark brown. Yellowish-buff supercilium and face. Mantle, scapulars and coverts with broad black subterminal bars boldly fringed yellowish-buff. Foreneck and breast whitish mottled pale grey. **In flight** Broad white band across secondaries extending onto bases of inner primaries, greater, outer median and primary coverts, contrasting with mostly black primaries and uniform brown mantle and inner wing, strongly blotched in juvenile. Lower rump and tail wholly white. Feet project well beyond tail tip.
CALL On breeding-grounds, rapid squeaking 'pet-OO-it'.
HABITAT AND BEHAVIOUR Breeds adjacent shallow standing or slow-flowing water, including damp areas overgrown with wormwood and swampy shores of brackish lakes. Nests in small colonies often in mixed company with Black-winged Stilts and pratincoles. Frequently feeds in shallow water. Gregarious, forming sizeable post-breeding flocks especially on migration.
MOVEMENTS Partial migrant. Middle East birds largely resident, undergoing local movements from flooded areas. Russian birds migratory, moving south from late August to winter in NW India, Pakistan, Afghanistan and also NE Africa, mainly Sudan. Spring passage commences March. Vagrant across most of Europe; also Malta, Tunisia, Libya and Nigeria.

A	B	C
D	E	F
G	H	I
J	K	L

A Northern Lapwing adult breeding
B Northern Lapwing adult non-breeding
C Northern Lapwing adult non-breeding
D Northern Lapwing first-winter non-breeding
E Northern Lapwing adult
F Sociable Lapwing adult breeding
G Sociable Lapwing adult non-breeding
H Sociable Lapwing juvenile
I Sociable Lapwing
J White-tailed Lapwing adult breeding
K White-tailed Lapwing adult
L White-tailed Lapwing juvenile

Charadriidae

Spur-winged Lapwing
Vanellus spinosus L 26.65 cm

A handsome pied *vanellus* of wetlands, patchily distributed in Greece, Turkey, the Middle East and Egypt, and south of the Sahara from Senegal east to Kenya and Ethiopia.

PLUMAGE **Adult** Forehead, lores and crown black with elongated nape feathers forming flattened crest. Face, sides of neck and hindneck brilliant white. Upperparts including mantle, scapulars and tertials greyish-brown. Primaries black. Chin, throat, breast, flanks and upper belly glossy black. Lower belly, vent and undertail coverts white. Bill black. Iris crimson. Legs black. Long black carpal spur. **Juvenile** Similar to adult with crown and upperparts narrowly fringed buff. Underparts tinged brown. **In flight** Striking black, white and brown pattern. Most flight feathers black contrasting with white panel across inner primary coverts, outer median and greater coverts and greyish-brown mantle and inner wing. Black carpal spur. Lower rump and uppertail coverts white. Tail black.

CALL Alarm note high pitched 'tick'; territorial call loud, screeching 'di-dridri-dri-drit', often heard at night.

HABITAT AND BEHAVIOUR Occupies wide variety of waterside habitat both fresh and saline including lakes, rivers, soda flats, mudflats, saltpans and estuaries. Also shortgrass meadows and irrigated farmland. Occurs usually in pairs or small parties up to 15. Territorial, adopting threatening posture towards intruders. Performs intricate nuptial display involving male circling around female with slow deliberate steps. Larger flocks up to 100 recorded outside breeding season.

MOVEMENTS Greek and Turkish population migratory, present on breeding-grounds March–October. Migrants regularly recorded on Turkish coast and Cyprus both spring and autumn, but wintering quarters uncertain. African birds largely sedentary, undergoing local movements in response to changing water levels.

River Lapwing
Vanellus duvaucelii L 30.50 cm

The oriental counterpart to Spur-winged Plover, breeding beside rivers in NE India and Nepal east through Burma to Thailand and Vietnam.

PLUMAGE **Adult** Superficially similar to Spur-winged Plover. Solid black crown, lores, chin and throat, with nape feathers further elongated to form pointed crest, usually not evident since flattened against hindneck. Rear cheeks, sides of neck and hindneck pale grey. Upperparts uniform sandy-grey. Primaries black. Upper breast sandy-grey shading into darker brownish-grey lower breast. Rest of underparts white with small, neat black belly patch. Bill black. Iris crimson. Legs black tinged brown. Long black curved carpal spur. **Juvenile** Similar to adult with upperparts fringed buff. Black feathering heavily mottled brown. **Flight** Pattern differs from Spur-winged Plover by presence of narrow black bar on innerwing formed by outer lesser and median coverts. White wing panel more extensive across base of innermost secondaries.

CALL Territorial call 'did-did-do weet', extremely similar to Spur-winged Plover.

HABITAT AND BEHAVIOUR Restricted to sand bars and shingle beds of flowing rivers, avoiding stagnant waters and 'jheels'. Normally occurs singly or in pairs. At rest adopts characteristic hunched posture, affording excellent camouflage against river sand and shingle. Performs elaborate nuptial display exposing striking piebald plumage.

MOVEMENTS Resident with occasional seasonal nomadic movements.

Grey-headed Lapwing
Vanellus cinereus L 35.55 cm

A large, heavy-looking *vanellus*, breeding in wetland habitat restricted to Honshu, Japan, Central Manchuria and Inner Mongolia.

PLUMAGE **Adult breeding** Entire head, neck and breast slate-grey, shading to broad blackish band on lower breast. Upperparts uniform brown with white tips to greater coverts visible on closed wing. Primaries black. Chin and throat whitish. Rest of underparts white. Bill longish, slender, bright yellow with distal third black. Iris bright red with narrow yellow eye-ring. Small, circular yellow wattles above base of bill. Legs yellow. **Adult non-breeding** Head, neck and breast brownish-grey with less distinct lower breast border. **Juvenile** Head, neck and breast brownish with lower breast border ill defined or absent. Upperparts neatly fringed buff. **In flight** Black primaries contrast strongly with broad white band across secondaries, greater and outer median coverts and brown mantle and inner wing. White lower rump, uppertail coverts and tail, with broad black subterminal tail band. Toes project beyond tail tip.

CALL Normal contact note a plaintive 'chee-it'.

HABITAT AND BEHAVIOUR Breeds in fairly wet regions including marshes, wet-meadows, river banks and rice fields. Territorial, swooping on intruders. Gregarious outside breeding season, forming flocks up to 50, favouring edges of 'jheels', wet grazing areas, and ploughed fields, often associating with Red-wattled Lapwings.

MOVEMENTS Asian population strongly migratory, moving south-west from early September to winter in SE China through Indo-China to NE India, returning to breeding-grounds April. In Honshu, southern birds resident whilst northern birds migratory. Vagrant N Russia, Kashmir, Malaysia and Indonesia.

	B
A	C
D	E
F	G

A Spur-winged Lapwing adult breeding
B Spur-winged Lapwing adult
C Spur-winged Lapwing adult
D River Lapwing adult non-breeding
E River Lapwing adult non-breeding
F Grey-headed Lapwing adult
G Grey-headed Lapwing adult

Charadriiidae

Long-toed Lapwing
Vanellus crassirostris L 30.50 cm
A black and white lapwing showing close associations with jacanas, specially adapted to aquatic habitat, breeding in S Sudan south to Botswana and east to S Mozambique, with isolated populations at Lake Chad, NW Angola and E Kenya.
PLUMAGE Adult White forehead, crown, face and neck. Black nape and hindneck extending down sides of neck to join black breast and upper belly, glossed blue. Upperparts dull greyish-brown. Rest of underparts white. Bill dark red tipped black. Iris red. Legs longish, dull red with toes especially middle one longer than other lapwings. **Juvenile** Black feathering tinged brown lacking bluish gloss. Upperparts mottled fringed brown.
CALL A loud clicking 'kick-kick-kick'; also when flushed a loud plaintive 'wheet'.
RACES Two are recognized: nominate *crassirostris* (northern part of range); *leucoptera* (S Tanzania southwards). **In flight** *crassirostris* shows mostly white innerwing coverts contrasting with black flight feathers. Uppertail coverts and basal third of tail white, rest of tail glossy bluish-black. Legs trail beyond tail tip. *Leucoptera* shows entirely white upperwing except for black outermost primaries. Intermediate forms occur showing mottled black and white wings.
HABITAT AND BEHAVIOUR Restricted to lakes, ponds and marshland with emergent floating vegetation, but also grass-covered floodplains, water meadows and flooded ricefields. Feeds on surface of vegetation, with long toes adapted for running about in manner similar to jacanas. Usually in pairs or small parties. Highly aggressive towards intruders.
MOVEMENTS Largely sedentary, with local movements dictated by habitat drying out.

Blacksmith Plover
Vanellus armatus L 29.20 cm
A highly distinctive pied *vanellus* named after its call, always found near water, common and widespread from Central Kenya south to Central Tanzania and SE Zaire to S Africa.
PLUMAGE Adult White cap and lower hindneck patch sharply contrasting with black nape, face, chin, throat, neck and breast. Rest of underparts white. Black mantle, back and lower scapulars. Grey upper scapulars, wing coverts and tertials. Primaries black. Bill black. Iris red. Legs longish, black. **Juvenile** Similar pattern to adult, but whitish forehead and crown admixed with brown and buff. Chin and throat whitish with all black feathers tipped buffish-brown. Scapulars barred dark brown irregularly edged buff, with coverts neatly fringed buff. **In flight** Black mantle, upper rump and flight feathers, except for white bases to innermost secondaries, contrast with grey upper scapulars and innerwing. White lower rump and uppertail with broad black tail band. Feet project beyond tail.
CALL Most familiar alarm note a metallic 'tink-tink', likened to noise of blacksmith's hammer striking anvil, varying in intensity and frequency depending on degree of alarm.
HABITAT AND BEHAVIOUR Habitually found on dry ground adjacent lakes, ponds, rivers and waterholes. Also swampy grassland, shallow floodplains, soda flats and mudflats. Forages on ploughed land, crop fields and around cattle. Usually singly or pairs but flocks up to 100 in non-breeding season. Alert, noisy and easily flushed, standing on elevated ground to obtain view of surroundings. Bathes by wading into deep water.
MOVEMENTS Resident, but subject to local movements in parts of range due to habitat flooding.

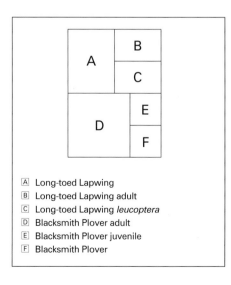

A Long-toed Lapwing
B Long-toed Lapwing adult
C Long-toed Lapwing *leucoptera*
D Blacksmith Plover adult
E Blacksmith Plover juvenile
F Blacksmith Plover

Charadriidae

Black-headed Lapwing
Vanellus tectus L 25.40 cm
The only crested wader south of the Sahara, found commonly on dry ground in the Sahel zone from Senegambia east to Ethiopia and Somalia.
PLUMAGE **Adult** White forehead with black lores, crown and long, wispy crest. White chin and throat extending as white stripe below and behind eye meeting on nape. Broad black patch on hindneck extending around sides of neck and throat, continuing as broad black stripe down centre of breast, lowest feathers elongated and loose. Upperparts uniform earth-brown. Rest of underparts white. Bill dull red distal third black. Small red wattles above lores. Iris yellow. Legs longish, bright red. **Juvenile** Similar to adult, crown and upperparts with dark subterminal lines narrowly fringed buff. Crest and elongated breast feathers shorter, tinged brown. Wattles reduced. Bill and legs duller pink tinged brown. **In flight** Broad white wing panel across primary coverts, bases to primaries and secondaries, contrasting with black tips to flight feathers and brown mantle and inner wing. Uppertail coverts white with black tail tipped white.
CALL Alarm notes include a harsh 'kwairr' and when flushed a piercing 'kir-kir-kir'.
RACES Two are recognized: nominate *tectus* (Senegal east to Ethiopia and NW Keyna) and *latifrons* (E Kenya to E Somalia), the latter with distinctly broader white forehead patch.
HABITAT AND BEHAVIOUR Frequents bare, dry ground or covered with short grass, from open desert and shortgrass plains to areas around human habitation including airfields and football pitches. Occurs in small groups 5–10 birds. Largely inactive during the daytime, feeding and calling mostly at night. Tame and approachable.
MOVEMENTS Sedentary, with only local movements during the rains.

Crowned Lapwing
Vanellus coronatus L 30.50 cm
A common *vanellus*, widespread across dry, open country in Ethiopia and Somalia south to Namibia and S Africa.
PLUMAGE **Adult** Black forehead, lores and supercilium extending behind eye meeting on nape. Black central crown encircled by white headband forming white 'V' at back of nape. Chin and throat whitish with rest of face and neck pale greyish-brown extending onto breast, shading to clear-cut blackish border on lower breast. Upperparts uniform earth-brown. Rest of underparts white with 'peak' between sides of breast and folded wing. Bill bright red with distal half black. Iris yellow. Legs

longish, bright pinkish-red. **Juvenile** Similar to adult with crown and front of headband brown with pale feather edgings. Upperparts with dark subterminal bars boldly fringed and notched warm buff. Border to lower breast mottled dark brown. Base of bill dull yellowish-green. Iris brown. Legs pale pink. **In flight** Slow, deliberate wingbeats with pattern similar to Black-headed Lapwing. White wing panel across primary and greater coverts contrasting with black primaries and secondaries and brown mantle and inner wing. White lower rump, uppertail coverts and tail, with broad black subterminal tail band.
CALL Very noisy. Alarm note 'krrt' rising in intensity. **In flight** a low, screeching 'kerrrrit'.
RACES Three are recognized: nominate *coronatus* (Ethiopia south to S Africa); *demissus* (Somalia) upperpart and breast feathers tipped buff giving paler, sandier coloration.; *xerophilus* (Namibia) paler, greyer coloration.
HABITAT AND BEHAVIOUR Found on grasslands, shortgrass savannah and cultivated land including airports, golf courses and open areas adjacent human habitation. Particularly favours recently burnt grassland. Gregarious, usually small flocks 10–40 birds. Active mostly from late afternoon when often performs communal display prior to flighting and feeding at dusk, calling noisily.
MOVEMENTS Resident, undergoing regular movements associated with habitat changes, especially dry season fires producing burnt grassland. Also responds to rains, moving to drier ground.

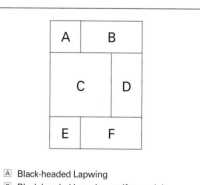

A Black-headed Lapwing
B Black-headed Lapwing *rarifrons* adult
C Black-headed Lapwing adult
D Crowned Lapwing adult
E Crowned Lapwing adult
F Crowned Lapwing adult

Charadriidae

Senegal Plover
Vanellus lugubris **L 24.15 cm**
A smallish, slim plover of open plains, patchily distributed in coastal W Africa, and a belt from Gabon east through Zaire to E Africa and south to Natal.
PLUMAGE Adult: Forehead, chin and throat white. Rest of head, neck and breast dark brownish-grey, shading to clear-cut black lower breast border. Upperparts including scapulars, coverts and tertials dark brown faintly glossed green. Primaries black. Rest of underparts white. Bill black sometimes tinged red at base. Iris dull orange-yellow. Legs reddish-brown. **Juvenile** Similar to adult, but head and breast mottled greyish-brown less well defined. Scapulars, coverts and tertials notched and fringed warm buff. **In flight** Clear white trailing edge across secondaries and tips of innermost primaries, strongly contrasting with black primaries and dark brown mantle and inner wing, paler in juveniles. Tail white with black inner terminal band.
CALL A clear piping 'tlu-wit'; also a melodious 'ki-ti-kooee', especially from night migrants.
HABITAT AND BEHAVIOUR Adapted to dry open grassland, lightly wooded savannah and cultivated ground, usually below 1500 m. Particularly partial to newly burnt grassland. Gregarious, usually small flocks 5–10 birds. Feeds in typical plover manner. Reluctant to fly when approached, preferring to walk away or often bobbing up and down before making short, quick runs. Active at night, feeding and migrating.
MOVEMENTS Partial resident. Undergoes regular movements, including seasonal appearance in certain areas, partly related to suitable burnt grassland for nesting.

Black-winged Plover
Vanellus melanopterus **L 26.65 cm**
Very similar to Senegal Plover, but larger and shorter-legged, preferring open plains at higher altitudes, with separate populations in NE, E, and S Africa.
PLUMAGE Adult Variable white forehead patch larger than Senegal Plover, often extending onto forecrown, lores and behind eye forming short indistinct supercilium. Chin and throat white. Rest of head, neck and breast slate-grey shading to sharply demarcated broad blackish band across lower breast. Upperparts uniform dark brown. White panel across greater coverts visible at rest. Primaries black. Rest of underparts white. Bill black, slenderer than Senegal Plover. Iris dull orange. Legs dark red. **Juvenile** Similar to adult with head, neck and breast pale brown, with darker brown border to lower breast. Crown streaked grey. Scapulars, coverts and tertials broadly fringed buff giving 'scaly' appearance. **In flight** Significantly different from Senegal Plover. Black primaries and tips to secondaries contrast with white panel across base of secondaries, greater and outer median coverts, and dark brown mantle and inner wing. Tail white with broad black subterminal band. Feet project less beyond tail than Senegal Plover.
CALL Variety of loud cries including a harsh 'tlu-wit'; common note when breeding and night flying plaintive 'titihoya'.
HABITAT AND BEHAVIOUR Breeds in short grassland on highland plateaux and mountain slopes, also open plains at lower elevations. Favours areas frequented by game animals and also recently burnt grassland. Gregarious, forming large post-breeding flocks, sometimes in excess of 1000, prior to migration. When approached tends to run away before taking to flight, calling loudly. In winter descends to fields, meadows and coastal flats.
MOVEMENTS Partial resident, undergoing altitudinal migration E and S Africa. Resident Ethiopia. Present Kenyan highlands January–August, wintering in plains 1000 m lower. In S Africa some birds move during non-breeding season from highlands to coastal plains, where now nesting Zululand.

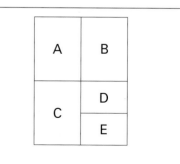

A Senegal Plover adult
B Black-winged Pover *minor* adult
C Black-winged Plover *minor* adult
D Black-winged Plover *minor* first-winter non-breeding
E Black-winged Plover *minor* juvenile

Charadriidae

Senegal Wattled Plover
***Vanellus senegallus* L 34.30 cm**
A large *vanellus* occupying a wide variety of habitat but usually associated with water, ranging from Senegambia east to Ethiopia and south to N Namibia and Natal.
PLUMAGE Adult Forehead and forecrown white bordered black. Face, sides of neck and hindneck pale greyish-brown streaked blackish-brown. Chin, throat and foreneck black. Upperparts greyish-brown tinged olive. Breast and upper belly greyish-brown. Lower belly, vent and undertail coverts white. Bill yellow, culmen tipped black. Legs long, bright yellow. Eye pale grey with yellow eye-ring. Large pendent yellow wattles, upper portion red. Black carpal spur. **Juvenile** Similar to adult but lacking black markings to crown, chin, throat and foreneck. Small whitish area to forehead obscured with brown streaking. Chin, throat and foreneck whitish streaked paler brown. Very small wattles and spur.
In flight Black flight feathers contrast with white panel across greater coverts and bases to secondaries. Lower rump, uppertail coverts and tail white, last with broad black subterminal band.
RACES Four are recognized: *senegallus* (Senegal east to Sudan and N Uganda); *major* (Ethiopia) slightly larger; *lateralis* (E Zaire east to W Kenya south to N Namibia and Natal) and *solitaneus* (occupying western part of range) blackish-brown band across belly. Bill tip solidly black.
CALL When flushed loud 'ke-weep, ke-weep'; when agitated, rapid 'peep, peep' becoming 'yip, yip'.
HABITAT AND BEHAVIOUR Varied, changing seasonally. Generally damp grassland near water, bare muddy or sandy ground adjacent pools, lakes and rivers, also dry short grassland and savannah far from water. After rains moves into wet grassland, temporary pools and ricefields. Usually occurs singly or in small groups. Very vocal during breeding season, often nesting near human habitation. During non-breeding season larger flocks form on temporary pools and burnt grassland.
MOVEMENTS Both sedentary and migratory, movements often both nomadic and in response to rain and resultant water levels. Vagrant Somalia, N and SE Kenya, Cape Province.

White-headed Lapwing
***Vanellus albiceps* L 29.85 cm**
Strikingly pied **In flight** favouring riverine habitat of W and C Africa south to NE Transvaal.
PLUMAGE Adult Broad white crown-stripe from bill to nape narrowly bordered blackish below. Rest of head, hindneck and sides of neck grey separated from brown mantle, upper scapulars and tertials by narrow white hindcollar. White bar across lower scapulars bordered below by black wing coverts. Small white spot anterior to eye. Chin, throat and entire underparts white. Bill yellow, distal third black. Legs yellow. Iris yellow. Long, hanging greenish-yellow wattles. Long black carpal spur. **Juvenile** Similar to adult. Brownish crown stripe. Upperparts mottled dark brown and buff. Very small wattles and carpal spur. **In flight** Predominantly white wings with black outer wing coverts and outer three primaries. Rump, uppertail coverts and base of tail white, the last with broad black terminal band. Call Rapidly repeated, high-pitched 'peuw'.
HABITAT AND BEHAVIOUR Breeds on large river beds, both sandy and shingly, especially with islands, occasionally on lake shores. Noisy and highly aggressive, readily taking to flight when disturbed. Occurs in small parties, up to 30 outside breeding season.
MOVEMENTS Largely sedentary, local movements dictated by rains when, depending on degree of flooding, moves up river to suitable habitat.

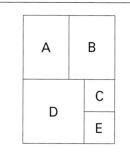

A Senegal Wattled Plover adult
B Senegal Wattled Plover *lateralis* adult
C Senegal Wattled Plover juvenile
D White-headed Lapwing juvenile
E White-headed Lapwing adult

Charadriidae

Yellow-wattled Lapwing
Vanellus malabaricus **L 26.65 cm**
A medium-sized *vanellus* with conspicuous bright yellow wattles and legs, preferring drier lowland habitat, endemic to Pakistan, India and Sri Lanka.
PLUMAGE Adult breeding Forehead, crown and nape black, bordered by white supercilium from behind eye almost meeting on nape. Chin and throat black. Rest of face, neck and breast mid-brown shading to clear-cut narrow black border to lower breast. Entire upperparts sandy-brown. Primaries black. Rest of underparts white. Bill black with yellow base. Large bright yellow wattles hanging down each side from base of bill joining and encircling yellow eye-ring. Iris pale yellow. Legs longish, bright yellow. **Adult non-breeding** Crown, chin and throat admixed with brown. **Juvenile** Similar to adult, with crown brown flecked paler. Upperparts with dark subterminal bars boldly fringed warm buff. Chin and throat white. Breast band mottled brown, less defined, lacking black lower breast border. Smaller, duller wattles. **In flight** Black primaries and tips to secondaries contrast with white panel across bases of secondaries and tips to greater coverts and uniform brown mantle and inner wing. Lower rump and tail white, with broad black central subterminal tail band.
CALL Normal contact note a plaintive 'dee-wit, dee-wit'; when alarmed a repeated 'twit-twit-twit'.
HABITAT AND BEHAVIOUR Generally frequents drier habitat than Red-wattled Lapwing, farther away from water, preferring barren wasteland, stubble fields and cultivated ground. Usually singly or in pairs, forming small parties outside breeding season. Raises crest feathers when excited or displaying. Quieter, less demonstrative than Red-wattled Lapwing.
MOVEMENTS Largely sedentary. Dry season visitor to parts of range, undergoing movements away from wettest areas during monsoon.

Red-wattled Lapwing
Vanellus indicus **L 33.00 cm**
A large, noisy, wattled *vanellus*, associated with open, well-watered country, breeding from Iraq east through Indian sub-continent to the Malaysian peninsula.
PLUMAGE Adult Forehead, crown and nape black. Chin, throat and breast also black, sharply defining white ear covert patch extending down sides of neck onto rest of underparts. Entire upperparts uniform brown faintly glossed green, with median and greater coverts tinged purple. Primaries black. Bill red with distal third

black. Small red wattles above base of bill joining and encircling red eye-ring. Iris red. Legs longish, bright yellow. **Juvenile** Crown mottled brown. Chin and throat whitish with greyish-brown breast. Wing coverts indistinctly fringed buff lacking green gloss. Wattles tiny. Iris dull reddish-brown. **In flight** Black primaries and secondaries contrast with white panel across greater and outer median coverts and brown mantle and inner wing. Lower rump and uppertail coverts white. Tail white with narrow black subterminal band, central tail feathers bordered brown.
CALL Extremely vocal. Various loud, penetrating calls resembling 'did-he-doit'.
RACES Four are recognized: *aigneri* (Iraq east to Pakistan); nominate *indicus* (India, Nepal); *lankae* (Sri Lanka); *atronuchalis* (Assam, Myanmar east to Malaysian peninsula), the last differing from other three similar races by black head completely encircling small white ear-covert patch. Narrow white hindneck collar joins white underparts.
HABITAT AND BEHAVIOUR Frequents damp meadows, irrigated fields, ditches, temporary pools and grassy glades of open forest. Normally in pairs or small family groups, but up to 30 in non-breeding season. Alert, noisy and strongly territorial, chasing off intruders with dashing powerful flight. Activity mostly crepuscular and nocturnal, especially on moonlit nights.
MOVEMENTS Mostly resident, but migratory in northern part of range in S USSR. In India undergoes altitudinal migration spring and autumn. Disperses widely during monsoon due to creation of suitable habitat. Vagrant Persian Gulf, Oman, Israel.

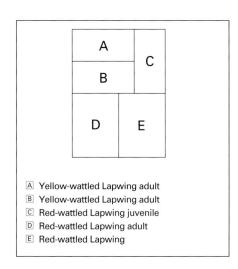

A Yellow-wattled Lapwing adult
B Yellow-wattled Lapwing adult
C Red-wattled Lapwing juvenile
D Red-wattled Lapwing adult
E Red-wattled Lapwing

Charadriidae

Spot-breasted Plover
Vanellus melanocephalus L 34.30 cm
A strikingly patterned *vanellus*, reasonably common but totally restricted to the northern and central highlands of Ethiopia. PLUMAGE **Adult** Forehead, crown and nape solidly black with extended lower nape feathers forming short crest. Bold white supercilium starting above and just anterior to eye curving backwards onto sides of nape. Face, sides of neck and hindneck pale greyish-brown. Upperparts uniform warmer olive-brown. Chin and throat black. Breast sides greyish-brown with centre of breast white, heavily spotted and streaked black. Rest of underparts white. Bill black, basal third of upper mandible dull yellow. Legs shortish, pale yellow. Small oval yellow wattle in front of eye joining narrow dull yellow eye-ring. Iris yellowish-grey. **Juvenile** Undescribed. **In flight** Conspicuous white bar across base of inner secondaries extending onto greater coverts, outer median and lesser coverts, contrasting with rest of black flight feathers and brownish mantle, scapulars and remainder of inner wing coverts. Rump, uppertail coverts and tail white, the last with black subterminal tail band. **Call** Typical *vanellus*; double 'ku-eep', with longer 'kree-kree-kre-krep-kreep-kreep'. HABITAT AND BEHAVIOUR Restricted to highland grassland, moorland and marshes up to 4100 m, in conjunction with giant lobelia, giant heath and tussock grass. Frequently recorded in the vicinity of cattle, flying considerable distance daily to find suitable areas grazing domestic cattle. Occurs singly and small parties, forming flocks up to 40 outside breeding season. Noisy, often very approachable. Flight erratic keeping close to ground. MOVEMENTS Resident with limited seasonal movements only.

Brown-chested Plover
Vanellus superciliosus L 22.85 cm
A small uncommon and migratory lapwing, with breeding restricted to grasslands of W Africa from Togo east through Nigeria and Cameroon to NE Zaire. PLUMAGE **Adult** Crown and nape black separated from grey face, sides of neck, hindneck and upper breast by very narrow pale rufous-white line extending backwards from eye to sides of nape. Forehead and lores dull rufous-brown. Chin whitish. Entire upperparts uniform olive-brown, narrowly fringed pale when fresh. Broad chestnut band across lower breast broadest in centre. Rest of underparts white. Bill black with pale yellow base to lower mandible. Legs reddish-brown. Small yellow wattle on lores continuing back just above eye. Iris yellow. **Juvenile** Crown dull brown with rufous-brown of forehead extending onto forecrown, continuing as broad supercilium to sides of nape. White line posterior to eye absent. Upperparts fringed pale rufous. Lower breast dull brown washed chestnut. **In flight** White diagonal bar extending across bases of inner secondaries, greater and outer median coverts separates remainder of black flight feathers from dark brown mantle, scapulars and rest of inner wing coverts. Rump, uppertail coverts and tail white, latter with broad black terminal band narrowing at sides. Feet project beyond tail tip. CALL Three high-pitched calls in succession, resembling rusty hinge. HABITAT AND BEHAVIOUR Breeds in open bare grassland and cleared ground especially recently burnt. In Nigeria favours 'orchard bush'. Wary, with rapid flight, frequently calling at night. Forms post-breeding flocks up to 50. During migration may occur on cleared areas within forest, wintering in both wooded and grassy savannah. Readily associates with Senegal Plover. MOVEMENTS Present on breeding-grounds during dry season. Leaves early June to winter in C Africa from S Zaire south to NW Zambia and east to W Kenya, returning to nest late November. Vagrant SE Tanzania.

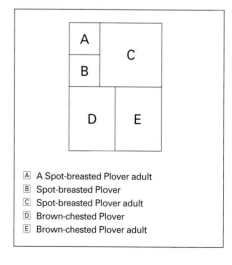

A A Spot-breasted Plover adult
B Spot-breasted Plover
C Spot-breasted Plover adult
D Brown-chested Plover
E Brown-chested Plover adult

Charadriidae

Southern Lapwing
Vanellus chilensis L 34.30 cm
A familiar lowland lapwing with racial plumage variation, common and widespread across S America excluding the Amazon basin and high Andes. **PLUMAGE Adult** Head variable grey with wispy blackish crest. Black forehead and throat variably bordered white. Mantle greyish-brown shading to bronzy-green upperparts. Distinct chestnut-bronze patch to anterior scapulars bordered glossy green on lesser coverts. Broad black breast band extending onto upper belly. Rest of underparts white. Bill dark red tipped black. Iris and eye-ring dark red. Legs longish crimson-red. Reddish carpal spur. **Juvenile** Similar to adult, lacking distinct face pattern. Shorter crest. Forehead and crown finely streaked dark brown and buff. Black throat line virtually absent. Upperparts duller olive-brown indistinctly barred, fringed buff. Dull sooty-brown breast band. **In flight** Conspicuous silvery-white band across outer median and greater coverts extending onto inner secondaries, contrasting with black f light feathers. White rump and uppertail coverts. Tail mostly black tipped white. Toes project slightly beyond tail tip. **CALL** When flushed loud, raucous 'parp-parp-parp, que-que-que', harsher in southern parts of range. **RACES** Four are recognized: *cayennensis* (northern S America to Amazon) cinnamon-brown head with whitish forecrown and face, black throat does not join black breast band; *lampronotus* (Amazon south to N Chile and N Argentina) brownish-grey head with faint, narrow white face line, black throat joins black breast band; *chilensis* (Argentina and Chile south to Chubut and Chiloe Is) and *fretensis* (S Argentina and S Chile] both similar with bluish-grey head and narrow clear face line. Black throat joins breast band. **HABITAT AND BEHAVIOUR** Breeds in damp meadows, fields, pampas and marshy plains. Performs slow butterfly display flight. Usually found in small parties 3–6 birds. Extremely noisy. Often assumes horizontal motionless stance. Forms flocks up to 200 birds outside breeding season, moving to wetlands, sloughs and tidal mudflats. **MOVEMENTS** Mostly sedentary. Southernmost population partially migratory, moving north during coldest parts of austral winter. Regular vagrant Falkland Is. Also Ecuador, Trinidad.

Andean Lapwing
Vanellus resplendens L 34.30 cm
Replaces Southern Lapwing at high altitude, breeding in the temperate and Puna zones of the Andes from SW Columbia south to N Chile and NW Argentina. **PLUMAGE Adult** Head and neck very pale ashy-grey, looking creamy-white at distance, shading to darker grey breast narrowly bordered blackish below. Variable dusky-grey lores continuing as narrow dusky-grey line through eye onto ear coverts. Upperparts uniform glossy brownish-green. Purple lesser coverts visible only close range, appearing blackish at distance. Throat whitish. Rest of underparts white. Bill longish, slender, basal half crimson-red, distal half black. Iris and eye-ring bright crimson. Legs shortish, crimson tinged orange. **Juvenile** Similar to adult. Head and neck slightly darker grey. Upperparts dull brownish-green narrowly fringed buff. Grey breast lacks blackish lower border. Iris and eye-ring dark reddish-brown. **In flight** Conspicuous white band across median and greater coverts, inner secondaries and bases of outer secondaries, contrasting with black primary coverts and remainder of flight feathers. Rump, uppertail coverts and base of tail white. Blackish-brown subterminal tail band fringed white. **CALL** Loud, harsh mobbing 'criee-criee-cree', rapidly repeated. **HABITAT AND BEHAVIOUR** Nests mainly at 3000–4500 m favouring grassy plains and open parts of marshes, often near shorelines of lakes and rivers. Both noisy and wary. Characteristically stands with raised wings on landing. Usually in small family parties, forming small flocks outside breeding season. **MOVEMENTS** Largely sedentary, descending to lower elevations during austral winter, rarely to sea-level including vagrant Peruvian Pacific coast and inner Amazon basin.

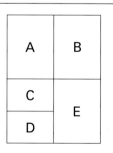

A	B
C	
D	E

A Southern Lapwing *lampronotus* adult
B Southern Lapwing *chilensis*
C Southern Lapwing
D Southern Lapwing juvenile
E Andean Lapwing adult

Charadriidae

Banded Lapwing
Vanellus tricolor L 26.65 cm
A common widespread *vanellus*, endemic to the short arid grasslands of S Australia and Tasmania.
PLUMAGE Adult Forehead and crown black contrasting with conspicuous rear white eye-stripe. Black band from lores extending through cheeks and down sides of neck to form broad 'U'-shaped breast band enclosing white chin, throat and upper breast. Upperparts brown faintly glossed green. Rest of underparts white. Bill bright lemon-yellow with dusky tip to upper mandible. Iris and eye-ring lemon-yellow. Small red wattles in front of eyes. Legs dull reddish-purple. **Juvenile** Crown brown flecked buff. Brownish-black neck and breast band with feathers tipped buff. Mantle, scapulars and coverts broadly fringed buff. Tertials barred brown and buff. Bill, legs and eyes duller. Wattles very small, dull. **In flight** Fast, clipped wingbeats. White tips to greater coverts form narrow white wing panel separating black flight feathers from uniform brown mantle and inner wing. White rump, uppertail coverts and tail with broad black subterminal tail band.
CALL Wild, plaintive notes including fast, repeated 'er-chill-char, er-chill-char'; also piercing 'kew-kew, kew-kew'.
HABITAT AND BEHAVIOUR Inhabits dry, shortgrass plains, stony wastes and airfields, often far from water. Usually in small parties, forming larger flocks during winter. Strongly territorial, flying at intruder, also using 'broken wing' distraction display. Foot patters to flush insects. Noisy, often calling while flighting at night.
MOVEMENTS Nomadic. Leaves drought-ridden areas, flying considerable distances to find suitable habitat, requiring rain before breeding.

Masked Lapwing
Vanellus miles L 34.90 cm
A large, wattled *vanellus*, common and increasing across agricultural areas as a result of human settlement, found in S New Guinea, N and E Australia and New Zealand.
PLUMAGE Adult Black crown. Mantle, coverts, scapulars and tertials uniform olive-brown. Underparts white. Bill bright yellow, paler towards tip with dusky tip to upper mandible. Iris and eye-ring yellow. Very large yellow wattles. Legs dull red. Yellow carpal spur. **Juvenile** Upperparts mottled and barred dark brown fringed buff. Wattles smaller. **In flight** Lacks white wing panel. Black flight feathers contrast with plain olive-brown mantle and inner

wing. White rump and uppertail coverts. Tail mostly black, narrowly fringed white. Legs project beyond tail tip.
CALL Extremely vocal. Loud, staccato 'keer-kir-kir-kik'.
RACES Two are recognized: nominate *miles* (New Guinea, NE Australia) black restricted to crown and nape. White hindneck and sides of neck join white underparts, large wattles extending above and behind eyes; *novaehollandiae* (SE Australia, New Zealand) black extending onto hindneck and down sides of neck forming black lateral breast patches, wattles confined to in front of eyes.
HABITAT AND BEHAVIOUR Widespread across open pastures and improved land as a result of human habitation, usually not far from water. Extremely territorial, aggressive and noisy, dive-bombing and striking intruder with carpal spur. Also performs 'broken wing' distraction display. Usually in small flocks especially during non-breeding season.
MOVEMENTS Mostly sedentary. Disperses during non-breeding season, undergoing considerable distances often frequenting lakeshores, tidal mudflats and estuaries.

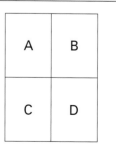

A Banded Lapwing adult
B Banded Lapwing adult
C Masked Lapwing *novaehollandiiae* adult
D Masked Lapwing adult

Charadriidae

European Golden Plover
Pluvialis apricaria L 27.20 cm
An attractive plover with highly variable breeding plumage, nesting on moorland and Arctic tundra in Britain, Iceland and N Europe east to the Taimyr peninsula.
PLUMAGE **Adult breeding** Brilliant white forehead and supercilium continuing as white patch down sides of neck onto breast sides and along flanks. Crown and upper parts blackish boldly spotted bright gold. Primary tips fall roughly level with tail tip. Face and underparts black with whitish vent and undertail coverts irregularly barred dark grey. Amount of black on face, neck, breast and flanks highly variable dependent on 'form' ('northern' or 'southern') and sex. Bill slim, black. Legs dark grey variably tinged green. **Adult non-breeding** Black coloration lost. Indistinct buffish supercilium. Dusky-grey ear covert patch extending just anterior to eye. Upperparts greyish-brown notched and spotted dull yellow. Breast mottled dull yellowish-brown with rest of underparts whitish-grey. **Juvenile** Very similar to non-breeding adult. Mantle and scapulars boldly spotted and fringed brighter yellow. Underparts especially flanks and belly finely barred grey. **In flight** Uniform dark upperparts, with thin wing bar across tips of greater coverts extending onto outer webs of primaries. Axillaries and most underwing coverts white.
CALL Flight note far carrying whistle 'tluu-ee'.
HABITAT AND BEHAVIOUR Nests on swampy heaths, highland moors and low lying coastal tundra. Performs plaintive 'butterfly' aerial display flight. Typical running gait interspersed with pauses in upright position. Highly gregarious outside breeding season, large flocks wary, quickly taking to flight. Winters largely on shortgrass fields, also lakeshores, saltmarsh, tidal shores and mudflats.
MOVEMENTS 'Northern' form highly migratory, majority of adults moving SW from late July to moult, arriving from early October to winter in Britain, southern North Sea south to Iberian peninsula and Mediterranean Basin. More easterly breeding birds winter Turkey east to Caspian Sea. Return passage in Europe peaks early May. British birds partially migratory, wintering adjacent breeding-grounds, returning from February onwards. Vagrant Canaries, Azores, Gambia, Greenland and Newfoundland.

Pacific Golden Plover
Pluvialis fulva L 24.75 cm
Separated from American Golden Plover in 1986, a long-distance migrant, nesting on the Siberian tundra from the Yamal peninsula east across the Bering Sea to W Alaska where it overlaps with *dominica*.
PLUMAGE **Adult breeding** Smallest, slimmest and proportionately longest legged of the three 'golden' plovers. White breast patch small. White flank line narrow, variably barred or mottled black, occasionally lacking. Upperparts generally spangled brighter than 'American' with larger, brighter gold spots to mantle and scapulars, often contrasting with whitish fringed coverts. Noticeable primary projection beyond tail tip, with 2–4 primaries visible beyond tips of tertials. Tip of longest tertial falls roughly level or just short of tail tip. Undertail coverts white variably barred black, more so in males, occasionally wholly black. Bill black. Legs greyish-black. **Adult non-breeding** Distinct buffish-yellow supercilium and yellow wash to face, occasionally paler and whiter. Small darkish loral smudge and dusky rear cheeks and ear covert patch. Crown heavily streaked dark brown. Upperparts dark brown spotted bright yellow, slightly paler on coverts. Underparts mottled greyish-buff with breast washed buffish-yellow. **Juvenile** Similar to non-breeding adult. Supercilium clear yellowish-buff. Upperparts spotted and fringed bright yellow. Breast buffish mottled bright yellow shading to whitish-grey underparts, finely barred on flanks and lower belly. **In flight** Thin inconspicuous wing bar. Toes project slightly beyond tail tip. Underwing coverts and axillaries dull grey.
CALL 'Chu-it' or 'chu-eet', readily separable from 'European' but very similar to 'American'.
HABITAT AND BEHAVIOUR Breeds on dry, well-vegetated slopes of Arctic tundra, more northerly in zone of overlap with European Golden Plover. Outside breeding season favours intertidal mudflats, beaches and reefs, also short grasslands and inland pools.
MOVEMENTS Strongly migratory. Alaskan birds migrate direct to Hawaii, Fiji and S Pacific Is, arriving New Zealand during October, with return passage from March. Siberian birds winter range extends from Ethiopia, India east across Indo-China, Indonesia and Australia. Few winter annually California. Vagrant S Africa, Europe west to Britain (increasing adult records late summer), New England, Chile.

A	B	C
D	E	F
G	H	I
J	K	L

A European Golden Plover (southern form) adult breeding
B European Golden Plover (northern form) adult breeding
C European Golden Plover adult non-breeding
D European Golden Plover juvenile
E European Golden Plover juvenile
F European Golden Plover
G Pacific Golden Plover
H Pacific Golden Plover
I Pacific Golden Plover adult breeding
J Pacific Golden Plover breeding male
K Pacific Golden Plover adult non-breeding
L Pacific Golden Plover juvenile

Charadriidae

American Golden Plover
Pluvialis dominica L 26.05 cm
Extremely similar in breeding plumage and overlapping in range with Pacific Golden Plover, breeding in Alaska east across Arctic Canada to Baffin Is and south to NE Manitoba.
PLUMAGE **Adult breeding** Middle-sized but longest winged of the three 'golden' plovers. White breast patch large, sometimes extending onto central breast, especially in males. White flank patch totally lacking (males), or narrow variably barred or mottled black (females and immatures). Upperparts less brightly spangled than Pacific with smaller, duller gold spots. Obvious long primary projection beyond tail tip, with 4–6 primaries visible beyond tips of tertials. Tip of longest tertial falls well short of tail tip. Undertail coverts typically wholly or partially black, highly variable. Bill black. Legs relatively long, greyish-black. **Adult non-breeding** Conspicuous whitish supercilium and greyish face contrasting with heavily streaked dark grey crown giving 'capped' appearance. Darker grey loral area with more prominent eye-stripe and ear covert patch also accentuates supercilium. Upperparts brownish-grey spotted dull yellow and white. Underparts whitish with breast and flanks mottled grey. **Juvenile** Similar to non-breeding adult. Mantle frequently very dark grey forming conspicuous darker triangular area. Breast, flanks and upper belly mottled and barred grey. **In flight** Longer winged than Pacific, with thin inconspicuous wing bar. Underwing coverts and axillaries dull grey.
CALL 'Phuu-ee' or 'phuu-uu-ee', very similar to 'Pacific'.
HABITAT AND BEHAVIOUR Breeds on high Arctic tundra, favouring disruptive ground coloration of lichen, gravel and rocks. Breeds alongside 'Pacific' in Alaska. Winters preferably on inland grassland and farmland, also wetlands, sloughs, coastal mud and sandflats. Quite tame and approachable.
MOVEMENTS Extremely migratory, travelling huge distances. Adults depart early August, using Great Circle route mostly non-stop south-east towards Hudson Bay, across Atlantic on elliptical course over Lesser Antilles to Argentinian Pampas. Juveniles mainly use coastal or Great Plains route. Return passage from late February largely through interior reaching breeding-grounds late May. Frequent transatlantic vagrancy to W Europe during autumn; also Greenland, W Siberia, W Africa and Australia.

Grey Plover
Pluvialis squatarola L 29.85 cm
A strikingly attractive plover with diagnostic black axillaries, breeding on the Arctic tundra across both N America from Alaska east to Baffin Is and Russia from the Kanin east to Chukotski peninsulas.
PLUMAGE **Adult breeding male** Brilliant white forehead and supercilium continuing as white patch down sides of neck onto sides of breast. Crown whitish. Upperparts brilliantly spangled black, silvery-grey and white. Primary tips extend just beyond tail tip. Face and underparts solid black except for white vent and undertail coverts. Bill heavy-looking, black. Legs blackish. **Adult breeding female** Upperparts sometimes brownish-black. Underparts tinged brown variably flecked white. **Adult non-breeding** Whitish forehead, lores and indistinct supercilium. Dark grey ear covert patch extending just anterior to eye. Crown and upperparts brownish-grey spotted and fringed white. Breast mottled and finely streaked brownish-grey. **Juvenile** Similar to non-breeding adult with upperparts darker grey spangled dull yellow. Breast and flanks heavily streaked and barred dusky-grey. **In flight** Broad long wing bar contrasting with blackish primaries and secondaries and dark grey mantle and inner wing. Squarish white patch to rump and uppertail coverts often irregularly barred grey. Tail white barred grey. Underwing coverts white with black axillaries.
CALL Flight note plaintive 'pee-uu-ee'.
HABITAT AND BEHAVIOUR Breeds on dry, grassy or lichen-covered tundra, preferring rocky slopes to low flat terrain. Performs butterfly song display flight. Characteristic hunched appearance. Relatively slow gait, often remaining motionless for short periods. Winters on tidal mudflats, estuaries and beaches, occasionally found inland during winter or on migration.
MOVEMENTS Migratory, adults moving south from late July followed by juveniles from mid September. Palearctic birds winter from W Europe, gathering at favoured estuaries to moult, south to Africa, Saudi Arabia, India, Indo-China, Indonesia and Australia. Nearctic birds winter on both Pacific and Atlantic coasts of N C and S America. Return passage from late February in S Africa through to early June on Wadensee. Non-breeding birds remain on wintering grounds. Vagrant Greenland, Iceland, Spitzbergen, Madeira.

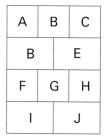

A	B	C
B		E
F	G	H
I		J

A American Golden Plover breeding male
B American Golden Plover breeding female
C American Golden Plover adult non-breeding
D American Golden Plover juvenile
E American Golden Plover adult
F Grey Plover breeding female
G Grey Plover adult non-breeding
H Grey Plover adult non-breeding
I Grey Plover breeding male
J Grey Plover first-winter non-breeding

Charadriidae

Eurasian Dotterel
Eudromias morinellus L 20.95 cm

An unusually tame plover, breeding in mountainous regions discontinuously across Scotland, N Scandinavia and N Eurasia east to the Chukotski peninsula, S Siberia, NW Mongolia and the Russian Altai, sporadically Central Europe and probably Alaska. **PLUMAGE Adult breeding female** Uniform blackish-brown cap with brilliant white supercilia meeting in 'V' on nape. Chin, throat and sides of face whitish, with dusk-grey lores and ear coverts, becoming dull ashy-grey on neck and upper breast. Upperparts dark grey fringed rich buff. Narrow white band bordered dark greyish above and below, separates grey upper breast from chestnut lower breast. Large black belly patch. Vent and undertail coverts white. Bill slim, blackish. Legs dull yellow. **Adult breeding male** Crown admixed with white. Neck and breast brownish-grey. White breast line less sharply defined. Black on belly reduced. **Adult non-breeding** Crown dark brown finely streaked buff, with creamy-buff supercilium. Upperparts fringed sandy-brown. Foreneck, breast and flanks mottled buffish-brown with indistinct whitish breast line. Rest of underparts white. **Juvenile** Upperparts darker brown with neat buff fringes to scapulars, coverts and tertials interrupted by dark wedge at tip. Neck and breast mottled buffish-brown with obscure buffish breast line. **In flight** Uniform darkish-grey mantle, rump and upperwing with white shaft to outer primary. Blackish subterminal tail band tipped white. **CALL** Fairly quiet. Usual flight notes soft trilling twitter. **HABITAT AND BEHAVIOUR** Typically breeds in northern tundra and montane regions with sparse, mossy vegetation and scattered boulders. Also breeds below sea-level on reclaimed Dutch polders. Reversed courtship roles, females calling and displaying, males incubating eggs and feeding young. Extremely approachable. Gregarious during winter, frequenting arid and semi-desert areas, barren, stony plateaux. **MOVEMENTS** Migratory, total population moving south from mid-July to winter in N Africa and Mediterranean Basin east to Iraq and Persian Gulf, returning to breeding-grounds mid-May onwards. On passage small 'trips' regularly pause at traditional sites. Vagrant Canaries, Iceland, Spitzbergen, Japan, Bermuda, Hawaii, W USA.

New Zealand Dotterel
Charadrius obscurus L 27.30 cm

A large, heavy-billed *charadrius*, now endangered, with a population of just 1400, totally restricted to New Zealand. **PLUMAGE Adult breeding** Forehead, face and supercilium variable from brilliant white to heavily washed buff-grey and even dull chestnut. Lores, ear coverts, crown and upperparts greyish-brown with mantle, scapulars, coverts and tertials fringed warm chestnut, especially when fresh. Underparts also highly variable from pale peach to rich chestnut admixed with white, males generally showing the brighter coloration. Vent and undertail coverts white. Bill longish, heavy, black. Legs grey sometimes tinged dull green. **Adult non-breeding** Upperparts generally paler grey-brown fringed whitish. Underparts whitish with grey mottling to breast and flanks. **Juvenile** Similar to non-breeding adult with noticeable darker brown cap. Upperparts darker brown fringed buff. Underparts variably warm tawny-buff with irregular grey mottling to breast. **In flight** Clear white wing bar and narrow white trailing edge to secondaries. Grey-brown rump with tail darker brown edged white. **CALL** Typical call a rippling 'trrrt' and also a rising 'weet'. **HABITAT AND BEHAVIOUR** Two distinct populations exist 1500 km apart. Small population about 60 birds breeds on exposed mountain tops of Stewart Is, nesting in stunted sub-Alpine vegetation often amongst rocky outcrops. Recent research shows predation, especially cats to be main reason for decline. Main population breeds around north coasts of North Island, preferring sandy beaches with shingle ridges, often adjacent brackish water. Highly territorial, often displaying broken wing distraction against intruders. Tame and approachable. **MOVEMENTS** Stewart Is population largely sedentary, moving to the coast post breeding, with small numbers crossing Foveaux Strait to winter at Awarua Bay, South Island. North Island birds undergo greater post-breeding dispersal around the coast, but colour banding indicates no movement to South Island.

Inland Dotterel
Peltohyas australis L 20.95 cm

A striking but somewhat scarce plover, restricted to dry inland plains from the coast of Western Australia east to western parts of Victoria and New South Wales. **PLUMAGE Adult breeding** Forehead, face, chin, throat and foreneck all warm buffish-white, interrupted by broad black vertical frontal bar extending down through eyes onto sides of face. Rear crown, nape and upperparts with dark brown feather centres broadly fringed buff giving very streaked appearance. Primaries black narrowly fringed buff. Conspicuous Y-shaped breast band continuing around sides of neck to form complete black hindneck collar. Small black vertical bar on side of nape joining neck collar. Underparts cinnamon-buff shading to chestnut belly. Whitish vent and undertail coverts. Bill slim, blackish tinged greenish-grey at base of lower mandible. Narrow white eye-ring. Legs dull greyish-yellow. **Adult non-breeding** All black areas lost. Darker feather centres to crown and upperparts paler giving mottled appearance. **Juvenile** Very similar to non-breeding adult. **Flight** swift and low, lacking wing bar. Dark flight feathers and primary coverts with paler cinnamon-buff outer webs to inner primaries forming indistinct panel. Rump and uppertail coverts brown. Tail dark brown fringed buff. Underwing coverts and axillaries rich cinnamon-buff. **CALL** Generally quiet. Flight note brisk, repeated 'quoick'. **HABITAT AND BEHAVIOUR** Found in flat, open arid country, stony deserts, and gibber plains all sparsely vegetated, occasionally ploughed wheat fields. Usually in small flocks up to ten birds, but up to 50 in non-breeding season. Most active at night when likely to be seen on dirt roads, feeding on nocturnal invertebrates. Fairly tame and approachable. When standing with back to observer exhibits excellent cryptic camouflage. If disturbed tends to run away, stopping to bob head. **MOVEMENTS** Nomadic with erratic north–south movements.

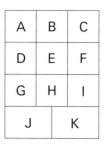

A	B	C
D	E	F
G	H	I
J	K	

A Eurasian Dotterel breeding male
B Eurasian Dotterel juvenile
C Eurasian Dotterel juvenile
D Eurasian Dotterel
E New Zealand Dotterel adult breeding
F New Zealand Dotterel adult non-breeding
G New Zealand Dotterel adult breeding
H New Zealand Dotterel adult non-breeding
I Inland Dotterel adult breeding
J Inland Dotterel adult non-breeding
K Inland Dotterel adult breeding

Charadriidae

Great Ringed Plover
Charadrius hiaticula L 19.05 cm
A smallish plover, common across the N Palearctic region, but also found in Greenland and NE Canada, where it overlaps with Semipalmated Plover.
PLUMAGE **Adult breeding male** White patch across forehead enclosed by black frontal bar and narrow black patch at base of bill joining black lores, cheeks and earcoverts. Narrow white rear supercilium. Crown and nape brown. White hindneck collar. Upperparts uniform brown with narrow pale fringes. Underparts white broken by black breast band continuing around base of hindneck. Bill orange tipped black. Legs bright orange-yellow. Webbing present between outer and middle toes. Faint yellowish orbital ring. **Adult breeding female** Browner coloration to both ear coverts and breast band. **Adult non-breeding** all black parts become brownish with buffish supercilium joining frontal bar. Large lateral breast patches barely meeting in centre. Bill and legs duller orange. **Juvenile** similar to non-breeding, with dark subterminal bar and buff fringes to mantle, scapulars and coverts. Bill blackish-brown with dull yellow base to lower mandible. Legs dull yellow. **In flight** Clear white wing bar extending onto outer primaries. White sides to dark rump and uppertail. Tail dark brown edged and tipped white.
CALL Usually an obvious rising 'too-li'.
RACES Two are recognized: nominate *hiaticula* (NE Canada to W Europe) and *tundrae* (N Scandinavia to N Russia), the latter being generally smaller and darker.
HABITAT AND BEHAVIOUR Nests mainly around coastal areas especially shingle beaches, but also Arctic tundra and inland lakes and gravel pits. Exhibits injury feigning display to ward off disturbance from nest site. In winter common along the coast, often forming sizeable flocks at high tide.
MOVEMENTS Largely migratory, moving south from mid- August returning during April/May. Nearctic birds migrate through Greenland, Iceland and W Europe to winter mainly in W Africa. N Palearctic birds also migrate through Europe, wintering largely in Africa. Some W European birds non-migratory. Vagrancy widely recorded, e.g., Azores, India, Singapore, Australia.

Semipalmated Plover
Charadrius semipalmatus L 17.80 cm
The American counterpart of Great Ringed Plover, extremely similar, generally more rounded and compact, breeding from Alaska east through N Canada to Baffin Is, where it overlaps and hybridizes with *C. h.*

hiaticula, Hudson Bay, Newfoundland and S Nova Scotia.
PLUMAGE **Adult breeding male** Very narrow white rear supercilium sometimes completely absent. Upperparts darker brown than *hiaticula* similar to *tundrae*. Generally both narrower white hindneck collar and black breast band. Bill averages shorter than Great Ringed Plover, stubbier. Diagnostic webbing present between all toes, extensive between inner and middle toes, clearly visible when foot splayed on shingle or sand. Narrow bright yellow orbital ring. **Adult breeding female** Black areas on head and breast tinged brownish. **Adult non-breeding** Sequence change as Ringed Plover. **Juvenile** Similar to non-breeding adult with dark subterminal bars and buff fringes to upperparts. Blackish loral line tends to narrow anterior to bill meeting culmen above gape. Bill coloration as Great Ringed Plover but legs duller. Orbital ring duller yellow. **In flight** White wing bar slightly narrower and shorter, with white on outer primaries restricted to shafts.
CALL Usual flight note diagnostic, disyllabic 'chu-wee'.
HABITAT AND BEHAVIOUR Nests on sandy and gravelly substrates including stony, pebbly ridges adjacent coastal beaches, sandbars and gravel bars of rivers and lakeshores. Winters on both muddy and sandy coastal beaches and inland lakes and pools.
MOVEMENTS Migratory, moving south from late August to winter from S USA south to S America and Hawaii, returning during April and May. Vagrant Tierra del Fuego, Azores, England.

Little Ringed Plover
Charadrius dubius L 15.25 cm
A small plover, widely distributed across Eurasia, Japan and south to N Africa, India and SE Asia, mainly differing from Great Ringed Plover in lack of wing bar, call and habitat preference.
PLUMAGE **Adult breeding male** Shape differs from Great Ringed in being proportionally smaller, slimmer with a noticeably attenuated rear end. Thin white line separates black frontal bar from brown crown. Bill blackish with yellowish base to lower mandible, noticeably thinner than Great Ringed. Legs pinkish sometimes tinged grey. Bright yellow orbital ring. **Adult breeding female** Breast band tinged brown. Slightly narrower orbital ring.
Adult non-breeding Black frontal bar, face mask and breast band become brownish with buffy wash to supercilium. **Juvenile** Ostensibly brownish with incomplete breast band often reduced to lateral patches. Noticeably buffish forehead with

mantle, scapulars, coverts and tertials showing dark subterminal lines neatly fringed buff. Orbital ring duller yellow with legs also yellow. **In flight** Wing bar virtually absent, reduced to insignificant white tips to greater primary and greater coverts.
CALL an obvious, often far carrying 'pee-uu' descending on the second syllable.
RACES Three are recognized: nominate *dubius* (New Guinea, Philippines); *jerdoni* (India and SE Asia) and *curonicus* (Britain, Eurasia across to Japan, N Africa), all exhibiting similar plumage but differing in length and bill colour.
HABITAT AND BEHAVIOUR Nests inland around fresh water especially stony rivers, lakes and gravel pits. Exhibits attractive display flight reminiscent of a butterfly. Outside the breeding season found primarily on muddy edges to both inshore waters and the coast. Mostly solitary, avoiding flocking with other waders.
MOVEMENTS *Curonicus* entirely migratory, commencing autumn passage from mid-July largely moving in south-south-west–south-south-east direction, wintering in Africa, India and SE Asia. Return spring passage from Africa starts late February. Vagrant to Azores, Cape Verdes, Aleutians and Australia.

A	B	C
D	E	F
G	H	I
J	K	L

A Great Ringed Plover *hiaticula* adult breeding male
B Great Ringed Plover *tundrae* adult breeding male
C Great Ringed Plover adult non-breeding
D Great Ringed Plover juvenile
E Great Ringed Plover adult
F Semipalmated Plover adult breeding
G Semipalmated Plover adult non-breeding
H Semipalmated Plover juvenile
I Little Ringed Plover *dubius* adult breeding
J Little Ringed Plover *dubius* adult non-breeding
K Little Ringed Plover juvenile
L Little Ringed Plover adult

Charadriidae

Long-billed Plover
Charadrius placidus **L 20.30 cm**
Differing subtly from Great Ringed Plover in structure, head and bare part coloration, breeding in the Amur Valley E Siberia south through Manchuria and E China and also Japan.
PLUMAGE Adult breeding White forehead bordered above by broad black frontal bar narrowing distinctly towards sides, lacking black patch at base of bill. Lores, cheeks and ear coverts dark greyish-brown. Longish, narrow white rear supercilium. Crown and nape brown. White hindneck collar. Upperparts uniform grey-brown narrowly fringed cinnamon-buff when fresh. Primaries clearly extend beyond tail tip. Underparts white interrupted by narrow black breast band continuing around base of hindneck. Bill long, slim and pointed, black with yellowish-orange base to lower mandible. Legs longish, pale yellowish. Narrow dull yellow orbital ring.
Adult non-breeding Very similar to adult breeding. Head and breast pattern duller admixed with brown. **Juvenile** Black frontal bar lacking. White forehead joins indistinct buffish-brown supercilium. Upperparts neatly fringed warm buff. Brownish lateral breast patches narrowly joining in centre. **In flight** Indistinct narrow greyish-white wing bar across tips of greater coverts barely extending onto inner greater primary coverts. Longish graduated tail greyish-brown narrowly edged white with clear darker brown subterminal bar.
CALL Clear 'peewee' similar to Little Ringed Plover; also musical 'toodulou'.
HABITAT AND BEHAVIOUR Nests on edges of lakes and river beds up to 1000 m covered by gravel, pebbles and stones, avoiding sandy areas. Generally non-gregarious. Performs aerial display flight with wings held vertically. Outside breeding season inhabits shingle river beds and mudflats.
MOVEMENTS Resident parts of S China and Japan from Honshu southwards. Otherwise migratory, wintering in China, Indo-China west to Nepal. Vagrant Malaysia, Brunei, Bali and Hong Kong (1994).

Wilson's Plover
Charadrius wilsonia **L18.40 cm**
A smallish, breast-banded plover with a heavy bill, breeding on the coasts of S USA, central and northern S America.
PLUMAGE Adult breeding male Black frontal bar with white forehead joining supercilium. Blackish loral patch from bill to eye. Crown, nape and ear coverts greyish-brown, variably tinged rufous. White neck collar. Upperparts uniform greyish-brown with pale feather edgings. Underparts white broken by broad black breast band. Bill black, longish and heavy, with both mandibles curving to a point. Legs bright pinkish-grey. **Adult breeding female** Black coloration lacking, becoming brown or rufous. White on forehead reduced, with supercilium washed warm buff. **Adult non-breeding** Both sexes resemble breeding female but lack any rufous coloration. Legs duller pinkish-grey. **Juvenile** Similar to non-breeding adult, but upperparts darker brown with dark submarginal lines and neat buff fringes producing 'scaly' effect. **In flight** Short white wing bar to dark upperwng with white sides to grey centred rump and uppertail. Tail black edged and tipped white.
CALL Alarm note a sharp 'kwit-it' with usual flight call an abrupt, weak 'wheet'.
RACES Four are recognized: nominate *wilsonia* (E USA and Mexico) usually lacks rufous; *rufinucha* (W Indies) crown rich rufous; *beldingi* (Baja California south to Panama) darker upperparts, more rufousy head, reduced supercilium and narrower breast band; *cinnamominus* (NE Columbia to NE Brazil) strongly rufous cap and rufous in breast band.
HABITAT AND BEHAVIOUR Breeds on sand dunes and sandy islands usually close to salt or brackish water. In winter also frequents mudflats. Very slow feeding action, with crabs forming major part of diet.
MOVEMENTS Partial migrant, present in many parts of range all year. *Wilsonia* more migratory, wintering south to Brazil and vagrant to Bermuda, Nova Scotia and Great Lakes. *Beldingi* also partial migratory, reaching Peru in winter, with vagrancy recorded in California.

Piping Plover
Charadrius melodus **L 18.40 cm**
Named after its call, this small Nearctic plover has declined significantly in numbers, breeding in the Great Plains and Lakes and E coastal N America.
PLUMAGE Adult breeding male White forehead and narrow white patch above and behind eye. Black frontal bar. Thin white neck collar. Dull reddish-yellow orbital ring. Rest of head, face and upperparts pale sandy-grey, with pale fringes to scapulars and wing coverts. Underparts white broken by black breast band, sometimes incomplete, continuing around base of hindneck. Bill short and stubby, bright orange, with sharply defined black tip. Legs orange tinged yellow. **Adult breeding female** Breast band and frontal bar become blackish-brown.

Adult non-breeding All black coloration is lost. Face generally pale with prominent dark eye. Breast band reduced to lateral breast patches. Dull eye-ring with bill wholly black. Legs duller yellow. **Juvenile** As non-breeding adult but upperparts with dark subterminal lines neatly fringed warm buff giving 'scaly' effect. **In flight** Strong wing bar contrasts with dark grey flight feathers and paler grey secondary coverts. White patch formed by bases of uppertail coverts with black tail tipped and edged white. '**Forms**' Two are distinguished: nominate *melodus* (coastal) usually with complete breast band and *circumcintus* (Prairies and Great Lakes), with mostly broken breast band.
CALL A melodious 'peep-lo'.
HABITAT AND BEHAVIOUR Coastal population nests on sandy, grassless beaches, with internal population favouring lakeshores, but both habitats extremely vulnerable to human disturbance. Outside the breeding season frequents beaches and edges of lagoons.
MOVEMENTS Population from Prairies, Great Lakes and N Atlantic coast migratory, leaving breeding-grounds late August to winter south to NE Mexico and Greater Antilles. Few non-breeders summer south of breeding range. Vagrant California, Ecuador and Lesser Antilles.

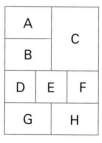

A Long-billed Plover adult
B Wilson's Plover adult non-breeding
C Wilson's Plover *wilsonia* breeding male
D Wilson's Plover adult non-breeding
E Piping Plover adult breeding
F Piping Plover juvenile
G Piping Plover adult non-breeding
H Piping Plover adult non-breeding

Charadriidae

Black-banded Sand Plover
Charadrius thoracicus **L 13.30 cm**
Clearly similar to Kittlitz's Plover but rare, found only in SW Madagascar.
PLUMAGE **Adult** Brilliant white supercilia narrowly meeting on forecrown extending backwards to join on nape enclosing dark brown crown finely edged buff. White forehead, black frontal bar and loral line continuing through eye down sides of neck meeting at base of nape. Upperparts dark brown narrowly fringed pale buff, slightly paler than Kittlitz's Plover. Chin and throat white with broad black breast band separating rest of whitish underparts richly suffused pale cinnamon-buff. Bill black. Legs black. **Adult non-breeding** Duller with black parts generally browner tinged buff. **Juvenile** Similar to non-breeding adult with head duller brown and white. Upperparts broadly fringed pale brownish-buff. Underparts whitish-grey with greyish breast band. Legs greyish. **In flight** Differs from Kittlitz's in white on more webs of inner primaries forming slightly bolder wing bar. White shafts to all primaries. Dark lesser coverts contrast less with median and greater coverts.
CALL A hoarse 'pit' similar to Kittlitz's; also rough 'twi-twi-twi'.
HABITAT AND BEHAVIOUR Strongly favours very dry coastal grassland, very seldom occuring far inland. Also found on sandy and muddy beaches, estuaries and edges of brackish pools. Usually found in pairs or small groups, but may form sizeable flocks at high-tide roosts. Decline in numbers may be attributable to recent arrival of Kittlitz's Plover with which it frequently associates. Commonly found feeding also with Great Ringed Plover and White-fronted Sand Plover.
MOVEMENTS Sedentary.

Kittlitz's Plover
Charadrius pecuarius **L 12.70 cm**
A small, long-legged plover, widely but patchily distributed on dry, open flats along the Nile Delta, sub-Saharan Africa and Madagascar.
PLUMAGE **Adult breeding male** White forehead and black frontal bar narrowly bordered above by white line. Black loral line continuing down sides of neck meeting on upper mantle. Brilliant white supercilia starting above eye curving downwards meeting on nape forming broad half collar. Crown and upperparts dark brown narrowly fringed and edged buff. Underparts white with breast and upper belly variably suffused pale sandy-rufous. Bill black. Legs long, greenish-black. **Adult breeding female** Virtually identical. Narrower black frontal bar. Black

loral line and black streak along sides of neck admixed with brown. **Adult non-breeding** Generally duller, lacking black coloration. Buffish face and hind collar. Upperparts variable pale to dark brown, blackish lesser covert panel evident. Underpart coloration highly variable, sides of breast sometimes suffused brown. Legs paler greenish-grey. **Juvenile** Similar to dull non-breeding adult. Upperparts broadly fringed buffish-brown. Underparts whitish with brownish lateral breast patches. **In flight** Blackish lesser coverts produce dark leading edge to wing with brownish mantle, median and greater coverts. White trailing edge to blackish secondaries, blackish primaries and primary coverts with narrow wing bar across tips of greater coverts extending onto webs of inner primaries. Broad white sides to blackish-brown rump and tail. Toes project noticeably beyond tail tip.
CALL Flight note plaintive 'tu-whit'; alarm note 'prrrt'.
HABITAT AND BEHAVIOUR Frequents variety of dry, flat ground, both coastal and inland, including edges of lakes, rivers, dams, dry saltflats, sandflats and tidal mudflats. Consistently found away from water. Often feeds in small mixed flocks with other calidrid species, alternately running at speed and stopping to peck. Gregarious outside breeding season forming small flocks up to 20 birds.
MOVEMENTS Largely sedentary, undergoing limited seasonal movements linked to rainfall, birds leaving during rains and flooding.

St Helena Plover
Charadrius sanctaehelenae **L. 15.25 cm**
Also known as 'Wirebird', very similar to Kittlitz's Plover but larger, longer billed and longer legged, totally restricted to the remote Atlantic island St Helena, nearly 3000 km west of Angola, recent survey indicating population of about 500 birds.
PLUMAGE **Adult** Differs from Kittlitz's Plover in black feathering frequently meeting across base of bill, upperparts indistinctly fringed buff, and underparts whitish, often lacking creamy-buff tones. Bill longer, black. Legs longer, black. **Juvenile** Head dull brown and whitish, lores very pale often whitish. Upperparts narrowly fringed buff. Breast washed dusky-grey. **In flight** wings appear noticeably rounded and broad. Wing bar virtually lacking with only buffish tips to outer greater coverts. Primary webs dark, very broad, only outermost primary shaft white. Leading edge of underwing, primary coverts and flight feathers all dusky-grey.

CALL Quiet, metallic 'wit-wit', resembling Little Stint.
HABITAT AND BEHAVIOUR Found on open grassland and plains, ploughed fields and even vegetable gardens, avoiding open shore. Usually seen in pairs, breeding mainly during dry season September–March when tends to favour short grass vegetation amongst regions up to 600 m. Suffers from predation, notably cats, rats and introduced Common Mynah.
MOVEMENTS Entirely sedentary.

A	B
C	D
E	F
G	H	I

A Black-banded Sand Plover adult
B Black-banded Sand Plover adult
C Black-banded Sand Plover adult
D Kittlitz's Plover adult breeding
E Kittlitz's Plover adult non-breeding
F Kittlitz's Plover juvenile
G St Helena Plover adult
H St Helena Plover juvenile
I St Helena Plover juvenile

Charadriidae

Kildeer Plover
Charadrius vociferous L 24.75 cm

One of the best known and widespread of all Nearctic waders, breeding from SW Alaska through Canada and the USA to Mexico, W Indies, Peru and NW Chile. **PLUMAGE Adult breeding male** White forehead extending as narrow band underneath eye, and short rear supercilium. Black frontal bar and black mask from bill across cheeks to join black ear covert patch. Crown and nape brown. Bright red orbital ring. White neck collar. Upperparts brown fringed rufous, with tail projecting well beyond folded wing tips. Underparts white broken by double black breast band, the upper broader and continuing around base of hindneck. Warm brown suffusion on breast sides between two bands. Bill black. Legs greyish tinged pink. **Adult breeding female** Face mask and breast band more brownish. **Adult non-breeding** Black areas become much browner. Duller red orbital ring. Upperparts extensively fringed rufous. **Juvenile** Similar to non-breeding adult but upperparts with darkish subterminal lines and pale buff fringes. **In flight** Bold white wing bar, with lower back, rump and uppertail conspicuous orange-rufous. Tail long, graduated, orange-rufous at base with black subterminal band tipped and edged white. **CALL** A rapidly repeated, shrill 'kill-dee'. **RACES** Three are recognized: nominate *vociferous* (Canada and USA) the largest; *ternominatus* (W Indies) smaller and greyer; *peruvianus* (Peru and NW Chile) also smaller with bright rufous feather fringes.
HABITAT AND BEHAVIOUR Often nests well away from water including dry upland, meadows and cultivated land and even roof tops. Performs high circular display flight uttering 'kildeer' call. More associated with water outside the breeding season, including mudflats, watercourses and open fields.
MOVEMENTS Nominate race migratory with long period of passage from July to November, wintering in W Indies (mixing with *ternominatus*) and C and northern S America. Spring passage commences February, thus the earliest American shorebird to return. Vagrant Hawaii, Galapagos Is, and W Europe especially November–April.

Three-banded Plover
Charadrius tricollaris L 17.80 cm

A distinctive long-winged, long-tailed plover, fairly common on inland wetlands in E and South Africa, with separate race in Madagascar.
PLUMAGE Adult White forehead joining prominent white supercilium extending behind eye meeting on hindneck, completely enclosing chocolate-brown crown and nape. Upperparts uniform dark brown. Tail tip extends well beyond folded wing tips. Chin and throat whitish. Lores, cheeks and rest of face pale grey bordered below by narrow black upper breast band. White band separates second much wider lower black breast band. Rest of underparts white. Bill scarlet tipped black. Conspicuous red eye-ring. Legs orangey-brown. **Juvenile** Similar to adult with face pattern less distinct. Forehead washed buffish-brown. Upperparts with dark subterminal lines narrowly fringed buff. **In flight** Characteristic jerky wingbeats. Dark brown mantle and upper wing alleviated by white trailing edge to secondaries, broadest on innermost, extending narrowly onto inner primaries. Narrow white wing bar across tips of greater and primary coverts. Alula and median primary coverts also tipped white. Centre of rump, uppertail coverts and tail dark brown bordered white.
CALL Alarm note loud 'wick-wick'; flight note high pitched 'pu-eet, pu-eet'.
RACES Two are recognized: nominate *tricollaris* (Africa); *bifrontatus* (Madagascar) differentiated by base of forehead grey with white band above. Lores, cheeks and face darker grey. Little white on chin and throat. **In flight** less white on secondaries and primary coverts.
HABITAT AND BEHAVIOUR Frequents pools and lakeshores, especially with muddy fringes, also saltmarsh and rivers with sandy or gravelly banks. Usually occurs in pairs or small family parties. Runs along water's edge taking short flights, bobbing tail on alighting. Also bobs when alarmed, calling frequently.
MOVEMENTS Mainly sedentary, undergoing local movements associated with rains. Occasionally moves farther afield to N Cameroon and N Nigeria as non-breeding visitor, especially during dry season. Vagrant Ghana, Mali and Egypt (March 1993, first Palearctic record).

Forbes's Plover
Charadrius forbesi L 20.30 cm

Similar to Three-banded Plover, differing chiefly in larger size, head pattern and habitat choice, found in dryish grasslands of W and C Africa from Senegambia east to W Uganda and W Tanzania and south to N Angola.
PLUMAGE Adult breeding Differs from Three-banded Plover in brown not white forehead, white rear supercilium not extending forwards beyond eye and upperparts darker chocolate-brown. Upper border to upper breast band merges into dark grey lores, ear coverts and sides of face. Throat brownish flecked white. Lower breast band distinctly broader than upper band. Undertail coverts barred dark brown. Bill dark brown, pinkish at base. Conspicuous red eye-ring. Legs yellowish to pinkish-brown. **Adult non-breeding** Supercilium washed buffish-brown. Breast bands generally dark brown. **Juvenile** Similar to non-breeding adult. Upperparts with dark brown subterminal bars narrowly fringed buff. Little barring to undertail coverts. **In flight** Appears very dark almost completely lacking wing bar, with just faint narrow pale tips to primary and greater coverts. Indistinct narrow white trailing edge to secondaries. Outertail feathers barred dark brown and white.
CALL Frequently repeated 'peeuw'; display song 'pleuw-pleuw-pleuw…'
HABITAT AND BEHAVIOUR Breeds during wet season March–September, nesting on rocky hillsides and granite outcrops. During dry season moves to grassy plains and newly burnt areas, forest clearings, golf courses, rice fields, and muddy edges of lakes and rivers. Occurs singly or in pairs, occasionally small flocks up to 20 birds. Like Three-banded Plover bobs head when alarmed, flying off in jerky, erratic movements.
MOVEMENTS Undergoes local seasonal movements, distinctly scarcer in eastern part of range.

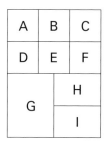

A	B	C
D	E	F
G		H
		I

A Killdeer Plover juvenile
B Killdeer Plover
C Killdeer Plover adult non-breeding
D Killdeer Plover adult breeding
E Three-banded Plover juvenile
F Three-banded Plover adult
G Three-banded Plover adult
H Forbes's Plover adult
I Forbes's Plover adult

Charadriidae

Kentish Plover
Charadrius alexandrinus L 16.50 cm
A small plover with a neck collar but incomplete breast band, showing distinct racial plumage variation, occurring widely throughout Eurasia, N Africa, India, SE Asia and the Americas.
PLUMAGE **Adult breeding male** Smaller than Great Ringed/Semipalmated Plovers. White forehead and supercilium. Black frontal bar and ear coverts. Crown, nape and lores extremely variable. White hindneck collar. Upperparts uniform grey-brown, distinctly paler in the American races. Bill black and slender. Legs longish, usually dark grey variably tinged brownish or yellowish, set well back giving characteristic 'chick' appearance. **Adult breeding female** Black areas become blackish-brown or brown with high degree of racial variation. **Adult non-breeding** Similar to dull female, lacking black coloration. **Juvenile** Similar to non-breeding with upperparts neatly fringed buff giving 'scaly' appearance. **In flight** All races show clear white wing bar and white sides to dark rump and tail.
CALL In Palearctic races flight call a soft 'twit', whilst a low 'krut' or 'ku-weet' in the Americas.
RACES Six are recognized: nominate *alexandrinus* (Eurasia, N Africa) and *dealbatus* (E China, Japan), with breeding males both showing bright rufous caps and black lores, the latter sometimes with pale legs; *seebohmi* (SE India, Sri Lanka) with breeding male lacking rufous cap, often showing white lores; *nivosus* (USA, Caribbean) and *occidentalis* (coastal Peru and Chile), together known as 'Snowy Plover', both shorter legged, with paler, greyer upperparts, breeding birds lack rufous cap, often showing white lores; *javanicus* (Java) little known.
HABITAT AND BEHAVIOUR Breeds on flat, sandy coastal beaches and also far inland by saline or brackish wetlands. Outside the breeding season favours the coast but can frequent inland lakes, especially saline. Distinctly fast feeding action. Also performs 'butterfly' display flight. Gathers in small flocks outside breeding season.
MOVEMENTS Inland and northern coastal populations migratory, with peak autumn movement early September, returning mainly March/April. Southern populations resident. Nearctic races vagrant north to British Columbia and Ontario and south to Panama. Palearctic races recorded Kenya and Zaire.

White-fronted Sand Plover
Charadrius marginatus L 17.80 cm
Resembling a shorter legged, longer tailed Kentish Plover with racial plumage variation, found in Africa both coastally and inland, from Senegambia to Somalia south to Cape Province, and Madagascar.
PLUMAGE **Adult breeding male** Brilliant white forehead and supercilium. Black frontal bar across forecrown with thin black eye-stripe from base of bill extending onto rear ear coverts. Crown, nape and upperparts warm greyish-brown variably edged rufous, with greater coverts tipped white. Blackish tail extending beyond folded wing tips. Underparts white with breast variably washed cream, buff or rufous, either as lateral patches or complete breast band, sometimes extending as pale rufous or whitish collar around hindneck. Bill black. Legs short, greyish tinged green. **Adult breeding female** Black on forecrown reduced. Paler underpart coloration. **Adult non-breeding** Black frontal bar admixed with brown or absent. Eye-stripe brownish-black. **Juvenile** Black frontal bar lacking. Lores dark brown. Underparts whitish lacking lateral breast patches. Upperparts greyish broadly fringed sandy-buff strongly tinged rufous. **In flight** Dark brownish-grey flight feathers with wing bar across tips of greater coverts extending onto webs of inner primaries. Broad white sides to dark greyish rump and tail. Toes do not project beyond tail tip.
CALL Soft 'wit' or 'woo-et'.
RACES Five are recognized: *marginatus* (S Angola to Cape Province) whitish collar, paler upperparts, liitle suffusion to underparts; *tenellus* (Natal to Ethiopia and Sudan, Madagascar) sides of lower neck, upper breast and collar tinged rufous; *mechowi* (Cameroon, N Angola to C Africa, Zaire) and *hesperius* (W Africa to C Africa) both with pale rufous collar; *pons* (S Somalia) whitish collar.
HABITAT AND BEHAVIOUR Prefers sandy coastal seashores, exposed sandy beaches adjacent lakes and large rivers, also saltpans, mudflats and estuaries. Usually in pairs or small parties. Feeds by alternately running very quickly and stopping to peck, sometimes in company with Sanderling and Curlew Sandpiper. Forms flocks up to 70 during non-breeding season.
MOVEMENTS Coastal birds largely sedentary, with local dispersion by immatures. Inland population of C and S Africa migrate to coast, movement largely dependent on rainfall and subsequent changing of water levels.

Malaysian Plover
Charadrius peronii L 15.25 cm
Similar to Kentish Plover but lacking a separate non-breeding plumage, resident on the coasts of Thailand and S Vietnam, Philippines, Malaysia and Indonesia.
PLUMAGE **Adult male** Brilliant white forehead and supercilium. Black frontal bar, narrow loral line and small isolated rear ear covert patch. Crown and nape greyish variably admixed bright rufous. Narrow white hindneck collar bordered black below extending around sides of neck to form black lateral breast patches, sometimes continuing across breast to form complete narrow breast band. Upperparts ashy-brown with darker feather centres. Rest of underparts white. Bill black tinged brown at base of lower mandible. Legs variable greenish-grey tinged yellow. **Adult female** Similar to male but black on head and breast largely replaced by pale rufous-brown. Lateral breast patches frequently joining to form complete breast band. White hindneck collar sometimes very narrow or occasionally lacking completely. **Juvenile** Similar to female, but lacking any black coloration to breast patches. Upperparts broadly fringed sandy-buff. **In flight** Dark brown mantle and upper wing with distinct wing bar across bases of secondaries and tips to greater coverts extending onto bases of inner primaries and tips of primary coverts. Broad white sides to dark rump, uppertail coverts and tail.
CALL Quiet 'chit', similar to Kentish Plover.
HABITAT AND BEHAVIOUR Frequents sandy shorelines, occasionally mudflats. Shows distinct preference for coral sand beaches. Usually occurs in pairs or small family parties.
MOVEMENTS Sedentary.

A	B	C
D	E	F
H	I	G
J	K	L

A   Kentish Plover *alexandrinus* breeding male
B   Kentish Plover alexandrinus breeding female
C   Kentish Plover adult non-breeding
D   Kentish Plover first-winter non-breeding
E   Kentish Plover juvenile
F   Kentish Plover (Snowy Plover) breeding male
G   Kentish Plover (Snowy Plover) breeding
H   White-fronted Sand Plover adult
I   White-fronted Sand Plover adult
J   malaysian Plover breeding male
K   Malaysian Plover breeding male
L   Malaysian Plover breeding female

Charadriidae

Chestnut-banded Sand Plover
Charadrius pallidus L15.25 cm
A small, short-tailed plover, very common but restricted to alkaline lakes in S Africa from SW Angola to Mozambique and also rift valley lakes on the Kenyan–Tanzanian border.
PLUMAGE **Adult male** White forehead narrowly extending around and above eye. Thin black loral line continuing onto ear coverts. Black frontal bar bordered above by chestnut head band extending around sides of neck joining across upper breast to form chestnut breast band. Upper border to breast band frequently admixed with black. Upperparts variable pale greyish-brown. Rest of underparts white. Bill pointed, black. Legs olive-grey. **Adult female** Similar to male, lacking black markings to head and breast band. **Juvenile** Lacks all black and chestnut coloration. Upperparts with dark subterminal lines narrowly fringed buff. Greyish breast band mostly reduced to lateral breast patches. **In flight** Narrow white wing bar extends onto inner primaries. White sides to dark rump, uppertail coverts and tail. Toes project slightly beyond tail tip.
CALL On take off and landing a quiet 'chuck'; also when defending territory an uncharacteristic 'chee-witch-ee-uu'.
RACES Two are recognized: *pallidus* (S Africa) larger, paler upperparts, with female lacking chestnut on head; *venustus* (E Africa) smaller, darker upperparts, with female showing pale chestnut eye-stripe.
HABITAT AND BEHAVIOUR Restricted to alkaline lakes, saltpans, coastal lagoons and estuaries, rarely visiting fresh water. Usually in pairs or small flocks up to 50 birds. Feeds along water's edge catching insects, frequently wading in shallow water. Calls extensively early morning. Relatively shy, flying low and fast.
MOVEMENTS Partially migratory, local movements associated with drying up of suitable habitat. In E Africa some commuting up and down Rift Valley. In S Africa inland birds disperse to coast after breeding, mixing with sedentary population. Vagrant north to Zambia.

Two-banded Plover
Charadrius falklandicus L 17.80 cm
The lowland relative to Puna Plover, breeding mainly adjacent the coasts of Chile, Argentina including Tierra del Fuego and the Falkland Islands.
PLUMAGE **Adult breeding male** Forehead and lores white. Black frontal bar with dusk-grey patch to cheeks and ear coverts narrowly extending down sides of neck joining upper breast band. Mid-crown,

nape and hindneck greyish extensively washed rufous. Rest of upperparts uniform greyish-brown. Narrow upper breast band often incomplete (especially Falkland Is population), reduced to lateral patches. Complete black lower breast band, widening in centre across upper belly. Rest of underparts white. Bill longish, slender, black. Legs black. **Adult breeding female** Black areas admixed with brown. Crown and hindneck duller rufous-brown. **Adult non-breeding** Black and rufous coloration replaced by dusky-grey. Nape warm buff-brown. Lower breast band frequently incomplete. **Juvenile** Similar to non-breeding adult. Upperparts with narrow dark submarginal lines fringed warm buff. Mottled greyish-brown lateral patches to upper breast. Greyish-brown wash to lower breast often incomplete. **In flight** Inconspicuous wing bar across tips of greater coverts and inner primaries. White fringe to greyish-brown uppertail coverts and darker grey tail.
CALL Flight note liquid 'wheet'.
HABITAT AND BEHAVIOUR Favours stony, gravelly beaches, also sandy beaches and flat, sandy areas adjacent lagoons, lakes and streams, and dry grass-covered slopes somewhat inland from coast. Also up to 1200 m in Andean foothills. Males perform impressive aerial display chases. Usually tame. Outside breeding season forms flocks up to 200 birds, wintering on sandy beaches and mudflats.
MOVEMENTS Falkland Is population resident. Mainland birds migratory, moving north to N Chile, Uruguay and S Brazil.

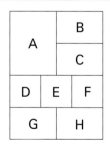

A Chestnut-banded Sand Plover *venustis* breeding female
B Chestnut-banded Sandplover breeding male
C Chestnut-banded Sandplover adult non-breeding
D Chestnut-banded Sandplover juvenile
E Chestnut-banded Sandplover adult
F Two-banded Plover breeding female
G Two-banded Plover breeding male
H Two-banded Plover juvenile

Charadriidae

Puna Plover
Charadrius alticola L 17.15 cm
A stocky 'neckless' plover, found in the Puna zone of the high Andes in S Peru, NE Chile, W Bolivia and NW Argentina. **PLUMAGE Adult breeding male** Brilliant white forehead and lores. Black frontal bar continuing down sides of neck. Indistinct whitish post-ocular spot. Mid-crown, nape and hindneck greyish-brown variably washed rufous. Rest of upperparts greyish-brown narrowly fringed warm buff. Small black lateral upper breast patches. Complete broad lower breast band greyish tinged chestnut. Rest of underparts white. Bill short, stubby, black. Legs black, set well back. **Adult breeding female** Black areas admixed with brown. Rufous coloration on head less extensive. **Adult non-breeding** Black and chestnut coloration replaced by dusky-grey. Large dark eye emphasized by plain-faced appearance. Indistinct mottled greyish upperbreast patch and lower breast band. **Juvenile** Chestnut and black coloration lacking. Buffish wash to forehead, lores and supercilium. Upperparts narrowly fringed buff giving 'scaly' effect. Upper breast patches lacking. Lower breast band warm chestnut-grey, often complete. **In flight** Greyish-brown mantle and upper wing with inconspicuous wing bar across tips of greater coverts and bases of inner primaries. White fringe to greyish-brown uppertail coverts and darker grey tail. **CALL** Flight note quiet, weak 'peet, peet'. **HABITAT AND BEHAVIOUR** Found above 3000 m, often considerably higher, favouring wide areas of short, open grassland adjacent fresh-or saltwater lakes. Feeds in small loose flocks in typical plover 'run, stop, peck' manner on wet, muddy shorelines. When approached prefers to run away very quickly rather than fly away. Sometimes crouches low on ground to avoid detection. **MOVEMENTS** Mostly sedentary. Regular small movement descends outside breeding season to Pacific coast, Peru.

Collared Plover
Charadrius collaris L 14.60 cm
A small plover, inappropriately named since lacks a hind collar, found in variety of sandy regions in C and S America from W Mexico east of the Andes to C Argentina and also C Chile. **PLUMAGE Adult male breeding** Broad black band across central crown and black lores enclose brilliant white forehead and forecrown. Rear crown, hindneck and ear coverts indistinct pale chestnut alleviated by small white post-ocular supercilium. Upperparts greyish-brown fringed tawny-buff. Underparts white with broad black central breast band. Bill longish, slim, black with orange tinge to base of lower mandible. Legs yellowish-pink. **Adult female breeding** Reduced chestnut on crown and hindneck. Black areas admixed with brown. **Juvenile** Black coloration initially lacking. Upperparts neatly fringed warm buff. Small chestnut-brown lateral breast patches gradually become black. **In flight** Greyish-brown mantle and upperwing with white tips to greater coverts extending onto inner and middle primaries forming narrow wing bar. Uppertail coverts and tail dark greyish-brown broadly fringed white. **CALL** Sharp, metallic 'chit' or 'chitik'. **HABITAT AND BEHAVIOUR** Found across a wide range of sandy and gravelly habitats including coastal beaches and estuaries, banks of rivers and ponds, and open sandy savannah. Feeds by running very fast with intermittent pauses. Ground display involves male puffing out chest while chasing female. Forms small, scattered flocks during non-breeding season. **MOVEMENTS** Largely sedentary. Chilean population mostly present outside breeding season.

Pied Plover
Vanellus cayanus L 22.20 cm
Resembling a large *charadrius*, this striking plover breeds in open country in S America from SE Columbia and Venezuela south to SE Brazil. **PLUMAGE Adult** White headband completely encircles greyish-brown crown. Black forehead extends as black mask through lores and sides of face, continuing onto hindneck and upper mantle and down sides of breast joining broad black breast band. Lower mantle, back, coverts and tertials greyish-brown. Outer mantle feathers and upper scapulars white, lower scapulars black, together forming two contrasting 'V's along upperparts. Rest of underparts white. Bill black tinged pink towards base. Legs long, orangey-red. Iris scarlet. Black carpal spur. **Juvenile** All black coloration replaced with greyish-brown. Whitish forehead. Scapulars and coverts fringed cinnamon-buff. **In flight** Black outer primaries and primary coverts contrast with white inner primaries and secondaries, outer median and greater coverts. Rest of coverts greyish-brown. Striking black and white scapular lines. Lower back, rump, uppertail coverts and tail white, the last with broad black terminal band narrowing at sides. Toes project beyond tail tip. **CALL** Mellow whistled 'kee-oo', second syllable lower in pitch.

HABITAT AND BEHAVIOUR Resides in savannah-type country in forested zones especially favouring sandy river banks and sandbars. Occurs in small groups up to ten. Feeds in typical plover-like manner. Performs peculiar undulating song display flight. **MOVEMENTS** Sedentary.

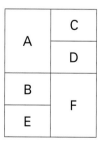

A	C
	D
B	F
E	

A Puna Plover adult
B Puna Plover breeding male and female
C Collared Plover adult
D Collared Plover juvenile
E Pied Plover adult
F Pied Plover adult

Charadriidae

Red-capped Plover
Charadrius ruficapillus L 15.25 cm

Closely related and similar to Kentish Plover but lacking a neck collar, widespread and common in wetland habitat throughout coastal and inland Australia and Tasmania.

PLUMAGE **Adult male** White forehead merging with short white supercilium extending just behind eye. Black frontal bar. Black lores and eye-stripe extending down sides of neck forming small black lateral breast patches. Crown and nape rich chestnut-red, with centre of crown variably flecked greyish-brown. Upperparts uniform greyish-brown. Entire underparts brilliant white. Bill black. Legs blackish tinged green. **Adult female** Often duller than male, with black parts brownish or blackish-brown. Crown invariably mottled greyish-brown. **Juvenile** Chestnut and black coloration replaced with brown. Upperparts with dark subterminal bars fringed buff. **In flight** Distinct white wing bar across tips of greater coverts and bases of inner primaries. White sides to dark brown rump, uppertail coverts and tail.

CALL Various. Usual flight note quiet 'weet', rapidly repeated; also short trill on breeding-grounds.

HABITAT AND BEHAVIOUR Frequents wide range of coastal habitat including beaches, tidal inlets and mudflats. Also salt lakes and margins of permanent lagoons in the interior. Feeds by running extremely fast, pausing to catch prey. Territorial, exhibiting 'rodent run' distraction display. Gregarious at all seasons, freely mixing with other small shorebirds.

MOVEMENTS Largely sedentary, but nomadic in the interior. Inland birds tend to move to the coast outside the breeding season when water dries up during the summer, returning in response to rains. Vagrant New Zealand (has bred South Island).

Red-kneed Dotterel
Charadrius cinctus L 18.40 cm

A striking, long-legged plover, resident and widely distributed on predominantly inland wetlands throughout Australia.

PLUMAGE **Adult** Entire head black faintly tinged dark green. Upperparts dark brown glossed green, slightly darker on upper mantle. Brilliant white chin, throat and sides of neck, enclosed by broad black breast band, extending down upper flanks, becoming chestnut on lower flanks. Sides of vent and undertail coverts spotted chestnut. Conspicuous long white flash along upper edge of flanks separating dark brown upperparts from black and chestnut breast and flank bar. Rest of underparts white. Bill longish, thin, dull pinkish-red tipped black. Narrow dull red eye-ring. Legs long with tibia to 'knee' joint dull pink, sometimes difficult to see in the field, tarsus bluish-grey. **Juvenile** Head dull greenish-brown, concolorous with upperparts. Mantle, scapulars and coverts narrowly fringed buff. Underparts white with ill-defined breast patches and flank bars. Bill duller pink tipped brownish.

Flight Swift and erratic. Broad white trailing edge to secondaries and inner primaries contrasts with blackish outer wing and dark brown mantle and inner wing. Broad white sides to dark brown rump, uppertail coverts and tail. Feet project noticeably beyond tail tip.

CALL Flight note sharp 'chet-chet'; also musical trill when disturbed.

HABITAT AND BEHAVIOUR Frequents muddy fringes of inland swamps and lakes usually avoiding the coast. Breeds almost colonially, unusually building substantial nest on wet ground, often susceptible to flooding. Stance characteristically horizontal with breast dipping forward. Feeds in wet mud, often wading in water. Swims well. When disturbed, uses effective disruptive camouflage, often bobbing head before flying off.

MOVEMENTS Resident. Nomadic in times of drought, moving considerable distance to find suitable habitat. First bred Tasmania 1967. Vagrant New Zealand.

A	C
B	
D	E

A Red-capped Plover breeding female
B Red-capped Plover juvenile
C Red-capped Plover breeding male
D Red-kneed Dotterel adult
E Red-kneed Dotterel adult

Charadriidae

Double-banded Plover
Charadrius bicinctus L 17.80 cm
Unique in migrating north after breeding, nesting on river beds and coastally throughout New Zealand, the majority on South Island.
PLUMAGE **Adult breeding male** White forehead and shortish narrow supercilium. Small black frontal bar. Black lores continuing as indistinct blackish-brown line down sides of neck across breast to form narrow black upper breast band. Crown and rest of upperparts warm greyish-brown. Broad chestnut-red lower breast band. Rest of underparts white. Bill pointed, black. Legs greenish-grey. **Adult breeding female** Generally duller, black parts admixed with brown. **Adult non-breeding** Lacks black and chestnut coloration. Creamy supercilium indistinct. Upper breast band faint, washed brownish. Lower breast band often lacking or reduced to lateral breast patches. **Juvenile** Breast bands both lacking, replaced with indistinct brownish-grey mottling across centre of breast. Conspicuous warm buff supercilium and nape. Upperparts with dark subterminal lines narrowly fringed buff. Legs yellowish-grey. **In flight** Dark grey mantle and upperwing with faint narrow wing bar across base of secondaries and tips of greater coverts extending onto bases of inner primaries. White sides to dark brown rump. Tail dark brown paler towards sides.
CALL Usual flight note abrupt repeated 'chip'.
RACES Two are recognized: nominate *bicinctus* (New Zealand); *exilis* (Aukland Is) slightly larger, duller breast bands and warmer brown upperparts.
HABITAT AND BEHAVIOUR Favoured breeding area is braided river beds on South Island; also coastal shellbanks and sand-dunes, lakeshores, pasture and ploughed fields across New Zealand. Performs trilling 'butterfly' display flight. Post-breeding flocks gather on short grassland and saltmarsh before moving to winter on coastal harbours, mudflats and estuaries. *Exilis* nests on mountain slopes.
MOVEMENTS *Bicinctus* migratory. Leaves during February moving to coast and mainly north to northern end of North Island, especially Manakau Harbour and Firth of Thames. Some migrate farther north to winter in SE Australia and Tasmania, returning to breed during August. *Exilis* is sedentary. Vagrant Fiji, South Pacific Is.

Black-fronted Plover
Charadrius melanops L 17.15 cm
The most widespread of Australia's waders, resident throughout the country

on suitable wetlands, having successfully spread comparatively recently to Tasmania and parts of New Zealand.
PLUMAGE **Adult** Prominent white supercilium starting just in front of eye meeting on nape, almost encircling brown crown. Unique vertical black frontal bar from centre of crown to forehead, joining black lores and broad black eye-stripe, also meeting on nape. Mantle and tertials brownish with dark brown feather centres. Upper scapulars deep purple forming solid dark patch on closed wing. Coverts brown heavily streaked whitish also forming prominent panel on closed wing, especially when worn. Broad black 'V'-shaped breast band extending around sides of neck and joining black eye-stripe at rear. Rest of underparts white. Bill scarlet tipped black. Scarlet eye-ring. Legs dull orange-yellow or pinkish. **Juvenile** Head pattern ill-defined. Crown brownish flecked white lacking black frontal bar. Lores and eye-stripe admixed with brown. Scapulars brown. Coverts chestnut streaked white. **In flight** Appears short-tailed, broad-winged with jerky wingbeats. Pale panel across coverts contrasts with black primaries and leading edge of wing. Dusky secondaries with prominent white shafts. Rump and uppertail coverts chestnut-brown. Blackish tail clearly fringed white.
CALL An abrupt 'tip' regularly repeated.
HABITAT AND BEHAVIOUR Frequents margins of rivers, creeks, fresh or brackish swamps and lagoons, especially with muddy or shingly surrounds. Also adapted to artificial wetlands including farm dams and sewerage works. Avoids open seashore. Usually solitary or in pairs, occasionally forming small flocks during winter. Foot patters when feeding. Well developed 'injury-feigning' display.
MOVEMENTS Resident. Occasionally undertakes local movements towards coastal wetlands if inland habitat becomes too dry.

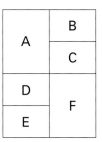

A Double-banded Plover adult non-breeding
B Double-banded Plover breeding male
C Double-banded Plover breeding female
D Double-banded Plover
E Double-banded Plover juvenile
F Black-fronted Plover adult

Charadriidae

Hooded Plover
Charadrius rubricollis L 19.70 cm
A palish plover, declining and largely restricted to undisturbed oceanic beaches of S Australia and Tasmania.
PLUMAGE **Adult** Entire head and neck black. Black hindneck collar extends up to sides of hood, narrowly enclosing broad white band across hindneck, also continuing onto breast sides, forming small black lateral breast patches. Upperparts pale grey faintly washed brown narrowly fringed white. Underparts white. Bill red tipped black. Eye-ring red. Legs shortish, pale orange. **Juvenile** Black parts all brownish tipped white. Upperparts greyish-brown with dark submarginal lines narrowly fringed buff giving 'scaly' effect. Chin, throat and underparts whitish washed very pale grey. Eye-ring orangey-red. Legs pale orange tinged brown. **In flight** Broad white wing bar extending onto outermost primaries, contrasting with black primary tips, outer secondaries and primary coverts, latter tipped white. Rump, uppertail coverts and tail blackish fringed white.
CALL Rather silent. Occasional deep 'kew-kew'.
HABITAT AND BEHAVIOUR Breeds on lonely sandy beaches; also on shores of salt lakes in SW Western Australia. Usually in small family parties, but flocks up to 100 encountered during winter. Feeds on all levels of beach, particularly favouring seaweed line. Fairly wary, moving slowly away when disturbed, bobbing head repeatedly, cryptic coloration affording excellent camouflage.
MOVEMENTS Largely sedentary. Undertakes some local movements from coast to inland salt lakes during winter.

Shore Plover
Thinornis novaeseelandiae L 20.30 cm
A dumpy, highly distinctive plover, extremely rare and numbering fewer than 130 birds, totally restricted to South East Is (Rangatira), Chatham Is, 800 km east of New Zealand.
PLUMAGE **Adult breeding male** Unique head and facial pattern. Black mask encompassing forehead, lores, sides of face, chin, throat and extending around hindneck as narrow neck collar. White head band totally encircling brownish crown. Upperparts brownish fringed pale. Underparts whitish with brown mottling to sides of breast. Bill longish, finely pointed, with deep red base and slightly drooping black tip. Legs rather short, thick set, orange. Red orbital ring. **Adult breeding female** Black mask mottled brown. Bill mostly black with red restricted to base.

Juvenile Face whitish with dark brown lores and eye-stripe forming facial mask. Crown and upperparts brown with darker brown subterminal bars heavily fringed warm buff giving distinct 'scaly' appearance. Bill dark grey tinged dull red at base of lower mandible. Legs dull yellow-brown. **In flight** Very plover-like with clear white wing bar extending onto outer primaries. White sides to dark brown rump and tail.
CALL Highly vocal. A clipped, ringing 'pieu', reminiscent of Oystercatcher and Little Ringed Plover. Also a rapidly repeated 'pit, pit, pit, pit'.
HABITAT AND BEHAVIOUR Inhabits flat rocky platforms adjacent the shoreline, nesting largely under boulders in vegetation above the high-tide line. Feeds by rapid pecking action, quite unlike a plover. Very tame and approachable. Exhibits 'butterfly' display action. Captive breeding scheme in operation at Mount Bruce Wildlife Centre, near Wellington, involving about 20 birds.
MOVEMENTS Sedentary. Attempts to move some birds to nearby Mangere Is resulted in them flying back almost immediately. Future aim of captive programme to release population into the wild on another predator-free island.

Wrybill
Anarhynchus frontalis L 20.30 cm
With a uniquely shaped bill among waders, this stocky plover breeds only in the braided river valleys of South Island, New Zealand, with a total population just exceeding 5000 birds (1994 census).
PLUMAGE **Adult breeding male** Broad white band across forehead joins short white supercilium extending just behind eye. Grey lores, ear coverts, crown and nape. Black frontal bar. Upperparts uniform grey. Underparts white broken by narrow black breast band. **Adult breeding female** Black frontal bar largely absent. Breast band narrower admixed with brown. **Adult non-breeding** Supercilium less distinct with black frontal bar absent. Black breast band largely indistinct, often reduced to grey smudges at sides. Bill black, tapering to a point. Appears straight viewed from the side, but from head-on clearly curves sharply to the right towards the tip. Legs black tinged dull green. **Juvenile** Similar to non-breeding adult but breast band absent, restricted to grey lateral breast patches. Upperparts grey neatly fringed white. **In flight** Thin white wing bar strongest on inner primaries alleviates plain grey upperwing, rump and tail, the last edged white.
CALL A loudish 'peep'. Feeding flocks maintain constant twittering sound.

HABITAT AND BEHAVIOUR Breeding restricted to large, stony, braided river beds. Bill especially adapted to extract prey from underneath stones. Fairly tame and approachable. Outside the breeding season favours harbours, sandy and muddy bays, where then feeds by normal pecking, running very fast between feeds and sweeping bill from side to side.
MOVEMENTS Migratory, moving along the coast from late December to winter mainly in the large harbours around Aukland, North Island (especially Manakau and Firth of Thames), returning to breed from late July. Small numbers remain in winter quarters all year round. Rare inland North Island.

A Hooded Plover adult
B Shore Plover breeding male
C Shore Plover breeding female
D Shore Plover juvenile
E Shore Plover adult
F Wrybill adult breeding
G Wrybill adult non-breeding
H Wrybill adult breeding
I Wrybill

Charadriidae

Lesser Sand Plover
Charadrius mongolus L 19.70 cm
A smallish plover, very similar to Greater Sand Plover, differing in more rounded headshape, bare part lengths and coloration, flight pattern and call, breeding discontinuously from sea-level in NE Siberia and Commander Is to high altitude in S Russia, Himalayas and Tibet.
PLUMAGE **Adult breeding male** Forehead variable, from white divided by thin black line to totally black. Crown pale brown tinged dull chestnut shading to brighter maroon-chestnut nape and hindneck. Black mask from bill base to ear coverts. Upperparts uniform dark brown. Underparts white with sides of neck and breast band maroon-chestnut extending onto upper belly, frequently bordered black above. Bill thickish, black, length not exceeding loral length. Legs longish with short tibia, dark grey, sometimes tinged greenish. **Adult breeding female** Black parts become rufous-brown, except sometimes around eye. **Adult non-breeding** All black and chestnut coloration lost. Whitish forehead and supercilium separates greyish-brown crown, lores and ear coverts. Hindneck and upperparts greyish-brown. Underparts white with extensive greyish-brown lateral breast patches sometimes joining in centre. **Juvenile** Upperparts especially scapulars and tertials fringed sandy-buff. Buffish-brown lateral breast patches. **In flight** Narrow inner wing bar, extending as parallel bar onto outer webs of inner primaries. White sides to dark rump. Tail appears uniform brown with narrow white sides and tip. Toes barely project beyond tail tip.
CALL Sharp 'chitik'.
RACES Five are recognized: (northern group) *mongolus* (E Russia) and *stegmanni* (E Siberia, Commander Is) larger, black line divides white forehead, blackish upper border to breast band; (southern group) *pamirensis* (S Russia); *atrifons* (Himalayas, S Tibet) and *schaeferi* (E Tibet) black forehead, sometimes with small white patches, shorter wings, longer bill and legs.
HABITAT AND BEHAVIOUR Ranges from sandy dunes at sea-level on Commander Is to mountain steppe and desert up to 5500 m in Tibet. Appears at inland wetlands during migration, wintering on tidal mud- and sandflats around coasts and estuaries.
MOVEMENTS Highly migratory, moving south from August returning May. Northern populations winter from Taiwan, south to Philippines to Australia. Southern birds winter from Persian Gulf and E Africa east to India, Thailand and Greater Sundas.

Often remains in winter quarters all year. Vagrant Europe west to Norway, E African lakes, W Alaska, Canada and USA.

Greater Sand Plover
Charadrius leschenaultii L 23.50 cm
A largish chunky plover with angular headshape and typically heavy bill, nesting in dry steppe in S Eurasia from Turkey east to Mongolia.
PLUMAGE **Adult breeding male** Similar to Lesser Sand Plover, black and chestnut areas slightly narrower. Breast band typically orangey-chestnut, extending around hindneck onto crown. Upperparts paler brown than Lesser, sometimes extensively fringed rufous. Bill stout, distinctly angled gonys, black, bill length exceeding loral length. Legs long, variable coloration, typically paler than Lesser, grey tinged dull green; tibia longer than Lesser. **Adult breeding female** Mask and forecrown greyish-brown, some black retained around eye. Crown, nape and breast band duller rufous. **Adult non-breeding** Similar plumage and coloration to Lesser. **Juvenile** Upperparts extensively fringed warm buff. Buffish-brown lateral breast patches may join in centre. **In flight** Inner wing bar slightly narrower than Lesser, but noticeably widening across inner primaries. Broader white border to lateral uppertail coverts and tail tip, with contrasting darker brown subterminal band. Toes project beyond tail tip.
CALL Soft trilling 'chirrri'.
RACES Three are recognized: *columbinus* (Turkey, Jordan east to Caspian shortest billed, rufous fringes to upperparts and flanks; *leschenaultii* (Russia, W China, Mongolia) intermediate bill length; *crassirostris* (Caspian east to Lake Baikal) longest billed, legs and wings.
HABITAT AND BEHAVIOUR Breeds at much lower altitudes than Lesser, favouring deserts, dry clayflats, sometimes devoid of vegetation. Rare inland except during migration, wintering on tidal sand- and mudflats, often mixing with Lesser.
MOVEMENTS Migratory, forming post-breeding flocks in July departing earlier than Lesser to winter in Persian Gulf, E Africa east to India, Indo-China, Taiwan, Philippines south to Australia. Spring passage also earlier than Lesser from April onwards. Some stay to winter around Caspian, with first-year birds remaining in winter quarters all year. Vagrant to W Europe more often than Lesser including Britain; also N Africa, Nigeria, Tanzania, Uganda.

A	B	C
D	E	F
G	H	I
J	K	L

A Lesser Sand Plover *mongolus* adult breeding
B Lesser Sand Plover *atrifons* adult breeding
C Lesser Sand Plover *mongolus* adult non-breeding
D Lesser Sand Plover *mongolus* adult breeding
E Lesser Sand Plover *atrifons* juvenile
F Lesser Sand Plover *mongolus* adult non-breeding
G Greater Sand Plover *columbinus* breeding male
H Greater Sand Plover *columbinus* female breeding
I Greater Sand Plover *columbinus* first-winter non-breeding
J Greater Sand Plover *columbinus* adult non-breeding
K Greater Sand Plover *leschenaultii* adult non-breeding
L Greater Sand Plover *leschenaultii* adult non-breeding

Charadriidae

Diademed Plover
Phegornis mitchellii L 17.80 cm
A small, scarce and highly charismatic wader of the high Andes, ranging from C Peru south to W Bolivia, N Chile south to C Argentina.
PLUMAGE **Adult** Blackish crown, forehead, face and throat separated by distinctive brilliant white supercilia or 'diadem' joining across forecrown. Narrow white crescent below eye. Hindneck rufous extending around sides of neck forming half collar. Entire upperparts greyish-brown, darker on mantle and tertials. Short creamy carpal bar invariably hidden by overlapping flank feathers. Broad white band across throat. Rest of underparts white, breast and upper belly narrowly barred dusky-grey, gradually diminishing on lower belly, vent and undertail coverts. Bill black, slim, drooping towards tip. Legs yellowish-orange. **Juvenile** Much duller, lacking white 'diadem' and rufous half collar. Head dull brownish-grey with inconspicuous buffish rear supercilium. Upperparts dark brown, spotted, barred and fringed warm cinnamon-buff. Underparts dirty brownish-white, barring confined to breast and flanks. **In flight** Distinctive stiff wingbeats on broad, rounded wings held below horizontal and short tail, appearing uniform dark grey apart from white fringes and tips to inner secondaries. Tail dark grey, outer feathers barred white, tips spotted white. Underwing coverts and axillaries mostly white.
CALL Usually silent, occasionally clear, plaintive plover-like 'pyeet'.
HABITAT AND BEHAVIOUR Breeds from 4000–5000 m in the Andean Puna zone, frequenting waterlogged bogs with matted cushion-plant vegetation, adjacent gravelly streams, rivers and lakes. Usually singly or in pairs, often tame and approachable but difficult to observe owing to size, quiet behaviour and slow movements. Feeds hidden in crevices and creeks in bogs with plover-like gait, probing with bill held vertically. Teeters like Common Sandpiper.
MOVEMENTS Mostly resident, descending during March to lower altitudes in southern part of range, returning to breeding-grounds October.

Tawny-throated Dotterel
Oreopholus ruficollis L 26.65 cm
An unmistakable and extremely attractive plover with characteristic upright stance, breeding both coastally and in the Andes from Peru south through Bolivia, Chile and W Argentina including Tierra del Fuego.
PLUMAGE **Adult** Broad creamy supercilium and forehead separating dark grey crown and narrow well-defined blackish line from

bill to eye continuing onto ear coverts, also bordered below by narrow creamy stripe. Chin white. Warm orangey-rufous wash across throat and foreneck. Hindneck and upper mantle slate-grey tinged rufous extending around sides of neck onto breast. Lower mantle, scapulars, coverts and tertials black centred broadly fringed tawny-buff giving distinct heavily streaked appearance. Belly and flanks warm buff shading to whitish vent with conspicuous black patch to central belly. Bill black, distinctly longish and slender, slightly drooping towards tip. Legs brightish pink. **Juvenile** Similar to adult. Brownish crown and greyish breast fringed buff. Throat buff. Upperparts dark grey narrowly fringed buff giving 'scaly' not streaked effect. Legs greyish. **Flight** fast, high and direct. Broad white bases to primaries and narrow white trailing edge to secondaries. Plain brown rump and uppertail coverts tinged rufous. Tail paler brownish-grey with darker grey subterminal band. Underwing coverts and axillaries white.
CALL In flight melancholy, falling, rapidly repeated 'durr, durr, durr', often combined with slower 'deuu, deuu'.
RACES Two are recognized: *pallidus* (N Peru) smaller, greyer; *ruficollis* (C Peru south through rest of range).
HABITAT AND BEHAVIOUR *Pallidus* breeds on arid coast favouring sandy 'lomas' zone. *Ruficollis* ranges from windswept tola heathland at sea-level to overgrazed grassland up to 4600 m in Puna zone of Andes, frequently some distance from water. When disturbed often remains motionless, adopting upright stance with neck stretched upwards. Sometimes stands with back to observer, striated upperparts affording excellent camouflage. Forms small loose flocks outside breeding season. During migration also found in lowland fields and meadows.
MOVEMENTS *Pallidus* sedentary. *Ruficollis* migratory in south part of range, moving north to Ecuador, Uruguay and S Brazil during March–April, returning August–September. Andean population descends to lower levels during winter. Vagrant Falkland Is.

Rufous-chested Dotterel
Charadrius modestus L 20.30 cm
A smallish handsome dotterel, breeding on dry grasslands of S Chile, S Argentina including Tierra del Fuego and the Falkland Is.
PLUMAGE **Adult breeding** Brilliant white supercilia joining on forecrown, terminating well behind eye in indistinct dull rufous spot. Crown dark brown. Forehead, lores, ear coverts, cheeks and

throat pale bluish-grey. Nape, hindneck and entire upperparts dark greyish-brown indistinctly and narrowly fringed buff. Chin whitish. Foreneck and breast rich rufous-chestnut broadly bordered black below. Rest of underparts white. Bill black. Legs greenish tinged grey. **Adult non-breeding** Head paler brown with forehead and supercilium creamy-buff. Upperparts brown with scapulars and coverts mottled and fringed buff. Chin and throat whitish. Neck and breast mottled brown. **Juvenile** Similar to non-breeding adult. Upperparts, especially mantle and scapulars very dark brown noticeably edged and fringed white. Neck and breast mottled dark brown. **In flight** Uniform darkish brown mantle and upperwing with indistinct white tips to inner secondaries. Broad white sides to dark brown rump. Dark brown tail edged white.
CALL Normal flight call sad, rippling 'pee-uu'
HABITAT AND BEHAVIOUR Favoured breeding-ground is dry grasslands and heaths, also open peat bogs and stony terrain, frequently at higher altitude. Performs noisy aerial display with wings raised high, uttering rattling call. Gait typical plover-like. Forms sizeable post-breeding flocks up to 200 birds, wintering on shingly coasts and adjacent flooded grasslands, frequently associating with Two-banded Plover.
MOVEMENTS Partially migratory. Most southerly breeding birds, especially from Tierra del Fuego, move north to N Chile, N Argentina, Uruguay and SE Brazil. Vagrant Peru and Tristan da Cunha.

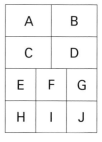

A	B
C	D
E	F	G
H	I	J

A. Diademed Plover adult breeding
B. Diademed Plover adult breeding
C. Diademed Plover adult breeding
D. Diademed Plover juvenile
E. Tawny-throated Dotterel adult
F. Tawny-throated Dotterel adult
G. Rufous-chested Dotterel male breeding
H. Rufous-chested Dotterel female breeding
I. Rufous-chested Dotterel juvenile
J. Rufous-chested Dotterel adult non-breeding

Charadriidae

Caspian Plover
Charadrius asiaticus L 19.05 cm
A highly migratory, fairly long-legged and long-winged plover, breeding on the steppes of C Asia from Kazakstan east to around Lake Balkhash.
PLUMAGE **Adult breeding male** Crown, nape and rear eye-stripe extending just anterior to eye all dark brown, contrasting with prominent long white supercilium, forehead, face and throat. Upperparts uniform dark brown. Wing tips project beyond tail tip. Upper breast rich chestnut narrowly bordered black below. Rest of underparts white. Bill slender, black. Legs variable greyish-green. **Adult breeding female** Breast band less distinct, mottled brown variably admixed with chestnut. **Adult non-breeding** Head and face pattern distinctly buffish and paler brown. Upperparts narrowly fringed buff. Breast band indistinct, mottled greyish-brown. Legs yellowish-brown. **Juvenile** Similar to non-breeding adult with upperparts fringed bright sandy-buff giving 'scaly' effect. Breast mottled sandy-brown. **In flight** Rapid wing beats on long, pointed wings. Uniform dark brown mantle and upper wing with narrow wing bar across tips of greater coverts extending and widening onto bases of inner primaries. Dark brown rump and tail, latter narrowly fringed white. Underwing coverts whitish. CALL Flight note sharp, whistled 'ku-whit'; also loud 'tyup'.
HABITAT AND BEHAVIOUR Breeds on dry steppes, semi-arid deserts, edges of lagoons and saltmarsh, often considerable distance from water. Breeds in small colonies. 'buzzing' territorial display flight. Winters on inland grasslands, plains and burnt grassland. Gregarious often forming dense flocks. Relatively tame and approachable. Gait courser-like. Active at night.
MOVEMENTS Strongly migratory, wintering from E Egypt and E Sudan south to SW Angola and S Africa. Autumn passage across Red Sea direct to E Africa, arriving from October, departing late February. Wanders considerably on wintering grounds. Vagrant across Europe (including Britain), W Africa, NW India, N Australia.

Oriental Plover
Charadrius veredus L 23.50 cm
The eastern counterpart of Caspian Plover, longer legged and longer necked, breeding on the arid steppes of N China from NW Mongolia east through Inner Mongolia to Manchuria.
PLUMAGE **Adult breeding male** Crown and ear coverts brownish flecked white . Rest of head, neck and face very pale, almost white, as remaining darker feather tips wear off.

Upperparts uniform dark brown. Wing tips extend beyond tail tip. Breast chestnut-orange bordered black below. Rest of underparts white. Bill black. Legs long, yellow tinged green. **Adult breeding female** Head and face washed darker. Breast suffused buffish-orange usually lacking black lower border. **Adult non-breeding** Whitish forehead, lores, supercilium, cheeks and throat contrast with brown crown and ear coverts. Upperparts narrowly fringed rufous. Underparts white with breast mottled brown forming indistinct breast band. **Juvenile** Similar to non-breeding adult. Upperparts with broader buff fringes. Breast buffish mottled brown. **Flight** Fast, powerful and erratic, appearing long-winged. Uniform dark brown mantle and upper wing with narrow very faint wing bar across tips of greater coverts and inner primary coverts. White shaft to outer primary. Dark brown rump and tail, latter narrowly fringed white. Toes project slightly beyond tail tip. Underwing uniform brown flecked white. CALL Flight note sharp 'chip, chip, chip'; also piping 'klink'.
HABITAT AND BEHAVIOUR Breeds on arid desert and mountainous steppes. Winters on inland plains, grassland, edges of lagoons, mudflats, airfields and edges of roadways. Gregarious outside breeding season forming sizeable flocks, sometimes exceeding 1000 birds. Tends to feed on plains at night, roosting with other shorebirds during day. Readily associates with pratincoles.
MOVEMENTS Strongly migratory. Moves south during September through E China to winter mostly in N and NW Australia, with smaller numbers in Indonesia. Further onward migration, with small numbers recorded annually in S Australia. Return passage through SE China peaks March–April. Vagrant New Zealand.

Mountain Plover
Charadrius montanus L 22.20 cm
A rare plover, incorrectly named since a species not of mountains but upland grass land, with range now severely restricted to the American Great Plains from Montana south to New Mexico and W Texas. 1991 survey indicates total population reduced to maximum 5600 birds.
PLUMAGE **Adult breeding** Brilliant white forehead and supercilium extending well behind eye contrasting with broad black forecrown and distinct black loral line. Rest of crown greyish-brown. Upperparts pale greyish-brown tinged buffish-ochre fringed similar. Ear coverts pale buffish-grey. Rest of face and underparts white, sides of neck and upper breast washed warm buffish-yellow. Bill longish, slim, black. Legs longish, pale brownish-yellow. **Adult non-**

breeding Similar to breeding, lacking black on lores and forecrown, becoming brownish. Ear coverts darker brown. Upperparts when fresh fringed warm buff. Sides of breast more extensive buffish-brown forming lateral breast patches sometimes joining in centre. **Juvenile** Similar to non-breeding adult. Upperparts darker greyish-brown with dark subterminal bars broadly fringed buff forming neat scaly pattern. Buffish supercilium. Crown, hindneck and sides of breast mottled dark brown and buff. **In flight** Appears long winged and uniform dark, alleviated by narrow white tips to greater coverts, white primary shafts and white bases to inner primaries. Tail greyish-brown with darker brown subterminal bar narrowly fringed white. Underwing coverts and axillaries white.
CALL Flight note low krrrk; various whistles, both plaintive and shrill.
HABITAT AND BEHAVIOUR Breeds on shortgrass upland plains, typically associated with blue grama and buffalo grass vegetation, feeding largely on insects especially grass-hoppers. Performs both 'butterfly' and 'falling leaf' display flights. Tame and approachable. Range declining owing to habitat loss from cereal production. Forms post-breeding flocks from mid-June, wintering on semi-desert and dry cultivated ground.
MOVEMENTS Migratory, arriving wintering grounds in C California and Texas south to S Lower California from mid-October, returning late March. Vagrant across USA from Washington, Massachusetts and Florida.

A	B	C
D	E	F
G	H	I
J	K	L

A Caspian Plover breeding male
B Caspian Plover breeding male
C Caspian Plover breeding female
D Caspian Plover adult non-breeding
E Caspian Plover juvenile
F Caspian Plover
G Oriental Plover breeding male
H Oriental Plover breeding female
I Oriental Plover adult non-breeding
J Oriental Plover juvenile
K Mountain Plover adult breeding
L Mountain Plover adult breeding

Scolopacidae

Black-tailed Godwit
Limosa limosa L 40.00 cm

Tallest of the godwits, with a distinctive flight pattern, breeding in predominantly temperate climates within the Palearctic. **PLUMAGE Adult breeding male** Dark loral patch with creamy fore-supercilium, becoming warmer buff behind eye. Crown rich brown finely streaked dark brown. Hindneck chestnut red, with mantle, scapulars and tertials blackish, heavily blotched chestnut and buff. Wing coverts largely grey fringed buff. Chin, throat, foreneck and breast chestnut, with variable amounts of chestnut and white on belly, with dark brown barring to flanks and belly. Bill long, virtually straight, blackish at tip, pinkish at base. Legs long, bluish-grey. **Adult breeding female** Chestnut paler with white flecking. Some retained grey scapulars and tertials. **Adult non-breeding** Dark loral line with prominent whitish supercilium. Upperparts grey-brown with wing coverts edged white. Neck, breast and flanks washed greyish, with rest of underparts white. **Juvenile** Crown cinnamon streaked brown. Upperparts dark brown fringed rich cinnamon-buff, giving 'scaly' effect. Underparts warm cinnamon-buff. **In flight** Clear white wing bar and white patch to rump and uppertail coverts contrasting with blackish remainder of wings and black tail. Underwing white.
CALL Usual flight call from migrating flocks 'wicka, wicka, wicka'.
RACES Three are recognized: *islandica* (Iceland, Norway, Scotland) intermediate in size, shorter bill, and more extensive chestnut on belly; nominate *limosa* (W Europe to W Asia) largest with chestnut paler and less extensive on belly; *melanuroides* (E Asia) smallest, distinctly darker above, and less extensive, paler chestnut below.
HABITAT AND BEHAVIOUR Breeds in damp grassland, wet-meadows and marshes. Males perform complicated 'ceremonial' display flights. Outside the breeding season prefers inland lakes and flooded grassland.
MOVEMENTS Migratory, with *islandica* returning to breeding-grounds from mid-March onwards, leaving from mid-June, mostly wintering in Ireland, Britain and W France. *Limosa* moves to south of the Sahara and N India, with huge wintering flocks recorded (100,000 in Mali). *Melanuroides* winters from E India south to Australia. Many non-breeders remain in winter quarters all year. Vagrancy widely recorded, e.g., Atlantic USA, S Africa, New Zealand, W Alaska.

Bar-tailed Godwit
Limosa lapponica L 38.75 cm

Shorter legged than other godwits, nesting in the high Arctic from Scandinavia to Alaska.
PLUMAGE Adult breeding male Head, neck and underparts generally striking deep chestnut-red. Indistinct loral line and supercilium. Mantle, scapulars and tertials dark brown extensively fringed and notched chestnut-buff. Wing coverts greyer-brown fringed white. Bill longish, slightly upcurved, with blackish tip and dull pink base. Legs long, dark grey, sometimes tinged greenish. **Adult breeding female** Generally lacks chestnut coloration, frequently remaining in non-breeding plumage. **Adult non-breeding** Distinct white supercilium, with dark loral line extending behind eye. Crown, hindneck and upperparts brownish-grey with thin dark shaft streaking and extensive white fringing especially on coverts. Underparts white with neck and breast washed grey-brown with fine dark streaking. **Juvenile** Upperparts blackish-brown fringed chestnut-buff, giving noticeable streaked appearance. Buff supercilium. Underparts white with neck and breast buff-brown finely streaked darker. **In flight** Lack of wing bar evident, with tail evenly barred white and grey-brown.
CALL Not very vocal, a harsh 'kirruc'.
RACES Two are recognized: nominate *lapponica* (Scandinavia to W Russia) shows white back, rump and underwing coverts; *baueri* (E Russia to Alaska) is larger, showing dark back and rump, and underwing coverts heavily barred dark brown.
HABITAT AND BEHAVIOUR Nests on marshy tundra, favouring open bogs and swamps with scattered willow and birch near the treeline. Performs intricate aerial display flights. Outside the breeding season frequents the coast, especially mudflats and estuaries. Avoids inland sites except occasionally on migration.
MOVEMENTS Autumn migration to coastal moulting sites commences during August, with onward migration October/November. Return to pre-breeding moult sites March/April and migrate during May to the breeding-grounds. Often seen moving offshore. *Lapponica* moves largely through the Baltic and North Sea to winter in W Europe, Mediterranean, W Africa and W India, often forming large flocks. *Baueri* winters from China south to Indonesia and Australia. Immatures often remain in winter quarters all year. Vagrancy widely recorded, e.g., USA, Spitzbergen, Madeira, Sri Lanka and S Ocean islands.

A	B

C	D	E
F	G	H
I	J	K

A   Black-tailed Godwit *limosa* breeding male
B   Black-tailed Godwit *limosa* breeding female
C   Black-tailed Godwit *limosa* adult non-breeding
D   Black-tailed Godwit *limosa* juvenile
E   Black-tailed Godwit *limosa* breeding male
F   Black-tailed Godwit *melanoides* breeding male
G   Bar-tailed Godwit *bauri* breeding male
H   Bar-tailed Godwit *lapponica* breeding female
I   Bar-tailed Godwit *lapponica* adult non-breeding
J   Bar-tailed Godwit *lapponica* juvenile
K   Bar-tailed Godwit *lapponica*

Scolopacidae

Hudsonian Godwit
Limosa haemastica L 40.00 cm
Distinguished by diagnostic flight pattern, this scarce godwit nests around the SW shores of Hudson Bay, NW Canada and W Alaska.
PLUMAGE **Adult breeding male** Obvious white supercilium extending behind eye, with dark grey loral line. Crown and rest of face grey finely streaked whitish. Mantle, scapulars and tertials dark brown notched buffish-yellow. Coverts mostly grey fringed white and buff. Underparts deep chestnut, with whitish lower belly and undertail coverts, heavily barred black. Streaked throat and barring on sides of breast extending onto flanks. Bill long, slightly upcurved, dark brown at tip shading to pinkish-orange base. Legs long, dark bluish-grey. **Adult breeding female** Generally paler underparts with extensive white blotching. **Adult non-breeding** Uniform grey-brown upperparts with pale fringed wing coverts. Dark grey forecrown with obvious white supercilium and blackish loral line. Greyish wash across breast contrasting with paler belly. **Juvenile** Upperparts dark grey brown evenly fringed buff giving 'scaly' effect. Underparts washed buffish-brown. **In flight** Unlike Black-tailed Godwit, thin white wing bar restricted to outer secondaries and inner primaries. Also narrow white band only across uppertail coverts, with largely black tail, thinly tipped white. Underwing coverts and axillaries black, with flight feathers largely dark grey with white bases forming a contrasting mid-wing panel.
CALL Usually silent on migration, but noisy when breeding including a variable 'ta-whit'.
HABITAT AND BEHAVIOUR Nests in meadows and sedge marshes at the edge of the treeline not far from the coast. Outside the breeding season, found on coastal mudflats, marshes and flooded grassland.
MOVEMENTS A long-distance migrant, with the bulk of the population gathering along the southern Hudson Bay area from July onwards. Migration almost direct to the main wintering grounds in S Argentina, with probable staging post in northern S America yet undiscovered. Spring passage during April/May, but on a broader, more westerly front. Transatlantic vagrant to Britain. Also New Zealand (regular), W USA, Pacific Mexico, Fiji and Galapagos Is.

Marbled Godwit
Limosa fedoa L 44.45 cm
A large, uniquely cinnamon coloured godwit, nesting on the N American prairies, with a remnant population on James Bay, Canada.
PLUMAGE **Adult breeding** Dark brown crown with long buff supercilium extending behind eye and dark loral line. Sides of face grey finely streaked buff. Hindneck cinnamon streaked dark brown. Mantle, scapulars and tertials blackish-brown with extensive chestnut notches giving distinctive speckled appearance. Wing coverts dark brown edged cinnamon-buff. Buffish-white foreneck. Underparts pale cinnamon, finely barred on breast, flanks and undertail coverts, producing the 'marbled' effect. Bill long, slightly upcurved, and distinctly bicoloured, with pinkish basal area and blackish tip. Legs long, bluish-grey. **Adult non-breeding** Upperparts also speckled but ground colour generally paler. Underparts pale cinnamon with reduced barring. **Juvenile** Similar to non-breeding adult but with paler fringing to upperparts. Underparts rich cinnamon-buff. **In flight** Upperwing cinnamon contrasting with blackish outer primaries and primary coverts. Rump, uppertail coverts and tail barred cinnamon and dark brown. Underwing uniform bright cinnamon.
CALL A noisy bird on the breeding-grounds, the typical call a loud 'ger-whit'.
HABITAT AND BEHAVIOUR Nests on the prairie wetlands, often adjacent pools, with an isolated population on the coastal marshland on James Bay. Perfoms typical godwit ceremonial display flight. Outside the breeding season, essentially coastal, favouring tidal mudflats, estuaries and coastal pools. Often relatively tame.
MOVEMENTS A short-distance migrant, moving to winter in California, Texas, Florida and Central America. Non-breeding birds often remain in the wintering grounds all year. Vagrant to Pacific S America, Galapagos Is, W Indies (regular) and Atlantic coast of N America.

Asiatic Dowitcher
Limnodromus semipalmatus L 34.90 cm
A rare wader more closely resembling Bar-tailed Godwit in shape and size than the Nearctic dowitchers, breeding sparingly across W Siberia, Mongolia and Manchuria.
PLUMAGE **Adult breeding male** Crown and eye-stripe chestnut-brown. Rest of head and neck chestnut-red. Mantle, scapulars and tertials blackish centred fringed chestnut and buff. Chin whitish with entire breast chestnut-red. Upper belly chestnut-red blotched white with lower belly and flanks white, the latter with prominent vertical brown bars. Bill typical dowitcher shape but wholly black and straight, deep-based and swollen at tip. Legs longish and dark grey, with webbing between all toes. **Adult breeding female** Generally duller chestnut with more white flecks. **Adult non-breeding** Prominent white supercilium with dark-grey crown, lores and ear coverts, finely streaked white. Upperparts darkish grey-brown fringed buffish-white. Underparts white with mottled grey-brown breast and grey-brown streaking on flanks. **Juvenile** Clear white supercilium contrasts with dark grey crown and eye-stripe. Mantle, scapulars and tertials blackish neatly fringed warm buff. Wing coverts paler grey fringed white. Underparts whitish with foreneck, breast and flanks suffused rich buff and streaked grey. **In flight** Paler band across primaries and inner secondaries, lacking white patch on back of Nearctic dowitchers. Rump and uppertail whitish heavily barred brown with tail mostly brown barred white. Underwing virtually pure white.
CALL A quiet nondescript 'chewsk' and a plaintive 'kiow'.
HABITAT AND BEHAVIOUR Nests on thinly vegetated grassy wetlands, with no apparent preference for fresh or saline habitat. Feeds using typical dowitcher 'sewing machine' action, often in deep water up to belly. Winters on intertidal mudflats and lagoons, frequently mixing with godwits.
MOVEMENTS Migratory, with known winter range extending from SE India through Thailand, Malaysia and Indonesia to NW Australia. Large flocks recently found in Sumatra (1500) and regular spring passage through Hong Kong (300) suggest more numerous than once thought. Vagrant SE Australia, Kenya and Aden.

A	B	C
D	E	F
G	H	I
J	K	L

A Hudsonian Godwit breeding male
B Hudsonian Godwit breeding female
C Hudsonian Godwit juvenile
D Hudsonian Godwit breeding male
E Marbled Godwit adult breeding
F Marbled Godwit adult non-breeding
G Marbled Godwit adult
H Marbled Godwit
I Marbled Godwit adult
J Asiatic Dowitcher adult breeding
K Asiatic Dowitcher adult non-breeding
L Asiatic Dowitcher

Scolopacidae

Little Curlew
Numenius minutus L 30.50 cm

A tiny, relatively scarce and unknown curlew, very similar to the nearly extinct Eskimo Curlew of N America, breeding in burned forested areas of N Siberia.
PLUMAGE **Adult** Distinctive head pattern with pale crown stripe and dark brown lateral crown stripes. Buffish supercilium, narrow and extending well behind eye, with dark brown eye-stripe also extending behind eye. Neck warm buff strongly streaked brown. Mantle, scapulars and tertials dark brown heavily notched buff-yellow. Wing tips fall level with tail tip. Breast warm buff finely streaked dark brown, shading to paler belly. Flanks lightly barred brown. Bill relatively short, with basal portion almost straight, but distal part evenly downcurved to tip; dark brown with pale yellow base to lower mandible. Legs dull bluish-grey. **Juvenile** Similar to adult, but scapulars and tertials with pale buff spotting. Coverts fringed pale buff. Eskimo Curlew differs in being slightly larger, shorter legged, with cinnamon underwing coverts. **In flight** Generally dark brown above with contrasting paler area across secondary coverts. Underwing coverts and axillaries buff barred brown. Toes project slightly beyond tail tip.
CALL Usual flight call a soft, musical 'te-te-te', somewhat reminiscent of Greenshank.
HABITAT AND BEHAVIOUR Favoured nesting site is grassy clearings, especially those affected by fire but rejuvenated, within larch, osier and birch forests of the sub-Arctic. Remarkable display flight with whistling sound emanating from wings and tail. Winters on inland grassland, both wet and dry, especially coastal black soil plains (N Australia). Highly gregarious, forming large flocks, sometimes in thousands.
MOVEMENTS Commences leaving breeding-grounds early August, returning towards the end of May. Migrates overland to E China, through Japan, Philippines and E Indonesia to winter mostly in Australia, but also New Guinea. Movements in Australia dictated by rainfall. Vagrant Britain, Sweden, Seychelles, Hong Kong (irregular in spring) and California.

Eskimo Curlew
Numenius borealis L 31.10 cm

Regarded by many as the world's rarest wader – indeed, possibly on the verge of extinction. Larger than Little Curlew, formerly nesting commonly in the Canadian NW Territories west to N Alaska and possibly east towards Hudson Bay. Six reported sightings in 1987, very recent wintering records, plus possible nest with eggs and adult bird in Canadian Arctic in 1992 renew positive speculation.
PLUMAGE **Adult** Very similar to Little Curlew from which great care is required to confirm positive identification. Differs in less strongly marked head pattern with indistinct buffish crown stripe and less well-defined buffish supercilium. Upperparts strongly notched and spotted buffish-yellow. Wing tips clearly extend beyond tail tip. Underparts washed cinnamon-buff with foreneck, sides of neck and breast heavily streaked dark brown. Flanks with bold dark brown Y-shaped chevrons. Bill shortish, evenly downcurved, with fleshy-pink base to lower mandible usually extending more than halfway towards tip. Legs shorter than Little Curlew, dark bluish-grey. **Juvenile** Similar to adult. Upperparts neatly fringed buff. Underpart coloration warm buff. **In flight** Differs from Little Curlew in cinnamon-buff underwing coverts and axillaries. Toes do not project beyond tail tip.
CALL Various soft, repeated mellow whistles. Calls from migrating flocks have been described as 'tee-dee-dee', somewhat resembling American Golden Plover.
HABITAT AND BEHAVIOUR Although almost certainly bred in Alaska and possibly E Siberia, only known breeding sites are from NW Territories, with first nest discovered in 1821. Clearly frequented barren Arctic tundra, feeding chiefly on insects and fruit. Was highly gregarious, during passage usually observed in flocks 30–50 but frequently recorded in thousands, favouring prairies, grasslands and ploughed fields, coastal marshes, mudflats and estuaries. Wintered on S American pampas. Unconfirmed reports include 2/3 birds wintering on wetland near Cordoba, Argentina during 1992 and 1993. Both the abundance and tameness of the bird made easy prey for shooters, flesh being described as great delicacy.
MOVEMENTS Highly migratory. Commenced leaving breeding grounds during July moving east to stage on Labrador coast before migrating south across western Atlantic Ocean to arrive from early September to winter in extreme S Brazil south to Argentina. Return passage more westerly route through Texas and Great Plains during March and April. Vagrant east to Bermuda, Greenland, British Isles and Falklands Is.

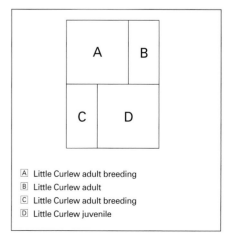

A Little Curlew adult breeding
B Little Curlew adult
C Little Curlew adult breeding
D Little Curlew juvenile

Scolopacidae

Bristle-thighed Curlew
Numenius tahitiensis L 41.90 cm

A rare curlew, total population estimated at 3200 pairs, differing from Whimbrel in brighter coloration, flight pattern and call, with breeding population concentrated on mountain tundra in W Alaska.

PLUMAGE **Adult** Head pattern similar to Whimbrel. Upperparts dark brown notched and spotted rich cinnamon-buff especially on wing coverts. Underparts dull buffish-cinnamon, breast and upper flanks heavily streaked brown. Bill thickish, more blunt-tipped than Whimbrel, dull flesh-pink tipped brown. Legs shortish, bluish-grey. Feather shafts to rear flanks and thighs elongated forming long shiny bristles, visible only in the hand. **Juvenile** Similar to adult. Wing coverts boldly spotted cinnamon-buff. Underparts buffish, with little or no streaking to breast. **In flight** Dark mantle and upperwing contrasting with bright cinnamon-chestnut rump, uppertail coverts and tail, last barred dark brown. Juvenile shows white tips to primary coverts and inner primaries. Underwing coverts and axillaries cinnamon barred dark brown.

CALL Diagnostic and far carrying, clipped 'pee-uu-ee', quite unlike Whimbrel.

HABITAT AND BEHAVIOUR Restricted to flat exposed tundra ridges on low mountain tops across Nulato Hills and C Seward peninsula. Preferred nest site in hummocky, dwarf shrub, vigorously defended against avian predators especially raptors, frequently using excellent camouflage. Adults and young form post-breeding flocks prior to heading for staging grounds. Winters on tiny Polynesian islands frequenting variety of habitat including sandy beaches, grassland and areas of lava, often feeding on eggs from seabird colonies. Undergoes flightless wing moult, unique amongst waders.

MOVEMENTS Highly migratory, adults commence leaving breeding-grounds from early July, with juveniles gone by early August to staging grounds on central Yukon Delta before migrating to winter in S Pacific including Marshall and Hawaiian Is, south to Tonga, Samoa, Marquesa and Tuamotu Is. Vagrant S Alaska, Vancouver Is, Washington, Norfolk and Kermadac Is and Japan.

Slender-billed Curlew
Numenius tenuirostris L 38.75 cm

A small curlew of the Siberian taiga zone, very rare and highly endangered.

PLUMAGE **Adult breeding** Similar size to Whimbrel but lacks crown stripe. May be confused with eastern race of Eurasian Curlew *orientalis*, but smaller and generally whiter on the breast, tail and underwing. Dark brown cap finely streaked, with whitish supercilium and dark loral line produce more contrasting head and face pattern than Eurasian Curlew. Upperparts dark brown notched and fringed buff-brown. Chin white. Underparts noticeably white with breast streaked brown. Sides of lower breast and flanks with black oval or heart-shaped spots. Bill, although shorter than Eurasian Curlew, of similar length proportionately, decurved, and tapering to fine point, brownish-black with pinkish-brown base to lower mandible. Legs bluish-grey. **Adult non-breeding** Generally more streaking on underparts, but reduced flank markings. **Juvenile** Similar to adult but flank spots replaced with brown streaks. **In flight** Back, rump, uppertail coverts and tail white, with brown streaking on uppertail, and tail barred brown. Blackish outer wing contrasts with extensive white notching across secondaries, greater coverts, and inner primaries, forming paler innerwing than Eurasian Curlew.

CALL Similar to Eurasian Curlew but shorter and higher pitched 'courl-ee'. Also flight alarm call 'kuu-ee'.

HABITAT AND BEHAVIOUR Nesting area, little studied, consists of swampy and boggy areas on the steppe and marshy tracts along the edges of forests. Non-breeding birds winter on mudflats, marshes and inland waters, often inshore from the coast. Records to date suggest flocking in sizeable numbers, often associated with Eurasian Curlew and Black-tailed Godwit.

MOVEMENTS Apparently commences autumn migration during August, moving south of due west, to winter in the Mediterrenean Basin, especially Morocco and Tunisia. Recent winter records are from the flooded marshland of Merja Zerga, Morocco, involving up to four adult individuals, with juveniles totally absent. However, a flock of four in January 1995 in Southern Italy, followed by ten in February at the same site, provides some positive encouragement. Clearly the species is very rare, still declining, and the subject of close study. Return spring passage commences during March, with irregular records from the Balkan States during May, especially Hortabágy, Hungary. Vagrant records include Oman, Canaries and Azores, Holland, Germany and Poland.

	B
A	
	C
D	E
F	G

A Bristle-thighed Curlew adult
B Bristle-thighed Curlew adult
C Bristle-thighed Curlew
D Bristle-thighed Curlew
E Slender-billed Curlew adult
F Slender-billed Curlew adult
G Slender-billed Curlew

Scolopacidae

Eurasian Curlew
Numenius arquata **L 54.60 cm**
Named after its call, this large curlew shows a conspicuous white back and rump, nesting widely across Eurasia in mostly temperate climates.
PLUMAGE **Adult breeding** Head, neck and breast buff-brown streaked dark grey-brown. Whitish chin. Virtual lack of supercilium and small loral spot give 'plain faced' appearance. Mantle and scapulars black centred with wamer buff-brown fringes and notches. Coverts notched and fringed paler, with tertials dark brown notched paler olive-brown. Belly whitish with heavy black streaking on flanks. Bill very long, decurved and dark brown, with pinkish base to lower mandible. Legs long and dull bluish-grey.
Adult non-breeding Generally duller, lacking warm buff tones, with greyish wash across underparts, and greyer-brown upperparts. **Juvenile** Strong buff wash across breast with underparts gererally more lightly streaked. Upperparts dark brown with contrasting buff notches and fringes. Bill distinctly shorter. **In flight** Extensive white across back and rump, with white tail irregularly barred pale brown. Wings dark brown with white notching secondaries, greater coverts and primaries.
CALL Familiar 'courlee-courlee'.
RACES Two are recognized: nominate *arquata* (Europe east to Urals), generally smaller with buffer underparts, underwing coverts and axillaries extensively barred brown; *orientalis* (Urals east to C Russia), larger with brown barring on lower rump, underwing coverts and axillaries virtually pure white.
HABITAT AND BEHAVIOUR Nests on open grassy or boggy moorland, dry heathlands, and also open arable land. Aerial display song one of the most attractive of all waders, the 'courlee' extending into a bubbling trill, often delivered on non-breeding quarters. Winters on estuarine mudflats and saltmarsh.
MOVEMENTS Mainly migratory, with post-breeding flocks arriving on the coast from late June onwards, and returning from mid-February. Some western birds do not move far, but most probably winter on their moulting grounds in Britain, W Europe and W Africa. Eastern birds more migratory, moving to the E Mediterranean, the Red Sea coasts and east across Asia to Japan and the Philippines. Many non-breeding birds remain in their winter quarters; Greenland, America, Borneo and Australia.

Whimbrel
Numenius phaeopus **L 43.20 cm**
A curlew of medium size with a well-defined head pattern, breeding widely across northern latitudes, and showing distinct racial variation **In flight**.
PLUMAGE **Adult breeding** Pale central crown stripe not always obvious, but long supercilium contrasting with dark grey lateral crown stripe and eye-line give distinctive face pattern, immediately separating from all other curlews except Bristle-thighed Curlew. Upperparts generally dark brown notched and fringed white. Chin white. Neck, breast and underparts warm buff-brown streaked dark brown. Bill longish and decurved over distal two-thirds, blackish-brown with dull flesh-pink base. Legs long, dull bluish-grey. **Juvenile** Similar to adult but upperparts generally darker, with clearer white spotting and fringing to scapulars and tertials. **In flight** Dark grey mantle and wings, darker than Eurasian Curlew, alleviated by white back and rump (except *hudsonicus* – *see* Races) Tail grey barred dark brown. Indistinct white notching across secondaries, greater coverts and primaries. Underwing coverts and axillaries variable white to barred dark brown and white.
CALL Diagnostic, far-carrying and rapidly repeated rippling titter.
RACES Four are recognized: nominate *phaeopus* (Iceland, Scotland, Europe to W Russia) unbarred white back and rump, underwing coverts and axillaries white narrowly barred brown; *alboaxillaris* (south of Urals), generally whiter above and below. Underwing white, unbarred; *variegatus* (E Russia) brown back and whitish rump heavily barred brown showing little contrast, underwing broadly barred brown and white; *hudsonicus* (Alaska and Canada) generally buffer-brown above and below, back and rump dark, underwing coverts and axillaries warm brown finely barred dark brown.
HABITAT AND BEHAVIOUR Breeds on sub-Arctic heaths and moorlands, where stunted bushes are present, usually adjacent to the tree-line. Occurs widely inland on migration, including wetland and grassland. Winters chiefly on the coast, especially rocky shores, but also sandy beaches.
MOVEMENTS Autumn passage commences in July with long flights often overland involving staging posts, with return passage from mid-March. Many non-breeders remain in the winter range. W Palearctic birds winter along coastal SW Europe, Africa, Persian Gulf and India, with vagrants to USA and Canada. Eastern race moves to SE Asia and Australia. *Hudsonicus* winters from California and the Gulf states south to S America, with vagrants to W Europe, Australia and New Zealand.

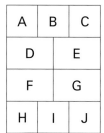

A	B	C
D		E
F		G
H	I	J

A Eurasian Curlew *arquata* adult breeding
B Eurasian Curlew *arquata* adult
C Eurasian Curlew *orientalis* adult
D Eurasian Curlew *orientalis* adult
E Eurasian Curlew *arquata* adult non-breeding
F Whimbrel *phaeopus* adult breeding
G Whimbrel *hudsonicus* adult
H Whimbrel *phaeopus*
I Whimbrel *hudsonicus*
J Whimbrel *variegatus* adult

Scolopacidae

Far Eastern Curlew
Numenius madagascariensis **L 63.50 cm**
The largest curlew with the longest bill of any wader, this long-distace migrant breeds in Siberia, Kamchatka, Mongolia and N Manchuria.
PLUMAGE **Adult breeding** Head, face and neck warm buff-brown, finely streaked dark brown. Faint supercilium and indistinct loral line with pale feathering around eye give distinct 'bare faced' appearance. Mantle and scapular feathers blackish centred with rich chestnut-buff notches. Tertials grey with blackish bars. Coverts grey-brown fringed buff. Underparts warm buff-brown, streaked dark brown across breast and flanks. Bill extremely long (longest in female), decurved and dark brown, with base of lower mandible dull flesh pink. Legs long, bluish-grey. **Adult non-breeding** Very similar, but upperparts lack rich chestnut-buff coloration. Mantle and scapulars notched and fringed paler brown. **Juvenile** Similar to adult but upperparts neatly fringed buff giving somewhat 'scaly' appearance. Bill distinctly shorter. **In flight** Uniform dark above with back and rump dark brown, lacking any white, immediately distinguishing from Eurasian Curlew. Secondaries, greater coverts, and inner primaries notched white. Underwing white extensively barred brown.
CALL A mournful 'curr-ee', flatter than Eurasian Curlew. Also a rapid 'kur-kur-kur-kur'.
HABITAT AND BEHAVIOUR Nests on mossy or swampy moorland and peatbogs, with a scattering of bushes as the preferred habitat. Bubbling courtship display song delivered on downcurved wings. Winters on mudflats, estuaries and sandy beaches.
MOVEMENTS Post-breeding flocks gather from early July, with migration through the Philippines and New Guinea, where some winter. Most move farther to winter in Australia, and also recently New Zealand. Many summer in their non-breeding range. Vagrant W Alaska and Aleutians (regular in spring), Thailand and Afghanistan.

Long-billed Curlew
Numenius americanus **L 57.15 cm**
This cinnamon-coloured curlew, the Nearctic counterpart of Far Eastern Curlew, inhabitats the old prairie country of the westerly states of the USA and S Canada.
PLUMAGE **Adult breeding** Cinnamon crown finely streaked dark brown. Faint buffish supercilium with dusky lores. Paler grey cheeks and ear coverts contrast with large dark eye to give 'bland face' appearance. Mantle, scapulars and coverts black with rich cinnamon-buff spots and fringes, giving distinct speckled effect. Tertials cinnamon barred dark brown. Entire underparts cinnamon, with neck and breast finely streaked dark brown, and heavier barring on flanks. Bill very long, decurved and dark brown, with dull flesh-pink base. Legs long, dull bluish-grey.
Adult non-breeding Extremely similar, but upperparts generally less speckled.
Juvenile Very similar to adult, but scapulars and coverts show buffer spots and fringes, with broader cinnamon bars on tertials. Bill distinctly shorter. **In flight** Generally dark above with dark brown back and rump. Secondaries, greater coverts and inner primaries cinnamon notched brown, contrasting with black outer primaries and primary coverts. Underwing rich cinnamon and almost unbarred.
CALL Usual flight call a plaintive 'currl-ee'.
RACES Two are recognized: nominate *americanus* (S USA) and *parus* (N USA), the latter smaller but with little plumage variation.
HABITAT AND BEHAVIOUR Nests on short grass prairies, especially on gravelly soil, with cactus and sage. Winters on coastal mudflats, estuaries and sandbars, but also inland on farmland. Overall a shy bird.
MOVEMENTS A short distance migrant, commencing leaving breeding-grounds early July to winter along the coasts of Texas, Louisiana, California, and Central America. Return passage begins during March, with many non-breeders remaining in their winter quarters. Vagrant NW Territories, W Indies and Venezuela.

Upland Sandpiper
Bartramia longicauda **L 29.85 cm**
A small headed, long necked and long tailed wader of short inland grassland. Breeding range extends from NW Alaska and Yukon, south-east through the Canadian Great Plains and Lake States, east to Virginia and Maryland.
PLUMAGE **Adult breeding and non-breeding** 'Bare faced' appearance with large dark eye. Supercilium, lores, and sides of face pale buff, with slightly darker ear coverts. Crown dark brown lightly streaked buff with indistinct crown stripe. Mantle, scapulars and tertials patterned pale olive-brown, barred dark brown and fringed buff. Coverts heavily fringed buffish-yellow. Tail clearly projecting beyond folded wing tips. Chin white. Breast and upper belly washed buff with heavy brown streaking. Rest of underparts whitish, with dark brown chevrons on lower belly and flanks. Bill short, thin and slightly decurved at tip; tip and culmen brown, with yellowish sides to base. **Juvenile** Scapulars and coverts dark brown with bold buff fringes, giving an overall 'scaly' effect. Tertials dark brown notched pale buff. Underparts show less prominent flank markings. **In flight** Looks dark, with blackish-brown primaries, back, rump and tail, with white sides to rump. Secondary coverts paler brown.
CALL Usual flight call a rapid 'guip-ip-ip'.
HABITAT AND BEHAVIOUR Mainly prairie grassland, but also wet-meadows and clearings in spruce muskeg in the northern parts of its range. Song display flight performed low over the ground at great height. Often tame, especially on migration. Winters on open fields and grassland, with migrants frequenting golf courses and airfields.
MOVEMENTS A long-distance migrant, with autumn departures commencing late August. Main passage is through the Great Plains and over E Central America, or crossing the Mexican Gulf to winter on the S American pampas. Return passage to S USA from early March onwards. Vagrancy widely recorded, e.g., Australia, New Zealand, Falkland Is, and east to Iceland, Britain and Europe.

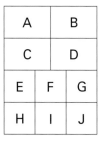

A	B
C	D
E	F	G
H	I	J

- A Far Eastern Curlew adult non-breeding
- B Far Eastern Curlew adult non-breeding
- C Far Eastern Curlew first-winter non-breeding
- D Far Eastern Curlew adult
- E Long-billed Curlew adult
- F Long-billed Curlew juvenile
- G Long-billed Curlew adult
- H Upland Sandpiper juvenile
- I Upland Sandpiper adult
- J Upland Sandpiper juvenile

Scolopacidae

Spotted Redshank
Tringa erythropus **L 30.50 cm**
With a unique black breeding plumage, this *tringa* breeds across the N Palearctic from Scandinavia east to N Siberia.
PLUMAGE Adult breeding male Head, neck and underparts entirely black. Narrow white eyelids. Mantle blackish with scapulars, coverts and tertials black, spotted and notched white. Undertail coverts blackish barred dark grey and white. Bill longer than Redshank, black with deep red base to lower mandible. Legs longish, dark red. **Adult breeding female** Underparts less black with white fringes. Vent often white. **Adult non-breeding** Blackish loral line contrasting with white fore-supercilium. Upperparts including forehead, crown and hindneck uniform pale grey with white fringes to scapulars. Coverts and tertials brownish-grey heavily notched and spotted white. Underparts white with greyish wash across breast and sides of upper flanks. Lower flanks lightly barred grey. Legs orange-red. **Juvenile** Distinct white fore-supercilium with darker brown upperparts boldly notched and spotted white. Underparts soft grey extensively barred brown. **In flight** Extensive white patch on back, mostly blackish wings with paler trailing edge and barred rump and uppertail. Feet project beyond tail.
CALL Usual flight call a distinctive 'chu-it'.
HABITAT AND BEHAVIOUR Nests in marshes, heathlands and lightly wooded regions close to the Arctic treeline. Outside the breeding season less marine than other *tringas*, preferring freshwater lakeshores and brackish lagoons, but also estuarine mudflats. Often forms dense feeding flocks in deep water, upending similar to Pied Avocet.
MOVEMENTS Females leave the breeding-grounds from mid-June, with males one month later and juveniles in August. Large flocks occur in important staging posts, e.g., Dutch Wadensee and Greek Evros delta, Black and Caspian Seas, before final departure to Mediterranean Basin, Persian Gulf, Indo-China and W, C and E Africa. Many non-breeders summer just south of breeding range. Vagrant to America, Aleutians and S Africa.

Common Redshank
Tringa totanus **L 27.95 cm**
A common medium-sized *tringa* nesting on a broad front across the Palearctic.
PLUMAGE Adult breeding Narrow white eye-ring and indistinct dark loral line from bill to eye. Head, neck and upperparts brownish with variable amounts of cinnamon and proportion of summer plumaged feathers notched and streaked blackish and buff-brown. Some wing coverts show narrow white fringes. Underparts white boldly streaked dark brown, with brownish wash across breast. Bill medium, straight, dark brown with orange base. Legs longish, dark orange-red. **Adult non-breeding** Upperparts uniform grey with narrow white fringing. Underparts white and finely streaked with breast washed grey-brown. Legs more orange. **Juvenile** Upperparts warm brown with extensive neat buff notching and fringing. Underparts streaked dark brown. Legs orange-yellow. **In flight** White secondaries and tips to inner primaries form clear white trailing edge contrasting with uniform dark upperwing. White lower back, rump and uppertail coverts. Tail white heavily barred brown.
CALL A loud, ringing 'tu-tu'.
RACES Six are recognized: nominate *totanus* (Ireland to W Russia); *robusta* (Iceland, Faroes) largest and more cinnamon coloured; *ussuriensis* (E Russia) also more cinnamon coloured; *terrignotae* (E China, Mongolia, Manchuria); *craggi* (NW Sinkiang); *eurhinus* (W China, Kashmir).
HABITAT AND BEHAVIOUR Breeds in grassy marshes and wet-meadows, coastal saltmarsh and swampy moorland, and also high grass steppe. Typical 'yodelling' song delivered on quivering downcurved wings. Outside the breeding season frequents mudflats, estuaries, lakes, reservoirs and sewage farms.
MOVEMENTS Least migratory of the *tringa* genus, present on the breeding-grounds April–August. Some W European populations stationary, those from Iceland and Faroes migrate to Britain. Scandinavian birds move down to the Mediterranean Basin, W and S African coasts. Central European population moves also to the Mediterranean, whereas eastern birds move to the E Mediterranean, Red Sea, Persian Gulf, Indo-China and east to the Philippines. Vagrant to Greenland, Spitzbergen, Cape Verde Is, Seychelles and Australia.

A	B	C
D	E	C
F	G	H
I	J	K

A Spotted Redshank adult breeding
B Spotted Redshank adult moult
C Spotted Redshank adult moult
D Spotted Redshank adult non-breeding
E Spotted Redshank first-winter non-breeding
F Spotted Redshank juvenile
G Spotted Redshank
H Common Redshank adult breeding
I Spotted Redshank adult non-breeding
J Spotted Redshank juvenile
K Spotted Redshank

Scolopacidae

Marsh Sandpiper
Tringa stagnatilis L 23.50 cm
The smallest, daintiest and longest legged of the 'shanks, breeding across SE Europe east through Russia to W Siberia and Ussuriland.
PLUMAGE **Adult breeding** Indistinct white supercilium and dark loral line from bill to eye. Crown, neck and ear coverts buffish-brown streaked darker. Upperparts rich patterned mixture of cinnamon-grey and dark brown, heavily notched and barred. Underparts white with brown streaking on lower neck and spotting on breast, extending to brown chevrons on flanks. Bill delicate, fairly long and thinly pointed, blackish, silvery-grey at base. Legs long, greenish-yellow or dull yellow. **Adult non-breeding** White forehead and supercilium with obscure dark eye-line. Crown and hindneck streaked grey-brown. Mantle, scapulars and tertials plainer grey fringed white, contrasting with darker grey wing coverts. Underparts white softly suffused grey with fine grey-brown streaking on breast sides. Legs dull olive-green. **Juvenile** Mantle and scapulars brownish-grey with dark subterminal bars and grey fringes. **In flight** Very similar to Greenshank, with uniform dark grey wings contrasting with elongated white patch across back, rump and uppertail coverts. Tail whitish barred pale brown. CALL A high-pitched metallic 'teu'.
HABITAT AND BEHAVIOUR Nests around grassy and muddy shores of predominantly freshwater pools in both steppe and boreal wetland. Wary, often feeding in water in large groups. Outside the breeding season found on inland wetlands and brackish pools but rarely on the coast.
MOVEMENTS Autumn passage commences early July, making long overland flights across broad fronts to mainly sub-Saharan Africa and India. Some Russian birds move south-west down through Europe, whilst others move east of the Black and Caspian Seas. Smaller numbers winter SE Asia and Australia. Spring passage begins mid-March through to early May. Vagrant to W Europe, Cape Verde Is, Seychelles, New Zealand and Aleutians.

Common Greenshank
Tringa nebularia L 31.75 cm
A large 'shank, breeding across the taiga and forest zones of the Palearctic, from Scotland, Norway, and east across Russia and Siberia to the Bering Sea.
PLUMAGE **Adult breeding** Crown, face and hindneck white heavily streaked brown. Narrow white eye-ring and dark loral line from bill to eye. Mantle, scapulars and wing coverts variable grey-brown and black, with dark submarginal lines, notched and fringed white. Tertials grey-brown notched dark brown and white, outer webs often appearing barred. Underparts white with heavy brownish-black streaking across foreneck, breast and flanks. Bill stout, uptilted, bluish-grey at base with blackish tip. Legs longish, dull greenish-yellow. Partial webbing between inner and middle toes. **Adult non-breeding** Crown and hindneck streaked finer. Upperparts more uniform grey fringed white. Underparts white with fine grey streaking across sides of upper breast. **Juvenile** Upperparts brownish-grey with extensive buff notching and white fringing. Breast washed buff finely streaked brown. **In flight** Very dark grey outerwing and slightly paler grey inner wing, contrasting with white back, rump and uppertail coverts. Tail pale grey finely barred brown. Underwing white finely barred brown. Toes project beyond tail tip.
CALL Often when flushed a ringing 'tuu-tuu-tuu'.
HABITAT AND BEHAVIOUR Breeds on open ground, varying from treeless moorland (Scotland), to open marshes, bogs and swampy clearings in coniferous forests, from near sea-level to 1500 m. Exhibits typical *tringa* 'switchback' display flight. Nervous, sometimes gathering into large flocks.
MOVEMENTS Commences leaving breeding-grounds mid-June, with Scottish breeders wintering largely in the British Isles. Passage largely south-south-west across Europe, with large numbers recorded in the Dutch Waddensee. Winters from Mediterranean Basin across Persian Gulf, China and south to S Africa, India, Indo-China, Indonesia and Australia. Vagrant Faroes, Azores, Newfoundland, Aleutians (regular), New Zealand and S Ocean Is.

Spotted Greenshank
Tringa guttifer L 29.85 cm
An endangered and rare wader, differing from Common Greenshank in shorter legs, white underwing and different call with heavily spotted underparts in breeding plumage. Nests largely on Sakhalin Is, but possibly also S Kamchatka and coastal Sea of Okhotsk.
PLUMAGE **Adult breeding** Dark brown crown. Indistinct white fore-supercilium and dark loral line from bill to eye. Rest of head and upper neck white heavily streaked dark brown. Mantle, scapulars and wing coverts dark brown notched and fringed white. Tertials dark brown heavily notched white, a useful separation feature from Common Greenshank. Underparts white with bold blackish spots on upperbreast, belly and flanks. Bill straighter than Common

Greenshank, indistinctly two-toned, blackish with basal half dull greenish or brownish yellow. Legs somewhat brighter yellow than Common Greenshank with distinctly shorter tibia. Partial webbing between all toes unique to *tringas*. **Adult non-breeding** Head paler grey-brown with fine streaking. Fore-supercilium and forehead whitish with indistinct darkish loral line. Dark brown lesser coverts contrast with more uniform grey upperparts, fringed white. Underparts white with lower neck and breast washed grey finely streaked. **Juvenile** Upperparts warm brown with buff notching to scapulars and tertials. Underparts white with indistinct brown flecking across breast. **In flight** Upperwing similar to Common Greenshank with paler grey tail. Underwing coverts and axillaries pure white. Toes do not project beyond tail tip.
CALL A piercing 'keyeu', usually repeated, less ringing and unlike Common Greenshank.
HABITAT AND BEHAVIOUR Nests in spruce and larch forests adjacent marshy coastal lagoons. Outside the breeding season favours coastal mudflats and deltas. Nervous bird with strong flight. Semipalmated toes assist feeding in deeper water, often up to belly.
MOVEMENTS Migration pattern poorly known. Winters from NE India east to Thailand and also Hainan. Regular spring migrant to Hong Kong and China, where flocks of 30-plus recorded. Vagrant Philippines and Australia.

A	B	C
D	E	F
G	H	I
J	K	L

A Marsh Sandpiper adult breeding
B Marsh Sandpiper adult non-breeding
C Marsh Sandpiper juvenile
D Marsh Sandpiper
E Common Greenshank adult breeding
F Common Greenshank adult non-breeding
G Common Greenshank juvenile
H Common Greenshank
I Spotted Greenshank adult breeding
J Spotted Greenshank adult non-breeding
K Spotted Greenshank adult breeding
L Spotted Greenshank

Scolopacidae

Greater Yellowlegs
Tringa melanoleuca **L 31.10 cm**
Similar to the Palearctic Greenshank, breeding in swampy muskeg regions across S Alaska and S Canada, Newfoundland, Labrador and Nova Scotia.
PLUMAGE Adult breeding Crown and hind neck dark grey-brown coarsely streaked white. Obscure whitish fore-supercilium and indistinct dark loral line. Rest of face grey-brown finely streaked white. Mantle, scapulars and tertials dark brown admixed with varying amounts of black, heavily fringed and spotted white. Wing coverts browner fringed white. Underparts white with coarse blackish-brown streaking across breast, becoming black chevrons on flanks and belly. Bill longer than Lesser Yellowlegs, stout and slightly uptilted, blackish with grey-green or yellow-green base. Legs bright yellow, occasionally orange. **Adult non-breeding** Head, face and neck paler grey-brown thinly streaked white. Upperparts darker brown-grey than Lesser Yellowlegs, notched and spotted white. Underparts white with foreneck, breast and flanks lightly washed and streaked brown. **Juvenile** Warm brown upperparts heavily notched and spotted buff. Underparts white with coarse brown streaks usually forming complete breast band, extending onto flanks and undertail coverts. **In flight** Similar to Lesser Yellowlegs with pale notching to secondaries.
CALL Almost identical to Common Greenshank, a triple ringing 'tu-tu-tu', readily distinguishable from Lesser Yellowlegs.
HABITAT AND BEHAVIOUR Nests in swampy muskeg or bog, along the edge of the coniferous forest, but also open marshy areas burnt over or grass-covered. Performs lengthy *tringa* 'switchback' display flight. Winters along muddy coasts and also inland waters, both fresh and brackish.
MOVEMENTS Autumn migration begins mid-July and both overland and coastal routes are involved, with some birds moving directly across the W Atlantic. Winters S USA, C America, W Indies and S America including Tierra del Fuego. Returns very early to breeding-grounds. Less prone to vagrancy than Lesser Yellowlegs, with records from Bermuda, Greenland, Iceland, Britain, Sweden and Japan.

Lesser Yellowlegs
Tringa flavipes **L 24.15 cm**
The smaller, more elegant and more numerous of the Nearctic 'shanks, nesting farther north across Central Alaska and most of Canada east to James Bay.
PLUMAGE Adult breeding Smaller size than Greater Yellowlegs often difficult to ascertain, especially on lone bird. Head, face and neck dark brown finely streaked white. Dark loral line and indistinct fore-supercilium. Mantle, scapulars and tertials blackish-brown fringed and notched white. Wing coverts greyish-brown fringed white. Underparts white with neck and breast heavily streaked brown, extending onto upper flanks. Bill shorter than Greater Yellowlegs, blackish, tinged dull brownish-yellow at extreme base. Legs long and bright yellow, occasionally orange-yellow. **Adult non-breeding** Upperparts paler brown-grey with pale spotting. Greater coverts and tertials more obviously notched white. Under parts white with breast washed grey-brown with indistinct fine brown streaking. **Juvenile** Warmer brown upperparts extensively notched and spotted buff. Under parts white with breast suffused grey finely streaked brown. **In flight** White patch to rump and uppertail coverts contrasts with dark brown barred tail and dark upperwing. Toes project beyond tail tip.
CALL Typical call a single 'tu' or double 'tu-tu', flatter and less ringing than Greater Yellowlegs.
HABITAT AND BEHAVIOUR Breeds in marshy bogs and open muskeg country, preferring drier habitat to Greater Yellowlegs. Reasonably tame and confiding. Exhibits typical *tringa* 'switchback' display flight. Winters on coastal mudflats, inland lakes, pools and flooded grassland.
MOVEMENTS Autumn migration later and spring migration earlier than Greater Yellowlegs. Large movements occur south-eastwards with the species abundant on the Atlantic coast and thus tendency to transatlantic vagrancy. Winters in Gulf States, C and S America. Vagrant to Azores, Europe, Japan, S Africa, Australia and New Zealand.

Willet
Catoptrophorus semipalmatus **L 36.20 cm**
Named after its call, this large, thickset wader has two distinct races breeding within separate regions of N America.
PLUMAGE Adult breeding Short, whitish supercilium and pale eye-ring give 'spectacled' appearance. Head and neck greyish streaked brown. Mantle, scapulars and tertials brownish-grey heavily barred dark brown and buff. Coverts largely grey. Underparts whitish with varying amounts of grey breast spotting and brownish flank barring. Bill straight, heavy, blackish-grey tip and bluish-grey base. Legs longish, stout, bluish-grey sometimes dull yellow-brown. Toes webbed. **Adult non-breeding** Upperparts pale brownish-grey narrowly fringed white. Underparts white with breast and flanks washed grey. Bill colour brighter.

Juvenile Upperparts darker brownish-grey fringed buff, with lower scapulars and tertials extensively notched buff. **In flight** Striking white wing bar contrasts strongly with black primaries and primary coverts and paler grey mantle and inner wing coverts. Equally striking underwing pattern. White rump and uppertail coverts with pale grey tail edged white.
CALL When disturbed a loud, rapidly repeated 'kip-kip-kip'. Flight call a triple 'wee-wee-wee'. Also a familiar, musical 'pill-will-willet'.
RACES Two are recognized: *semipalmatus* or Eastern Willet (Nova Scotia south to N Mexico and W Indies) and *inornatus* or Western Willet (SW Canadian prairies and adjacent US states), the latter larger with paler breeding plumage and reduced barring on flanks.
HABITAT AND BEHAVIOUR *Semipalmatus* is ostensibly coastal, nesting on saltmarsh, especially salt hay, whereas *inornatus* prefers lakes and ponds within prairie marshes. A noisy and aggressive bird. Winters on the coast, especially mudflats and estuaries.
MOVEMENTS Northern populations strongly migratory, with birds arriving late April, and leaving late June; southerly breeding birds more sedentary. Eastern birds move down Atlantic coast to winter in the Caribbean, and C and N S America. Westerly birds migrate along the Pacific Coast mostly wintering from California to Peru and Galapagos Is. Vagrant Alaska, Azores, Finland and Norway.

A	B	C
D	E	F
G	H	I
J	K	L

A   Greater Yellowlegs adult breeding
B   Greater Yellowlegs adult non-breeding
C   Greater Yellowlegs juvenile
D   Lesser Yellowlegs adult breeding
E   Lesser Yellowlegs adult non-breeding
F   Lesser Yellowlegs juvenile
G   Lesser Yellowlegs adult
H   Lesser Yellowlegs juvenile
I   Willet adult breeding
J   Willet adult non-breeding
K   Willet juvenile
L   Willet male breeding

Scolopacidae

Green Sandpiper
Tringa ochropus L 22.20 cm

A rather small, darkish and white wader, breeding across Scandinavia and Eurasia east to the Sea of Okhotsk, using old tree-nests of other birds.

PLUMAGE **Adult breeding** Distinct white fore-supercilium joining narrow white eye-ring. Black loral line from bill to eye. Crown and hindneck heavily streaked brown. Upperparts dark brown heavily spotted white. Underparts white with coarse brown streaking across breast extending onto upper flanks. Bill olive-green at base becoming black towards tip. Legs greyish-green appearing black at distance. **Adult non-breeding** Paler brown head and breast with generally smaller spotting on upperparts. **Juvenile** More obvious supercilium contrasting with dark head and loral line. Upperparts browner with less obvious buff spotting. Breast more finely streaked. **In flight** Uniform dark upperwing contrasts strongly with white rump and uppertail. Remainder of tail white barred brown. Underwing black. Wood Sandpiper differs in being smaller, slimmer, with shorter bill and longer legs, different flight pattern and call. Solitary Sandpiper also similar but differs in smaller size, wings extending beyond tail tip, more distinct eye-ring, and white sides to dark rump and tail.

CALL Noisy, invariably calling when flushed, a clear high pitched 'ku-wit-a-wit'. Often given from migrating birds overhead.

HABITAT AND BEHAVIOUR Breeds in marshy areas within forests, preferring those of pine, using old nests of birds especially thrushes and Wood Pigeon. Winters on inland fresh waters including small pools and even ditches. Avoids intertidal mudflats. Rather nervous, easily flushed.

MOVEMENTS Adults leave the breeding-grounds from mid-June, migrating largely overland. Winters in S Europe and Mediterranean Basin, tropical Africa, and S Asia east to China, Philippines and Borneo. Vagrant Aleutians (spring), Madeira, S Africa and N Australia.

Solitary Sandpiper
Tringa solitaria L 19.70 cm

The Nearctic counterpart of Green Sandpiper, breeding across the boreal forests of Alaska and Canada, using old tree-nests of other birds.

PLUMAGE **Adult breeding** Distinct white fore-supercilium with dark loral line from bill to eye. Clear white eye-ring. Crown and hindneck dark brown thinly streaked white. Upperparts dark brown with buffish-white spotting across mantle, scapulars, wing coverts and tertials. Tips of primaries extend slightly beyond tail. Underparts white with heavy brown streaking across breast and flanks. Bill greenish at base becoming black towards tip. Legs greyish-green. **Adult non-breeding** Upperparts paler grey-brown with reduced spotting. Foreneck and breast finely streaked brown. **Juvenile** Upperparts warmer brown with buffish spotting. Underparts white with buffish wash across breast and thin brown streaking. Legs sometimes tinged yellow. **In flight** Uniform dark upperparts including rump, affording diagnostic distinction from Green Sandpiper. Tail brown with white bars to sides.

CALL Usual call a high 'tuu-tuu-weet', similar to Green Sandpiper, but less frequent.

RACES Two are recognized: nominate *solitaria* (eastern parts) and *cinnamomea* (western parts), the latter slightly larger, with richer buff-brown spotting in breeding plumage.

HABITAT AND BEHAVIOUR Frequents muskeg country usually in wet open areas with scattered trees adjacent bogs and lakes. Utilizes old nests of Rusty Blackbird and American Robin. Generally nervous; bobs when alarmed. Outside the breeding season found on inland lakes including temporary pools and ditches. Avoids the open shore. As its name suggests, not gregarious.

MOVEMENTS Strongly migratory, moving largely overland, with adults moving from early July, both races intermingling in winter quarters. Some overwinter in SE USA, but majority winter in C and S America including Argentina. Vagrant Greenland, Iceland, W Europe (autumn) and S Africa.

Wood Sandpiper
Tringa glareola L 19.70 cm

A common, highly migratory *tringa*, breeding across the N Palearctic excluding the high Arctic from Scandinavia east to the Kamchatka peninsula, and, rarely, in Alaska.

PLUMAGE **Adult breeding** Conspicuous white supercilium extending to rear of ear coverts with bold blackish loral line from bill to eye. Thin whitish eye-ring. Crown dark brown heavily streaked white. Upperparts dark brown heavily barred pale brown with whitish spotting across mantle, median and greater coverts, scapulars and tertials. Lesser coverts plainer dark brown fringed white. Chin and throat white with rest of underparts white with greyish breast heavily streaked and spotted dark brown. Upper flanks also streaked dark brown. Bill shortish, olive or yellowish-green at base becoming blackish towards tip. Legs greenish-yellow, appearing pale at distance. **Adult non-breeding** Upperparts paler brown with less obvious spotting. Breast washed greyish with indistinct thin streaking. Flank barring absent. **Juvenile** Upperparts warmer brown with distinct white spotting and buff fringing. **In flight** Brown upperwing paler than Green Sandpiper, contrasts with with white rump and uppertail coverts. White outer primary shaft. Tail brown narrowly barred white. Feet project beyond tail. Underwing dark brown.

CALL Invariably when flushed a clear, often repeated 'chiff-chiff-chiff'.

HABITAT AND BEHAVIOUR Centring on the boreal climatic zone, breeds in bogs and marshes within coniferous forests, generally not using nests of other birds. Outside the breeding season, found on inland lakes, pools and marshes, generally avoiding the shore.

MOVEMENTS Adults commence migrating towards the end of June, with juveniles a month later, moving in a broad front mainly overland across Europe and the Middle East. Western populations winter largely in tropical Africa with some on the Mediterranean coasts. Eastern birds winter on the Persian Gulf, India, SE Asia and Australia. Vagrant W Aleutians (regular in spring), Azores, Bermuda, Greenland and Iceland.

A	B	C
E	F	D
G	H	I
J	K	L

A — Green Sandpiper adult breeding
B — Green Sandpiper adult non-breeding
C — Green Sandpiper juvenile
D — Green Sandpiper adult
E — Solitary Sandpiper adult breeding
F — Solitary Sandpiper adult moult
G — Solitary Sandpiper juvenile
H — Wood Sandpiper adult breeding
I — Wood Sandpiper adult non-breeding
J — Wood Sandpiper juvenile
K — Wood Sandpiper
L — Wood Sandpiper juvenile

Scolopacidae

Terek Sandpiper
Xenus cinereus L 24.15 cm
The only small wader with an upturned bill, breeding mainly across the middle and higher latitudes of Russia and Siberia, spreading westwards through Finland and Norway.
PLUMAGE **Adult breeding** Indistinct white fore-supercilium with dark loral line extending behind eye. Crown and hind neck grey finely streaked brown. Mantle, coverts and tertials greyish-brown with thin black shaft streaks and pale fringes. Broad shaft streaks form conspicuous black line along scapulars. Underparts white with finely streaked lateral breast patches, sometimes joining across the centre of breast. Bill longish, upturned and blackish at tip, orange at base. Legs variable, from dull greenish-yellow to bright orange. **Adult non-breeding** Upperparts plainer, brownish-grey with extensive pale fringing. Dark scapular lines virtually absent or lacking altogether. Underparts white with thin streaking across breast sides. **Juvenile** Upperparts dark brown with indistinct ubterminal bars and buffish-orange fringes to scapulars, coverts and tertials. Thin black scapular line usually present. **In flight** Striking white trailing edge to secondaries and dark outerwing contrast with paler mid-wing panel. Rump, uppertail coverts and tail greyish, edged and tipped white.
CALL Usual flight call a fluty, rippling 'twit-twit-twit-twit'.
HABITAT AND BEHAVIOUR Nests in wet grassland, alongside lakes and rivers and marshy openings within the Eurasian conifer forest. Recent westward spread has shown preference for more open habitat. Winters on coastal lagoons, mudflats, mangroves and creeks. Highly active when feeding, often running and then lunging at prey with near horizontal bill.
MOVEMENTS Adults commence autumn migration early July. Returning birds arrive mid May in Finland, mid-June in Russia. Due to range expansion, migrants now more often recorded in W Europe and W Africa. Winters from S Red Sea to S Africa, Persian Gulf and eastward to Australia. Annual in New Zealand. Vagrant to Tasmania and Alaska.

Common Sandpiper
Actitis hypoleucos L 20.30 cm
A common wader with a distinctive flight, found in a variety of wetland habitats, breeding from the British Isles, across C and S Eurasia to Japan and outlying islands.
PLUMAGE **Adult breeding** Indistinct whitish supercilium and eye-stripe extending to ear coverts. Whitish eye-ring. Head, hindneck and mantle olive-brown with fine dark brown shaft streaks. Scapulars, wing coverts and tertials similar but also show irregular dark brown bars and tipped buff. Underparts white with thin brown streaking across breast, most obvious on sides forming white 'peak' between folded wing and breast sides. Bill short, straight, pinkish with black tip. Legs duller pinkish-brown. Tail extends noticeably beyond folded wing tips. **Adult non-breeding** Upperparts plainer dark brown with little dark shaft streaking. Wing coverts show thin pale fringes. Underparts white with brownish lateral breast patches. Centre of breast largely unstreaked. Bill dark brown, greenish at base. Legs variable but usually dull yellowish, often tinged olive. **Juvenile** Similar to non-breeding adult with mantle and scapulars fringed buff. Wing coverts strongly barred dark brown and pale buff. Tertial pattern diagnostic with alternate dark brown and buff notches along outer web. **In flight** Wing bar from middle primaries becoming stronger and extending across to inner secondaries. Outer webs of outer tail feathers broadly edged white.
CALL Often heard on migration and when breeding a loud, descending 'tswee-wee-wee'.
HABITAT AND BEHAVIOUR Found breeding along fast-flowing rivers, but also edges of lakes and ponds. Exhibits teetering gait and distinctive flight, with flickering wingbeats and short glides on downcurved wings. Noisy song is a rapid 'kitlee-wee-it, kitlee-wee-it'. Winters on almost every type of wetland, including the open shore.
MOVEMENTS Autumn migration commencing in mid-June is mainly overland, wintering in S Europe and the Mediterranean Basin, C and S Africa, Persian Gulf east to Japan, Indonesia and Australia. Vagrant to Alaska (regular) and New Zealand.

Spotted Sandpiper
Actitis macularia L 19.05 cm
With diagnostic breeding plumage, this wader breeds widely across N America from Alaska through Canada to Newfoundland and south to most USA states.
PLUMAGE **Adult breeding male** Upperparts similar to Common Sandpiper but with less shaft streaking. Underparts white heavily spotted black; white 'peak' and breast streaking absent. Tail projecting slightly beyond folded wing tips. Bill short, straight, pinkish with black tip. Legs pinkish-brown. **Adult breeding female** Similar to male with spots both larger and blacker. **Adult non-breeding** Upperparts plainer with much reduced shaft streaking and barring. Wing coverts fringed pale. Bill dark brown with paler greenish-brown base. Legs variable from greyish-yellow to yellow-ochre. **Juvenile** Differs from Common Sandpiper in that strongly barred pale buff and dark brown coverts contrast more markedly with plainer mantle and scapulars. Tertials usually plain with buff notching reduced to tips. **In flight** Wing bar virtually absent on inner secondaries and less white in outer tail feathers.
CALL Typical flight call a rising series of 'pit' notes, with others similar or even identical to Common Sandpiper.
HABITAT AND BEHAVIOUR Very similar to Common Sandpiper.
MOVEMENTS Migrates over a broad front across N America, with adults departing during July. Apart from small numbers in S USA, most birds winter in W Indies, C America and S to N Argentina. Vagrant to W Europe (bred Scotland 1975), Azores, Madeira, Tristan da Cunha and W Pacific Is.

A	B	
C	D	E
F	G	H
I	J	K

A Terek Sandpiper adult breeding
B Terek Sandpiper adult non-breeding
C Terek Sandpiper adult breeding
D Common Sandpiper adult breeding
E Common Sandpiper adult non-breeding
F Common Sandpiper juvenile
G Common Sandpiper adult
H Spotted Sandpiper adult breeding
I Spotted Sandpiper adult non-breeding
J Spotted Sandpiper juvenile
K Spotted Sandpiper

Scolopacidae

Grey-tailed Tattler
Heteroscelus brevipes L 25.40 cm
Positively identified from Wandering Tattler by length of nasal groove and call, breeding in mountains of E Siberia west to the Putorana Mountains and south to Lake Baikal.
PLUMAGE **Adult breeding** Distinctive long white supercilia virtually meeting across nape contrasting with blackish loral line extending behind eye. Crown, hindneck and entire upperparts slate-grey tinged brown, initially mostly tipped white. Wing tips fall level with tail tip. Face, sides and front of neck white finely streaked grey. Underparts white with breast, flanks and limited extent undertail coverts sides lightly barred grey. Bill medium, straight, olive-grey to blackish with basal third of lower mandible tinged yellow. Length of nasal groove diagnostic, extending just over half way to bill tip. Legs shortish, bright yellow with scales on tarsi scutellated. **Adult non-breeding** Similar to breeding but underparts lack barring. Neck, breast and flanks washed soft grey. **Juvenile** Similar to non-breeding adult. Scapulars, coverts and tertials clearly notched white. Sides of tail also notched white. **In flight** Appears virtually uniform grey, with darker blackish-grey outer primaries and greater primary coverts. Indistinct pale tips to outer greater coverts and greater primary coverts. Uppertail coverts faintly barred whitish.
CALL Usual note diagnostic disyllabic, upward inflected 'tu-weep'.
HABITAT AND BEHAVIOUR Favours mountain streams with islands covered in willow scrub or dwarf birch and open spaces with mosses and lichens. Nests both on the ground and in old tree-nests of other birds. Freely perches in trees. 'Teeters' when walking. Outside breeding season found on coastal mudflats, sandflats and estuaries and to lesser extent rocky coasts, often forming communal high-tide roosts on mangroves and breakwaters.
MOVEMENTS Migratory, mostly moving south during August to winter in China, Philippines, SE Asia, Australia and New Zealand. Spring passage during April and May. Vagrant Alaska, California and Wales.

Wandering Tattler
Heteroscelus incanus L 27.30 cm
Darker than its American counterpart, nesting in the Alpine zone of S Coastal, Central and W Alaska east to the Yukon and NW British Columbia, and probably also Anadyrland and the Chukotski peninsula of E Siberia, overlapping with Grey-tailed Tattler.

PLUMAGE **Adult breeding** Narrow white supercilium with blackish loral line extending through and behind eye. Crown, hindneck and entire upperparts plain, dark slate-grey. Wing tips extend beyond tail tip. Face, sides and front of neck white heavily streaked dark grey. Underparts heavily barred dark grey including undertail coverts, except for central belly and vent. Bill blackish, basal third tinged yellow. Length of nasal groove diagnostic, extending almost two-thirds to bill tip. Legs shortish, bright yellow, with scales on tarsi reticulated. **Adult non-breeding** Similar to breeding but underparts lack barring. Neck, breast and flanks plain slate-grey. **Juvenile** Similar to non-breeding adult. Scapulars, coverts and tertials narrowly fringed whitish. Sides of tail faintly notched whitish. Breast and flanks faintly barred. **In flight** Appears long winged, almost uniform dark slate-grey with darker blackish-grey outer primaries and greater primary coverts. Indistinct pale tips to outer greater coverts and greater primary coverts and sometimes uppertail coverts.
CALL Usual flight note diagnostic, rippling series of six to ten notes, rapidly accelerating but decreasing in volume.
HABITAT AND BEHAVIOUR Breeds along mountain streams with gravelly banks, often adjacent swift waters and quiet pools. 'Teeters' when walking, frequently 'freezing' when alarmed. Outside breeding season favours rocky shorelines and to lesser extent gravelly or sandy beaches, sometimes on ponds well away from salt water.
MOVEMENTS Migratory, moving south from August to winter along Pacific coast from S California south to Ecuador, Galapagos Is, Hawaii, Central and S Pacific Is, Australia and New Zealand. Returns to breeding-grounds late May. Vagrant Japan (regular), S Canada, Peru, Chatham Is.

Tuamotu Sandpiper
Prosobonia cancellata L 15.85 cm
A most unusual looking, insectivorous wader, reminiscent of Upland Sandpiper, extremely rare and restricted to a few atolls within the Tuamotu Archipelago, with numbers possibly as low as 200.
PLUMAGE Indistinct creamy supercilium faintly streaked brown separates dull brown lores and ear-coverts from darker brown crown and hindneck. Upperparts dark brown variably spotted and blotched whitish, buff and pale brown. Wing coverts tipped whitish-buff. Tail noticeably long projecting well beyond folded wing tips. Underparts creamy-buff streaked mid-brown across throat, foreneck and sides of

neck, with breast, belly, flanks and undertail coverts barred mid brown. Bill longish, black and pointed, very similar to insectivorous passerine. Legs variable greyish to yellowish-brown. **In flight** Wings appear broad and rounded with whitish tips to greater coverts and paler buffish-brown panel across median coverts. Tail long, dark brown variably barred pale buffish-brown.
CALL Frequently uttered high-pitched piping.
HABITAT Probably restricted to predator-free atolls of Rangiroa, Moraine, Tahanea and Anuanu Runga 2 within the archipelago. Found on all types of habitat within the atolls, often calling continuously as forages for insects amongst vegetation and coral rubble along shorelines. Number of 'populations' surviving on atolls free from introduced predators, especially rats and cats, is crucial to the birds continued existence.
MOVEMENTS Sedentary with some possible inter-atoll exchange of birds.

A	B	C
D	E	F
G	H	I
J	K	L

A Grey-tailed Tattler adult breeding
B Grey-tailed Tattler adult non-breeding
C Grey-tailed Tattler juvenile
D Grey-tailed Tattler adult
E Wandering Tattler adult breeding
F Wandering Tattler adult non-breeding
G Wandering Tattler juvenile
H Wandering Tattler adult
I Tuamotu Sandpiper adult
J Tuamotu Sandpiper adult
K Tuamotu Sandpiper juvenile
L Tuamotu Sandpiper

Scolopacidae

Ruddy Turnstone
Arenaria interpres **L 23.50 cm**
A small, stocky wader with a distinctive piebald plumage, breeding around virtually the entire Arctic coastline.
PLUMAGE **Adult breeding male** Pattern variable, with head white finely streaked black. Black mask through eye, neck, collar and upperbreast, enclosing white breast patch. Chin and rest of underparts white. Upperparts mainly chestnut-orange, with blackish patch across lower scapulars. Bill short, slightly uptilted and black, with paler base to lower mandible. Legs short and bright orange-red. **Adult breeding female** Head generally duller with more black crown streaking. **Adult non-breeding** Darkish brown head with distinctive duller upperparts lacking chestnut-orange colour. Buffish chin and dark grey breast enclosing pale patch on side. Rest of underparts white. Legs dull orange-red. **Juvenile** Pale brown head with neat brownish upperparts uniformly fringed buff giving 'scaly' effect. Legs dull yellowish-brown. **In flight** Strikingly pied, with bold white wing bar, elongated white patch on back and white uppertail coverts. Black tail tipped and edged white. Also white patch across inner wing coverts and tertials.
CALL A clear rapid 'tuk-a-tuk'. Also when flushed a sharp 'tchit-ik'.
RACES Two are recognized: nominate *interpres* (Ellesmere Is, Greenland, Eurasia and NW Alaska), generally larger, with more crown streaking and paler coloration to upperparts, and *morinella* (NE Alaska east to Baffin Is).
HABITAT AND BEHAVIOUR Nests on tundra usually close to the sea, often on sloping, stony ground with sparse vegetation. Relatively tame. Distinctive feeding action, turning over stones and seaweed to catch prey. Winters mainly on stony or rocky coasts, but also sandy beaches and mudflats with pebbles and seaweed.
MOVEMENTS Adults commence leaving breeding-grounds early August, returning late May. Nominate race winters from California to S America, but NE Canada and Greenland birds cross Atlantic to winter in W Europe and NW Africa. Palearctic birds winter on more tropical coasts from Africa east to Australia. *Morinella* winters in S America and Pacific islands. Vagrant to southern Ocean Is.

Black Turnstone
Arenaria melanocephala **L 23.50 cm**
Differing from Ruddy Turnstone in darker chin and legs, with a breeding range restricted to W and S Alaska.
PLUMAGE **Adult breeding male** Head largely black with fine white streaking. Large white spot at base of bill, and indistinct pale crescent above eye. Upperparts blackish-brown lacking any chestnut coloration, with pale fringes to lower scapulars, coverts and tertials. Chin black. Throat and breast black extensively flecked white. Rest of underparts white. Bill black. Legs dull blackish-brown tinged red. **Adult breeding female** Smaller spot at base of bill, and generally less streaking on head. Black streaking extending onto upper flanks. **Adult non-breeding** Head, nape, breast and upperparts generally all dark, lacking white streaking. White spot at base of bill absent. Coverts, scapulars and tertials with indistinct pale fringing. **Juvenile** Upperparts and breast generally browner, with neat buff fringes to coverts, scapulars and tertials. **In flight** Differing from Ruddy Turnstone by broader wings, wider wing bar across bases of secondaries, and narrower white patch across uppertail coverts.
CALL A trill-like 'skurr', less harsh and higher pitched than Ruddy Turnstone.
HABITAT AND BEHAVIOUR Breeds on grass-covered shorelines adjacent brackish pools on the coastal tundra. Aerial display flight not dissimilar from Snipe, including audible note from vibrating tail feathers. Winters on rocky coastlines, especially those of outlying reefs and islands.
MOVEMENTS Less migratory than Ruddy Turnstone, moving south to winter from SE Alaska to Sonora, Mexico, with one-year-old birds remaining south of breeding-grounds. Vagrant inland to W States, Yukon, and Wrangel Is, Russia.

Surfbird
Aphriza virgata **L 24.15 cm**
An unusual calidrid with a plover-type bill, showing certain similarities to Great Knot, nesting in the mountains of Alaska and adjacent Yukon territory.
PLUMAGE **Adult breeding** Distinctive. Entire head, neck and upper breast heavily streaked blackish-brown and white. Mantle and upper scapulars dark grey edged chestnut and white. Lower scapulars show paired buffish-orange spots tipped black and white, becoming more obvious as tips wear off. Wing coverts and tertials brownish-grey fringed pale. Underparts white with heavy chevrons on lower breast extending onto flanks. Bill short, dark brown, with orangey-yellow patch to base of lower mandible. Legs rather short, dull yellow. **Adult non-breeding** Head, breast and upperparts uniform slate-grey with pale fringing. Chin and rest of underparts white with brownish-grey chevrons on flanks. Bill base yellow. Legs brighter yellow. **Juvenile** Similar to non-breeding adult, but upperparts browner with dark submarginal line and extensively fringed buff. Breast strongly mottled brown. **In flight** Prominent white wing bar across dark flight feathers. White rump and uppertail contrasting with black tail finely tipped white.
CALL Not very vocal. Occasional shrill whistle 'kee-wee-argh'.
HABITAT AND BEHAVIOUR Breeds on Alpine tundra above 1200 m, often on mountain sides and other rugged country occupied by mountain sheep. Winters on wave-tossed and seaweed-covered rocks adjacent to the tideline. Gregarious, forming large flocks on migration. Often very tame.
MOVEMENTS Strongly migratory, with adults leaving the breeding-grounds from mid-July, moving almost exclusively down the Pacific coast to winter from SE Alaska continuously to the southern tip of S America including Tierra del Fuego. Non-breeders remain on the wintering grounds all year. Rare spring visitor to Texas. Vagrant Pennsylvania.

A	B	C
D	E	F
H	I	G
J	K	L

A Ruddy Turnstone *morinella* adult breeding
B Ruddy Turnstone *interpres* adult breeding
C Ruddy Turnstone adult non-breeding
E Ruddy Turnstone
E Ruddy Turnstone juvenile
F Black Turnstone adult
G Black Turnstone adult
H Surfbird adult moult
I Surfbird adult breeding
J Surfbird adult non-breeding
K Surfbird
L Surbbird juvenile

Scolopacidae

Wilson's Phalarope
Phalaropus tricolor L 22.85 cm
The largest of the phalaropes, breeding extensively across the prairies of N America.
PLUMAGE **Adult breeding female** As with all phalaropes, female shows brighter coloration. Crown and hindneck soft grey. Small white patch anterior to eye. Black mask from bill to eye extending down sides of neck shading to deep chestnut on sides of mantle. Upperparts grey alleviated by chestnut across edges of mantle and scapulars. **Adult breeding male** Distinctly duller lacking chestnut. Head, face and upperparts dark brown. Underparts whitish with orangey wash across breast. Bill longest of all phalaropes, needle-like and black. Legs black. **Adult non-breeding** White face with grey mask through eye extending to back of nape. Upperparts uniform pale grey fringed white. Underparts clean white. Legs yellow. **Juvenile** Dark brown upperparts boldly fringed buff. Underparts white with buffish wash to sides of breast and flanks. Legs pinkish-yellow. **In flight** Uniform dark wings contrasting with squarish white patch to rump and uppertail coverts. Tail grey. Toes project beyond tail.
CALL Usually silent but occasionally a soft 'ungh' given in flight.
HABITAT AND BEHAVIOUR Breeds around shallow ponds and lakes on the American prairies, close to wet-meadow vegetation. Unlike the other phalaropes does not winter at sea, but on inland wetlands, lakes and marshes, occasionally mudflats. Often very tame.
MOVEMENTS Migratory with females departing from mid-June ahead of males and juveniles. Migration is largely overland across W USA to Mexico and across the E Pacific to NW S America, and south to winter on the Argentinian pampas and also the high Andean lakes. Return passage to S USA from mid-April. Vagrant to S Africa, Australia and New Zealand and Alexander Is, most southerly record of any wader.

Red-necked Phalarope
Phalaropus lobatus L 18.40 cm
The smallest and daintiest of the phalaropes, breeding across the entire northern Holarctic region from the Aleutians to the east coast of Siberia.
PLUMAGE **Adult breeding female** Dark grey head and face alleviated by small white spot above eye. Elongated orange neck patch starting behind eye running down sides of neck and joining at base. Upperparts dark grey with rich golden-brown lines to edges of mantle and upper

scapulars. Lower scapulars, wing coverts and tertials edged rufous-buff. White chin and throat. Slate-grey breast and flanks with rest of underparts white. Bill black, needle-like. Legs dark grey with toes lobed. **Adult breeding male** Generally duller around the head and face with more subdued neck patch. **Adult non-breeding** Whitish head with black patch extending through and behind eye. Upperparts grey edged white forming distinct lines along mantle and upper scapulars. Underparts white. **Juvenile** Dark brown mask through eye. Crown, hindneck and upperparts dark brown, with orange-brown edges to mantle, scapulars and tertials. Underparts white with pinkish-buff wash to foreneck and upper breast. **In flight** Conspicuous white wing bar and white sides to blackish rump, with dark grey tail.
CALL Most often heard is a soft 'twick', with family parties of birds often giving a fast repeated 'pri-pri-pri-pri'.
HABITAT AND BEHAVIOUR Typically adjacent freshwater pools with the female playing no part in the incubation process. Feeds by swimming, spinning erratically. Very tame and confiding.
MOVEMENTS Migration extensively overland, with females departing towards the end of June, ahead of males and juveniles during July and August. European and W Siberian populations migrate south-east towards staging posts around the Caspian and Black Seas, where huge numbers occur, moving on to winter in the Arabian Sea. Canadian populations migrate south-west to the Pacific and winter off the Peruvian coast. Alaskan and E Siberian birds winter in the E Indies. Breeding-grounds re-occupied from late May. Vagrant to S Africa, Australia and New Zealand.

Grey Phalarope
Phalaropus fulicarius L 20.95 cm
A pelagic wader except when nesting or storm driven, breeding across Arctic N America from Alaska to Hudson Bay, Greenland, Iceland and Spitzbergen, and W Siberia east to the Chukotski peninsula.
PLUMAGE **Adult breeding female** Blackish crown, hindneck, base of bill and chin. White sides to head surrounding dark eye. Upperparts blackish-brown edged rich chestnut-buff. Rest of neck and underparts deep chestnut-red. **Adult breeding male** Duller with streaked crown and ill-defined face pattern and variable amounts of white on underparts. Bill markedly broad based and less pointed than Red-necked, yellow tipped black. Legs brownish or greyish-yellow with lobed toes. **Adult non-breeding** Head and underparts white with blackish cap and dark mask through eye,

amount varying considerably. Upperparts uniform soft grey with wing coverts and scapulars fringed white. Bill becoming black with legs greyish. **Juvenile** Rich dark brown upperparts broadly fringed buff. Underparts white with pinkish-buff suffusion to face, neck and sides of breast. **In flight** Noticeably broader and longer winged than Red-necked, with white wing bar and white sides to dark rump, and grey sides to darker centred tail.
CALL A clear 'whit', not unlike Sanderling.
HABITAT AND BEHAVIOUR The most Arctic of the phalaropes, breeding adjacent pools on flat, marshy tundra. Female performs circling display flight, but plays no part in the incubation process. Lobed toes adapted for swimming.
MOVEMENTS Migrates exclusively by sea routes, wintering largely off the coasts of Chile, W and S Africa. Females depart early July followed by males and juveniles a month later. Migration is largely in a south-easterly direction. 'Wrecks' occur off the W European coast during autumn from severe Atlantic depressions, occasionaly being forced inland. Returns to breeding-grounds late May. Vagrant to inland parts of northern continents; also Australia, New Zealand, Argentina and Antarctic peninsula.

A	B	C
D	E	F
G	H	I
J	K	L

A Wilson's Phalarope juvenile
B Wilson's Phalarope adult breeding male
C Wilson's Phalarope adult breeding female
D Wilson's Phalarope adult
E Red-necked Phalarope adult breeding male
F Red-necked Phalarope adult breeding female
G Red-necked Phalarope juvenile
H Red-necked Phalarope adult
I Grey Phalarope adult breeding male
J Grey Phalarope first-winter non-breeding
K Grey Phalarope adult breeding female
L Grey Phalarope adult non-breeding

Scolopacidae

Eurasian Woodcock
Scolopax rusticola L 34.30 cm

A large woodcock, widely distributed in temperate woodlands across the Atlantic Is, Eurasia east to Sakhalin Is, and Japan, also China, N India and N Burma, the Caucasus and Turkistan.
PLUMAGE Adult Steeply sloping buffy forehead, crown and nape transversed with blackish bars, first bar equal in width to second one, separated by several narrow buffy-pink bars. Face mottled buffish-brown with converging dark grey facial bars across lores and cheeks. Eye encircled with feathering. Large pale area between eye and cheek bar. Upperparts cryptic plumage of rufous, black, brown and buff giving overall rufous coloration, with greyish 'V's along edge of mantle and upper scapulars. Wing coverts and tertials with oval patches of blackish and chestnut, spotted and tipped whitish and buffish yellow. Underparts warm buffish-grey strongly barred dark greyish-brown. Bill pinkish-horn, darker towards tip. Legs very short, dull pinkish-grey. **Juvenile** Extremely similar to adult. Tail shorter with duller whitish-grey terminal spots. Pale tips to primary coverts equal width and concolorus with rest of chestnut-brown feather barring (narrower and paler in adult). **In flight** Wings broad, relatively long and pointed. Chestnut-brown and black mantle and upperwing. Rump and long uppertail coverts reddish-brown., subterminal tail band mainly black notched bright chestnut on outer webs, with silvery-grey terminal spots. Underside of tail tipped silvery-white.
CALL Rarely calls when flushed. During 'roding' croaking 'quorr-quorr-quorr', followed with distinctive 'tsiwick'.
HABITAT AND BEHAVIOUR Breeds chiefly in woodland, both broad-leaved and coniferous with undergrowth of bramble, bush or fern and ground cover of decaying leaves. Adjacent open rides or glades essential for males 'roding', calling and displaying on slow deliberate wingbeats at dawn and dusk in search of females. Usually solitary. Wintering habitat similar, also small woods, fields and gardens, even intertidal mudflats during persistant freezing conditions.
MOVEMENTS Largely migratory, some wintering in W Europe, most birds moving south or south-west to winter in Mediterranean Basin, Iraq, Iran, India east through Indo-China and Ryuku Is. Onward south-west movements occur with onset of severe cold weather. Return passage commences from early March. Vagrant Iceland, Greenland, Spitzbergen, USA, Sri Lanka and Malaysia.

Amami Woodcock
Scolopax mira L 35.55 cm

Separable from Eurasian Woodcock by head, face and tail pattern and call, inhabiting subtropical forests of Amami-oshima, Tokunoshoma, Okinawa and Tokashika-jima in the Nasei-Shoto chain of islands, Japan.
PLUMAGE Generally more olivaceous less rufous coloration than Eurasian Woodcock. Gentle sloping forehead with high peaked crown. First blackish crown bar distinctly narrower than second one. Dark grey facial bars across lores and cheeks lie almost parallel, with smaller pale area between eye and cheek bar. Pink bare patch of skin surrounds eye, particularly noticeable behind eye. Upperparts darkish-olive brown, greater coverts and tertials showing pale cinnamon-brown triangles, lacking bold oval pattern of Eurasian Woodcock. Underpart pattern and coloration similar to Eurasian. Bill deeper based, dull horn, lacking dark tip of Eurasian. Legs longer, dull brownish tinged dull yellow or grey. **In flight** Very similar to Eurasian with small narrower cinnamon triangles across primaries. Tail uniform dark brown notched paler brown at edges tipped silvery-grey but lacking black subterminal band of Eurasian. Undertail shows less sharply defined silvery spots.
CALL When flushed occasional snipe-like 'jeh-jee'.
HABITAT AND BEHAVIOUR Found in montane forest favouring damp shady areas of forest floor. Seldom seen except along forest tracks at night, probing into earth and vegetation adjacent roadside. Lacks 'roding' display but displays on the ground, male hanging quivering wings loosely at side whilst gently bobbing head. When disturbed runs for cover or takes flight, quickly dropping to cover again or landing on forest branches.
MOVEMENTS Sedentary.

American Woodcock
Scolopax minor L 27.90 cm

The smallest of the woodcocks, breeding in woodlands across E and S USA.
PLUMAGE Adult Buffy-grey forehead and forecrown, crown and nape black with buffy-orange transverse bars. Face warm buffish-orange with black loral line extending narrowly onto ear coverts, and blackish bar across cheeks joining on hindneck. Mantle, scapulars and tertials chestnut and black fringed chestnut, grey and buff. Conspicuous silvery-grey 'V's along edge of mantle and upper scapulars, with less well-defined 'V's along upper edge of lower scapulars. Wing coverts

mottled dull chestnut-brown tipped greyish-buff. Tail clearly extending beyond tips of tertials and hidden primaries. Entire underparts unbarred, rich orangey-buff. Bill dull greenish or yellowish-brown, darker olive-brown towards tip. Legs dull fleshy-grey. **Juvenile** Extremely similar to adult. Pale tips to underside of middle secondaries contrast markedly with dark brown subterminal bars (adults only show slight contrast). **Flight** Wings broad, square-ended. Plain brown primaries, primary coverts and outer secondaries unbarred, contrasting slightly with barred inner secondaries and warm chestnut wing coverts. Outer three primaries shorter and narrower, producing mechanical 'song'. Rump and uppertail coverts orangey-buff mottled dark brown in centre. Tail tipped pale grey. Undertail tipped bright silvery-white. Underwing coverts and axillaries rich buffish-orange.
CALL Male utters muffled 'chuk-oo', followed by louder 'peent'; twittering aerial display 'song'.
HABITAT AND BEHAVIOUR Favours young plantations, deciduous or mixed, with herbaceous ground cover, adjacent scattered openings and clearings with low, scrubby vegetation for male to perform musical aerial display song over 'station' at dawn and dusk. Mostly crepuscular and nocturnal. Walks with body swaying from side to side, probing for earthworms. Winter habitat includes smaller plantations, pine uplands and gardens.
MOVEMENTS Partially migratory. Summer resident in northern part of range, wintering October–March in southern parts of breeding range south to Gulf States. Vagrant west to Colorado, Montana, also Bermuda.

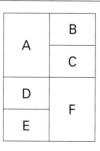

A Eurasian Woodcock adult non-breeding
B Eurasian Woodcock adult breeding
C Eurasian Woodcock adult non-breeding
D Amami Woodcock
E Amami Woodcock
F American Woodcock

Scolopacidae

Dusky Woodcock
Scolopax saturata L 30.50 cm
A small, dark, rare woodcock restricted to montane forest in Java, Sumatra and New Guinea.
PLUMAGE Head rufous-brown with narrow black bars across forehead and several broad black bars across crown and nape. Face variably dark brown and whitish with blackish loral line and rear cheek bar. Entire upperparts including scapulars, wing coverts, and tertials blackish broadly notched and fringed rufous. Chin variable buffish or white. Underparts strongly barred dark brown. Foreneck and breast suffused paler rufous-brown, rest of underparts variably washed whitish. Bill dark flesh and swollen at base tapering to blackish tip. Legs dark grey. **In flight** Appears rounded winged with uniform dark rufous-black flight feathers, mantle and inner wing. Tail similar coloration tipped dark silvery-grey. CALL Contact note harsh 'kkrrr'; during roding nasal 'queet' and rapid 'quo-quo-quo-quo'. RACES Two are recognized: *saturata* (Java, Sumatra) brownish supercilium, buffish chin, whitish area to underparts restricted to upper belly; *rosenbergii* (New Guinea) whitish spot anterior to eye, whitish chin and malar region, entire belly whitish contrasting with bold dark brown barring. HABITAT AND BEHAVIOUR Found at altitudes 1500–3000 m, especially where small patches of forest adjoin open areas of alpine grassland. Performs horizontal roding display at dawn and dusk above both forest and clearings. On the ground tame and reluctant to fly. MOVEMENTS Entirely sedentary.

Celebes Woodcock
Scolopax celebensis L 32.40 cm
A large, very rare woodcock, with no confirmed sighting since 1931. Differs from Eurasian in largely plainer, unbarred under parts and longer bill and legs, restricted to the mountains of Sulawesi, Indonesia.
PLUMAGE Sandy-buff forehead and face. Several broad transverse blackish bars across crown and nape. Converging dark grey facial bars across lores, ear coverts and rear cheeks. Upperparts black finely spotted, barred and fringed ochre and rufous. Under parts ochre-buff faintly barred blackish on sides of breast and flanks. Bill long, bluish-grey. Legs longish, slate-grey. **In flight** Appears broad, rounded winged. Flight feathers notched with small ochre triangles and spots. Tail blackish indistinctly notched pale chestnut tipped silvery-grey. CALL Undescribed. RACES Two are recognized: *celebensis* (C Sulawesi) and *heinrichi* (NE Sulawesi) both virtually identical.

HABITAT AND BEHAVIOUR Found in mature montane forest above 2000 m elevation. Seldom seen, hiding in thick undergrowth along mountain ridges in areas of open ground. Highly terrestrial, taking flight to escape danger, rapidly dropping again. May be more widespread within suitable habitat than records suggest. MOVEMENTS Sedentary.

New Zealand Snipe
Coenocorypha aucklandica L 22.85 cm
The larger of the two 'semi-snipes', highly endangered and totally restricted to the sub-Antarctic islands of New Zealand.
PLUMAGE **Adult male breeding** Small, 'neckless', proportionally longer billed and longer legged than Chatham Islands Snipe with highly variable plumage coloration according to race. Darkish brown crown and loral stripe with buffish-brown supercilium and crown stripe, latter not reaching base of bill. Upperparts very variable, mantle and scapulars from mid-brown to black centres with irregular brown to tawny-buff bars variably fringed narrow whitish-buff to broad yellowish-buff. Tertials virtually cloak short primaries with very short tail projection giving characteristic 'squat-ended' appearance. Underpart colour also highly variable from pale buff-yellow to darker grey-brown, lightly to heavily barred brown. Bill longish, dark brown with slightly paler base. Legs dull yellowish to greenish-grey. **Adult female breeding** Slightly larger with proportionally longer bill. **Juvenile** Very similar to adult. *Huegeli* generally greyer toned with greyish base to bill. **In flight** Similar to Chatham Islands Snipe, when flushed dashing off low and fast on whirring rounded wings, taking to cover very quickly. CALL Series of repeated whistles 'chup-chup'. Female call lower pitched 'chur'. RACES Three are recognized: *Aucklandica* (Aukland Is group) largest, palest, with unbarred buffish belly; *meinertzhagenae* (Antipodes Is) darkest, yellowish-buff underparts; *huegeli* (Snares Is group) underparts dark, uniformly barred. HABITAT AND BEHAVIOUR Favours clumped woodland interspersed with low thickish undergrowth. During daytime usually remains hidden in tussock grass, undergrowth or holes in rocks. Mostly active at dusk and night-time, probing in soft edges of wooded clearings and scrub for earthworms, insects and arthropods. Highly territorial. Very tame and approachable. MOVEMENTS Totally sedentary.

Chatham Islands Snipe
Coenocorypha pusilla L 20.30 cm
The smallest 'semi-snipe', restricted to the Chatham Is, probably now numbering in

excess of 500, and currently still regarded as a separate species from similar New Zealand Snipe.
PLUMAGE **Adult male** Very small, short-winged and short-tailed 'neckless' snipe. Separated from New Zealand Snipe by range, smaller size and shorter bill. Facial markings less pronounced than on typical *gallinago* snipe. Upperparts warm brown with black submarginal markings and fringed white. Underparts buffish-brown with breast and flanks streaked and mottled darker brown. Very short wings and tail give characteristic 'squat ended' appearance. Bill very short, brownish with dull reddish base. Legs dull yellowish-brown. **Adult female** Slightly larger with paler, less patterned upperparts and longer bill. **Juvenile** Upperparts less defined. Underparts warm yellowish-buff with reduced breast streaking. Base of bill and legs both duller coloration. **Flight** When flushed flies low and fast on short rounded wings quickly landing again. CALL A number of soft, low 'chirrups' precedes a series of plaintive whistles 'wit, wit, wit', rapidly repeated up to ten times. Female call apparently lower pitched. HABITAT AND BEHAVIOUR Restricted to South East Is, Mangere, Little Mangere and Star Keys in the Chatham group, having suffered badly from predation, especially by cats. Numbers now increasing due to predator-free island reserves. On South East Is found in 'bush' areas. Actively probes leaf mould on the forest floor, running rapidly between feeding. Nests amongst tussock grass adjacent bush. Tame and approachable. Calls mostly at dusk but also during the daytime. Exhibits nocturnal drumming display. MOVEMENTS Sedentary, with occasional localized movements between islands.

		B
	A	
		C
		E
D		
		F

A New Zealand Snipe
B New Zealand Snipe
C New Zealand Snipe
D Chatham Islands Snipe
E Chatham Islands Snipe
F Chatham Islands Snipe

Scolopacidae

Common Snipe
Gallinago gallinago L 26.00 cm

A familiar, medium-sized snipe, with a circumpolar distribution from N USA and Canada, British Isles and Europe east across Eurasia to the Kamchatka peninsula, and also N India and N Afghanistan.

PLUMAGE **Adult** Buff central crown stripe to dark brown crown. Dark brown loral line broadens towards bill base, appearing wider than buff supercilium. Mantle, scapulars and tertials brownish-black variably streaked and barred, with broad, creamy edges to mantle and lower border to upper scapulars forming conspicuous 'V's. Broad creamy-buff edges to outer webs of lower scapulars contrasts with brownish inner webs. Coverts dark brown fringed and spotted whitish-buff. Pale brown tertial bars frequently narrower than darker brown bars producing overall dark patterned tertials. Primaries visibly extend beyond tertials. Tail extends well beyond primaries. Underparts white with breast washed buff strongly streaked dark brown and flanks barred brown. Bill medium, straight, dark brown with basal half dull reddish-brown. Legs greenish-yellow. **Juvenile** Extremely similar to adult. Coverts more neatly fringed buffish-white.
FLIGHT Agile, erratic, usually distant and high. Clear, broad white trailing edge to secondaries and inner primaries. Indistinct wing bar to tips of greater coverts and greater primary coverts. Faint pale panel to median coverts. Longish tail grey-brown, subterminally rich chestnut, tipped white. Underwing coverts and axillaries variable (*see* Races)
CALL When flushed, hoarse 'scaap'; 'song' monotonous, repeated 'chipper-chipper-chipper'.
RACES Three are recognized: *gallinago* (Palearctic) central white band to underwing coverts. Axillaries narrowly barred brown; *faeroensis* (Iceland, Faroes, Shetland and Orkney) more rufous breast and upperparts; *delicta* (Nearctic – Wilson's Snipe) underwing coverts darker, finely barred brown. Axillaries broadly barred brown.
HABITAT AND BEHAVIOUR Breeds in marshes, bogs, swampy meadows, wet areas adjacent lakes and rivers and marshy patches of tundra. Performs aerial 'drumming' display. When disturbed, uses zig-zag 'towering' escape flight. Winters in similar marshy areas, sometimes forming largish flocks or 'wisps'.
MOVEMENTS Both migratory and sedentary. *Gallinago* winters largely north of equator mostly in W Europe, vagrant Bear Is. *Faeroensis* winters south to British Isles with *delicta* reaching Columbia and Venezuela, vagrant to Bermuda and Britain.

African Snipe
Gallinago nigripennis L 26.65 cm

Longer billed but extremely similar to Common Snipe, inhabiting highland marshland from Ethiopia south to Namibia and S Africa.

PLUMAGE **Adult** Blackish crown with buff central crown stripe. Loral line broadens towards base of bill, wider than fore-supercilium. Mantle and scapulars blackish, darker than *gallinago*, extensively streaked and barred rufous. Conspicuous creamy-buff mantle and upper scapular 'V's. Creamy-buff edges to outer webs of lower scapulars with blackish-brown inner webs. Buffish-olive spotted median and greater coverts contrast with plain blackish lesser coverts. Blackish-brown bars to tertials generally wider than paler brown bars producing very dark patterned coloration. Very short primary extension beyond tertials. Tail extends well beyond folded wing. White belly and vent contrast strongly with dark upperparts. Foreneck, breast and flanks boldly streaked and barred very dark brown. Bill appreciably longer than *gallinago*, dark brown with basal half greenish to fleshy-brown. Legs greenish to yellowish-brown. **Juvenile** Mantle and scapular 'V's somewhat narrower. Coverts fringed whitish-buff.
FLIGHT slower, fluttery, less 'zig-zagging' than *gallinago* on more rounded wings. White trailing edge to secondaries. White tips to greater primary and greater coverts contrasting with blackish upperwing more conspicuous than *gallinago*. Faint pale panel to median coverts. Underwing coverts and axillaries variably white lightly barred blackish.
CALL When flushed abrupt 'skaap', quieter and less rasping than *gallinago*.
RACES Three are recognized: *aequatorialis* (E Africa); *nigripennis* (C Africa) upperparts slightly paler brownish-black, coverts more buffish; *angolensis* (S Africa) longer billed.
HABITAT AND BEHAVIOUR Breeds in upland bogs, edges of swampy lakes and seasonally flooded grassland, in E Africa largely above 1500 m up to 4000 m. Occurs singly or in small scattered parties. Performs typical snipe 'drumming' display, lower pitched than *gallinago*.
MOVEMENTS Largely sedentary. Local movements associated with drying up of temporary flooded areas. Descends to lower altitudes in non-breeding season.

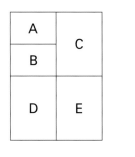

A Common Snipe adult
B Common Snipe juvenile
C Common Snipe adult non-breeding
D Common Snipe
E African Snipe

Scolopacidae

Pintail Snipe
Gallinago stenura L 26.00 cm

Unique with 28 tail feathers, the outer 'pins' not readily visible in the field, separable from Common Snipe with care, breeding in forested areas from NW Russia east across Siberia to W Anadyrland and the Sea of Okhotsk.

PLUMAGE **Adult** Central buff crown stripe occasionally meeting bill base. Broad fore-supercilium wider than narrow dark brown loral line. Edges to mantle and lower border to upper scapulars narrower than *gallinago*, still forming conspicuous 'V's. Narrow whitish edges to outer webs of lower scapulars continues along inner web, diagnostic distinction from *gallinago*. Lower lesser and median coverts spotted whitish-buff showing as pale covert panel. Pale brown tertial bars often wider than dark brown bars producing overall paler, brighter tertials. Tertials almost cloak primaries, with very short tail projection beyond folded wing combining to give 'squat' rear end. Underparts white, with breast streaked dark brown, flanks barred brown. Bill shortish, dark brown, basal half greyish-green. Legs greyish-green. **Juvenile** Very similar to adult. Upperparts more vermiculated with narrower mantle and scapular 'V's. Coverts fringed whitish-buff. Flight less erratic and extensive than *gallinago*. Indistinct greyish trailing edge to secondaries and innermost primaries. Distinctive pale median covert panel. Toes clearly project beyond shortish tail. Under wing coverts and axillaries appear uniform dark, with broad dark brown bars and narrow white bars.

CALL When flushed, nasal 'squak' weaker, less rasping than *gallinago*.

HABITAT AND BEHAVIOUR Favours damp somewhat drier sites than *gallinago* , including grassy marshlands in taiga, damp meadows along river valleys, sphagnum bogs and dwarf birch-covered tundra. Males perform aerial display in group or 'tok', vertically diving, metallic calls merging with whistling sounds from outer tail feathers. When flushed 'towers' less than *gallinago*. Winters on marshy areas and rice paddies.

MOVEMENTS Migratory, moving south across broad front from late July to winter in SE China, Taiwan south to India, Indo-China, Malaysia and the Sundas, with return passage commencing late February. Breeding-grounds re-occupied from May onwards. Vagrant Oman, Somalia, Kenya, W and NW Australia, Hawaii.

Swinhoe's Snipe
Gallinago megala L 27.95 cm

A largish, heavy looking snipe, possibly overlooked due to its great similarity with Pintail Snipe, inhabiting open forested regions in Central Siberia and probably also S Ussuriland and Sakhalin.

PLUMAGE **Adult** Largish head with eye set well back. Buffish crown stripe invariably does not meet base of bill. Broad fore-supercilium wider than dark brown loral line. Edges to mantle and lower border to upper scapulars forming conspicuous 'V's. Whitish-buff edges to outer webs of lower scapulars continuing along inner web. Lower lesser and median coverts broadly spotted whitish-buff creating distinctive mid-wing panel contrasting with plainer greater coverts. Pale bars to tertials at least equal width to dark brown bars. Primary tips extend noticeably beyond tertials, with tail projecting well beyond primary tips, producing more elongated rear end. Underparts white with barring on flanks sometimes extending across breast giving very dark brown coloration. Bill longish, dark brown, basal half greyish-green. Legs thickish, yellowish-green. **Juvenile** Very similar to adult. Coverts and tertials fringed whitish-buff. **Flight** Slow, heavy, direct, reminiscent of Eurasian Woodcock. Inconspicuous grey trailing to secondaries and inner primaries. Distinctive pale median covert panel. Toes project slightly beyond tail tip. Dark brown and white barred underwing coverts and axillaries.

CALL reluctant to call. Flight note 'squok' usually uttered just once, flatter than Pintail.

HABITAT AND BEHAVIOUR Breeds in clearings and margins of well-wooded regions both coniferous and deciduous, river valleys and well-forested plains. Aerial display flight involves soaring upwards whilst singing, then plummetting downwards, producing strange sound likened to twirling metal object. Winters in marshy areas and paddy fields, singly or in loose groups.

MOVEMENTS Migratory, moving south from mid-August on broad front to winter in S China and Taiwan, India, Indo-China and east to Philippines, Indonesia, New Guinea and Australia. Spring passage from early April arriving breeding-grounds mid-May onwards. Vagrant Maldives.

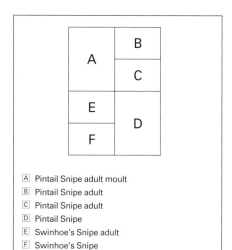

A Pintail Snipe adult moult
B Pintail Snipe adult
C Pintail Snipe adult
D Pintail Snipe
E Swinhoe's Snipe adult
F Swinhoe's Snipe

Scolopacidae

Japanese Snipe
Gallinago hardwickii L 29.20 cm

A large, highly migratory snipe, very similar to Swinhoe's Snipe, with breeding area confined to Japan, Kuril Is and S Sakhalin. **PLUMAGE Adult** Broad buffish fore-supercilium wider than blackish loral line. Conspicuous 'V's to edges of mantle and lower border to upper scapulars. Creamy-buff edge to outer web of lower scapulars extending onto inner web. Median coverts spotted pale buffish-brown forming pale panel on closed wing. Wider barring to tertials, appearing colder brown and blackish-brown. Tertials virtually cloak primaries, with long tail projection beyond folded wing. Underparts similar to *megala*, with breast washed greyer-brown strongly streaked blackish. Bill longish, blackish with basal half greenish-brown. Legs dull green. **Juvenile** Very similar to adult. Coverts fringed whitish-buff. Flight heavy, fairly direct with little 'zig-zagging', appearing relatively long winged and long tailed. Inconspicuous narrowish grey trailing edge to secondaries and inner primaries slightly broader than *megala*. Distinctive pale median covert panel contrasting with blackish-brown lesser and greater coverts. Tail showing slightly more white to outer feathers than *megala*. Dark brown and white barred underwing coverts and axillaries with dark bars slightly wider than pale bars giving underwing pattern somewhat darker than *megala*. **CALL** when flushed abrupt, rasping 'khrek'. **HABITAT AND BEHAVIOUR** Breeds in dryish areas with well-drained soil up to 1400 m, often far from water, including wet glades of open pine forest, river valleys and dry meadows. Usually solitary. Aerial display flight involves circular movements and 'drumming' whilst calling harshly. In winter reverts to edges of marshland and swamps, alpine bogs and tussock pasture, singly or loose flocks. **MOVEMENTS** Strongly migratory, recorded on passage Taiwan, Philippines and New Guinea *en route* to SE Australia and Tasmania, arriving from late July, peaking in Victoria and New South Wales December–January. Most departed by mid-April. Some remain in winter quarters all year. Vagrant NW Australia, New Zealand.

Magellan Snipe
Gallinago paraguaiae L 26.00 cm

Extremely similar to Common Snipe, widespread across most lowlands of S America from Trinidad south on east side of the Andes, and also N Chile south to Tierra del Fuego and Falkland Is.

PLUMAGE Adult Very careful separation required where overlaps slightly in range with wintering *delicta* race of Common Snipe. At rest identification features may include more evenly barred dark and pale brown tertials and richer chestnut-brown subterminal tail band. Vent and undertail coverts washed whitish-buff. Tail tip extends well beyond tips of primaries and tertials. Bill averages slightly longer, dark reddish-brown with dull fleshy-green base. Legs dull green. **Juvenile** Similar to adult with lesser and median coverts neatly fringed buff. **In flight** Clean white trailing edge to secondaries and inner primaries. Underwing coverts and axillaries finely barred brown and white, generally paler than *delicta*. **CALL** Squeaky, slightly rasping 'dzheet', distinguishable from Common Snipe. **RACES** Two are recognized: *paraguaiae* (Trinidad and northern S America east of Andes south to N Argentina) with colder brown upperparts, prominent breast streaking and shorter primaries, longer bill detectable in the field, shorter, broader wings giving more rounded flight silhouette; *magellanica* (C Argentina and C Chile south to Tierra del Fuego, Falkland Is) warmer brown upperparts, less prominent breast streaking and longer primaries, white in outer tail feather. **HABITAT AND BEHAVIOUR** Ranges from savannah and chaco through to pampas and Patagonian steppe. *Paraguaiae* breeds in marshy bogs, rushy shore meadows; *magellanica* favouring peat bogs and tussock grass. Strongly territorial, males performing typical 'winnowing' aerial display flight, somewhat more prolonged and pulsating than *delicta*. When flushed, rises steeply, levelling out into slightly undulating flight, dropping soon to cover. Outside breeding season favours typical marshland habitat. **MOVEMENTS** *Paraguaiae* largely sedentary. Southern *magellanica* population moves north during austral winter towards N Argentina and Uruguay. Summer resident Falkland Is.

Puna Snipe
Gallinago andina L 23.00 cm

A small snipe, sometimes considered as race of Magellan Snipe, largely restricted to the Andean Puna zone from N Peru south to N Chile, W Bolivia and NW Argentina.

PLUMAGE Adult At rest, short bill and short, bright legs along with habitat preference readily distinguish this small compact snipe. Dark blackish-brown mantle and scapulars contrast more strongly with rest of upperparts than Magellan Snipe. Bill noticeably short, dull greenish-yellow darker towards tip. Legs short, bright yellow. Characteristic 'bounding' flight on short rounded wings very apparent. Contrasting paler grey outer wing with white outer web to two outermost primaries. White trailing edge to secondaries and inner primaries. Tail broadly tipped rufous with extensive white to outer tail feather. Toes do not project beyond tail tip. Underwing coverts and axillaries whitish finely barred brown. **CALL** When flushed fairly high-pitched 'bjheep'. In flight rapidly repeated then slowing down 'djak,djak'. **RACES** Two are recognized: *andina* (Peru south to N Chile, W Bolivia and NW Argentina); *innotata* (Loa River, Puna zone, N Chile) with white outer webs to all primaries. Underwing coverts and axillaries virtually pure white. **HABITAT AND BEHAVIOUR** *Andina* found 3000–4500 m, favouring boggy parts of the Puna including cushion plant bogs, boggy creek margins and rushy parts of puna grassland. Runs extremely fast through vegetation making detection on ground very difficult. Performs hoarse, wheezy 'winnowing' aerial display flight. Rises from ground without 'towering' or zig-zagging, assuming characteristic low, bounding almost undulating flight before dropping quickly to cover. *Innotata* restricted to lower elevations of Loa River confines. **MOVEMENTS** *Andina* descends to lower elevations during winter, occurring on plains of N Argentina alongside Magellan Snipe.

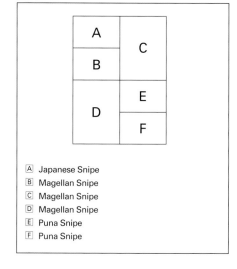

A Japanese Snipe
B Magellan Snipe
C Magellan Snipe
D Magellan Snipe
E Puna Snipe
F Puna Snipe

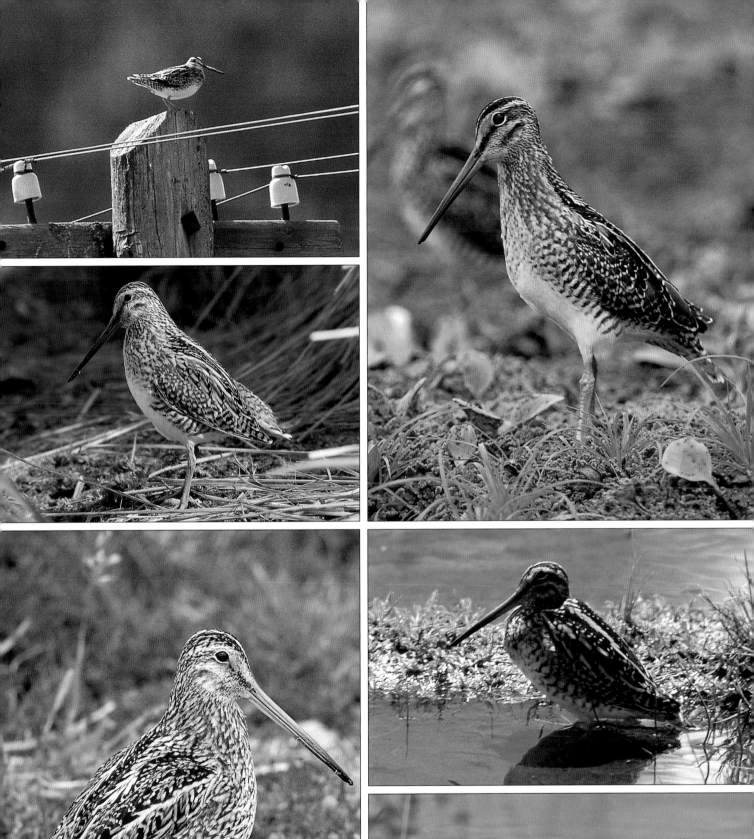

Scolopacidae

Solitary Snipe
Gallinago solitaria **L 30.50 cm**
A large, scarce snipe, with breeding distribution patchily spread across the mountain ranges of E Asia.
PLUMAGE **Adult** Head markedly pale, whitish-grey. Narrow white crown stripe to gingery-brown crown. Gingery-brown loral line extending onto ear coverts and lower cheek panel. Mantle, scapulars and coverts barred and fringed white, rufous and black producing vermiculated pattern. Mantle and lower border to upper scapulars narrowly but conspicuously edged white forming typical snipe-like 'V's, lacking creamy or buff coloration. Tertials boldly barred pale brown and dark brown. Tail clearly extends beyond folded wing tips. Breast mottled whitish washed pale gingery-brown especially at sides, contrasting with unbarred white belly and heavily barred greyish-brown flanks. Bill yellowish to olive-brown, blackish towards tip. Legs dull greenish-yellow. **Juvenile** Extremely similar to adult. Upperparts slightly more vermiculated and narrowly fringed rufous-buff. Belly somewhat barred. **In flight** Appears large, heavy and slow. Inconspicuous narrow white trailing edge to secondaries and inner primaries. Narrow wing bar formed by white tips to greater primary and secondary coverts. Pale panel across median coverts. Tail with bold subterminal chestnut band narrowly tipped white. Underwing coverts and axillaries equally barred brown and white.
CALL When flushed loud 'pench', similar to Common Snipe.
RACES Two are recognized: *solitaria* (most of range); *japonica* (E part of range) extremely similar and validity uncertain.
HABITAT AND BEHAVIOUR Nests above timber line from 2400–4600 m, favouring boggy, gravel-bottomed mountain streams with grassy hummocks, rhododendron scrub and Alpine meadow vegetation. Performs aerial swooping 'drumming' display. Winters at lower elevations, descending to heavy cover along mountain streams, edges of reed-fringed ponds, rarely on the coast, but usually associated with water.
MOVEMENTS Largely sedentary, undergoing regular altitudinal and further distance migrations. Winters regularly N India, Pakistan and Japan. Vagrant Indian coast, Hong Kong.

Wood Snipe
Gallinago nemoricola **L 30.50 cm**
A large dark snipe, rarely observed, reminiscent of both Solitary Snipe and Woodcock, breeding in the Himalayas east to E Assam, S Tibet and N Burma.
PLUMAGE **Adult** Very narrow whitish-cream crown stripe to dark brown crown. Darkish brown loral line, ear coverts and lower cheek panel enclose whitish face washed and diffusely streaked dark brown. Blackish mantle and scapulars fringed greyish with prominent creamy-yellow 'V's. Wing coverts dark brown variably spotted and fringed paler buffish-grey. Tertials virtually cloak primaries, broadly barred dark brown and paler buffish-brown. Tail extends beyond tertials. Foreneck, sides of neck and upper breast washed buffish-brown streaked darker brown shading to whitish lower breast, belly, vent and undertail coverts heavily barred dark brown. Bill dull reddish-brown darkening towards tip. Legs greenish-grey. **Juvenile** Similar to adult. Narrow whitish fringes to mantle, scapulars and coverts producing neater, scaly appearance. **In flight** Appears large on broad rounded wings. Inconspicuous narrow grey trailing edge to secondaries. Pale panel across median and greater coverts with indistinct wing bar formed by pale tips to greater and primary coverts. Tail greyish with chestnut subterminal band barely tipped white. Underwing appears all dark with fine dark brown barring to underwing coverts and axillaries.
CALL when flushed occasional croaking 'tok-tok'.
HABITAT AND BEHAVIOUR Breeds in highly wooded regions of Himalayas from 1400–4600 m, usually associated with thick cover. When flushed flies off slowly with wavering flight reminiscent of Eurasian Woodcock, quickly dropping back to cover. Performs 'beating' display flight. Winters at lower elevation favouring swampy ground with thick matted grass and vegetation.
MOVEMENTS Partially migratory, with part of the population moving south to Pakistan, India, S Burma and N Bac Phan. Vagrant Thailand, Sri Lanka.

Madagascar Snipe
Gallinago macrodactyla **L 30.50 cm**
Closely resembling Noble Snipe in size, bill length and plumage characteristics, found only in E Madagascar and Mauritius.
PLUMAGE **Adult** Superficially shows similar head and face pattern to Common Snipe. Larger size and upperpart pattern more closely resemble Noble Snipe with slightly wider creamy-buff 'V's to outer mantle and lower borders of upper and lower scapulars. Wing coverts greyish-brown spotted and tipped olive-brown. Primaries barely extend beyond tertials, but clear tail projection beyond folded wing. Sides of neck, foreneck and breast washed buff strongly streaked and mottled dark brown.

Barring on flanks more extensive than Common Snipe continuing onto sides of belly. Bill long, blackish, slightly paler towards base. Legs slate-grey. **Juvenile** Very similar to adult. Mantle and scapular 'V's slightly narrower. Wing coverts fringed warm buffish-olive. **In flight** Wings appear broad and rounded, with very narrow inconspicuous greyish trailing edge to secondaries, difficult to see in the field. Rump and uppertail coverts dull greyish-brown, tail narrowly tipped white. Toes project beyond tail tip. Underwing coverts and axillaries appear largely dark because brown bars wider than white bars.
CALL hoarse note when flushed, similar to Common Snipe.
HABITAT AND BEHAVIOUR Occupies grassy and sedgy marshes and swamps on the humid eastern part of the island, from sea-level to 2000 m amongst mountain forests. Performs aerial 'bleating' display. Flight slow and deliberate.
MOVEMENTS Sedentary.

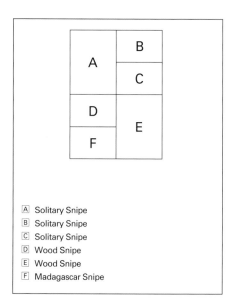

A Solitary Snipe
B Solitary Snipe
C Solitary Snipe
D Wood Snipe
E Wood Snipe
F Madagascar Snipe

Scolopacidae

Jack Snipe
Lymnocryptes minimus L 17.80 cm
The smallest of the snipes, lacking a central crown stripe, breeding in boreal marshland from N Norway east across Russia and Siberia to the Kolmya Delta.
PLUMAGE **Adult** Buffish-yellow 'split' supercilium enclosing thin blackish line. Glossy brownish-black crown lacks central crown stripe. Broad dark brown loral line extending narrowly behind eye, with diffuse brownish line across lower cheeks. Rest of face, chin and throat buffish-white. Mantle and upper scapulars brownish-black glossed purplish-green. Lower scapulars dark brown, chestnut and buff. Conspicuous golden-buff 'V's along outer edges of mantle and lower border to upper scapulars. Wing coverts warm brown fringed buff. Underparts whitish with foreneck, breast and flanks washed and streaked brown. Inner tail feathers relatively broad and rounded. Undertail coverts white with distinct blackish subterminal shaft streaks. Bill shortish, basal two-thirds variable pinkish or dull green, distal third dark brown. Legs yellowish-green. **Juvenile** Inner tail feathers relatively narrow and pointed. Undertail coverts whitish with indistinct yellowish-brown to greyish-brown subterminal shaft streaks. Legs greyish-green. **In flight** Thin white trailing edge to secondaries and inner primaries. Flight feathers dark brown with inconspicuous white tips to greater and primary coverts.
CALL Invariably silent, occasional low 'gah' when flushed.
HABITAT AND BEHAVIOUR Nests amongst marshes and bogs in coniferous forest, willow, alder and birch woods. Song delivered both on ground and **In flight** reminiscent of distant galloping horses. Characteristically bobs body when feeding. Often freezes when disturbed using superb camouflage. When flushed rarely flies far avoiding 'towering'. Usually solitary.
MOVEMENTS Migratory, with late autumn passage from mid-September south to British Isles, W and S Europe, Caspian, India, SE Asia and tropical Africa, with arrival often not until mid-November. Early spring passage from mid-February, breeding-grounds re-occupied from mid-April onwards. Vagrant Azores, Zambia, Tanzania and California.

Noble Snipe
Gallinago nobilis L 31.75 cm
Similar to Magellan Snipe but larger and longer billed, inhabiting both temperate and paramo regions of the northern Andes from W Venezuela south through Colombia to Ecuador.

PLUMAGE **Adult** Exhibits typical *gallinago* features including broad pale central crown stripe, creamy-white edges to outer mantle and lower border to upper scapulars forming conspicuous 'V's, and broad creamy edges to outer webs of lower scapulars. Very short primary projection beyond tertials, with short tail projection beyond folded wing. Neck and breast washed pale chestnut-brown, latter contrasting with large unmarked white belly patch. Bill very long, greenish-horn at base, blackish towards tip, distinctly two-toned. Legs greyish-green. **Juvenile** Very similar to adult. Mantle and scapulars narrowly edged buff. **In flight** Wings appear broad, clearly lacking pale trailing edge to secondaries. Rump and uppertail coverts tinged rufous, tail narrowly tipped white. Feet project well beyond tail tip. Underwing coverts and axillaries finely barred dark brown producing overall dark brown underwing.
CALL When flushed nasal 'dzhit' or 'tzhi-tzhi-tzhi'.
HABITAT AND BEHAVIOUR Favours grassy bogs, wet savannah, rushy pasture and reed-marsh, and montane forest of the northern Andes from 2000–3000 m. Flight slow, heavy and direct. Sometimes several gather together on communal 'lek' type display ground. Also performs low 'bleating' circular display flight.
MOVEMENTS Sedentary.

Cordilleran Snipe
Gallinago stricklandii L 29.20 cm
A large woodcock-like snipe, lacking white in the tail, with two separate populations, northern race inhabiting the Andes from Venezuela south to Peru, southern race favouring marshy areas at altitude in S Chile south to sea-level on Tierra del Fuego.
PLUMAGE **Adult** Dark chestnut-brown crown with very indistinct, thin buffish central crown stripe. Typical *gallinago* face pattern, warmer buff and brown than Magellan Snipe. Upperparts variegated buffish-yellow, blackish-brown and cinnamon-chestnut. Yellowish outer webs to outer mantle feathers forming indistinct 'V's. Scapular 'V's lacking. Primary tips extend beyond tertials with tail projecting beyond folded wing tips. Throat unmarked creamy-white. Underparts variable rich warm buff to cold greyish-brown with chevrons and bars – see 'Races'. Bill brownish-horn at base becoming blackish towards tip, swollen at base, slightly drooping towards tip. Legs grey tinged yellowish-brown. **Juvenile** Extremely similar to adult. Upperparts tipped and edged pale buff. **In flight** Broad, rounded

wings lack white trailing edge. Tail greyish-brown barred buffish-brown lacking both chestnut and white coloration. Underwing coverts and axillaries narrowly barred greyish and buffish-brown.
CALL When flushed, explosive 'tzhic'.
RACES Two are recognized: *jamesoni* (W Venezuela, Colombia, Ecuador, Peru, W Bolivia) larger unmarked throat patch, barred greyish-brown foreneck, breast and flanks, becoming unbarred whitish on belly and undertail coverts; *stricklandii* (S Chile, S Argentina south to Tierra del Fuego including Cape Horn, Falkland Is) warm yellowish-buff underparts with heavy dark brown chevrons, clearer unmarked central belly.
HABITAT AND BEHAVIOUR *Jamesoni* inhabits marshy paramo grassland upto 3500 m, often with bamboo, mossy dwarf forest and cushion-plant bogs. *Stricklandii* occurs in wet, grassy areas above timberline through open, boggy forest to coastal moorland. Aerial display commences after sunset continuing into night, roding in circles with loud 'whee-tcheu' calls, then diving with audible winnowing from wings or tail. Also displays on ground uttering monotonous 'djyc' calls.
MOVEMENTS *Jamesoni* resident. *Stricklandii* partially migratory in southern part of range.

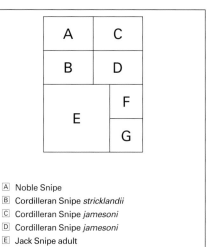

A	C
B	D
E	F
	G

A   Noble Snipe
B   Cordilleran Snipe *stricklandii*
C   Cordilleran Snipe *jamesoni*
D   Cordilleran Snipe *jamesoni*
E   Jack Snipe adult
F   Jack Snipe juvenile
G   Jack Snipe juvenile

Scolopacidae

Great Snipe
Gallinago media L 27.95 cm
A bulky medium-sized snipe, decreasing as a breeding species across boreal regions of Fenno-Scandinavia east through Russia and Siberia to the Yenesei river and south to the Baltic States.
PLUMAGE Adult Buff crown-stripe with loral line more constant width, slightly narrower and paler than *gallinago*. Sides of face profusely spotted light brown. Dark brown upperparts with mantle and scapular 'V's less prominent than *gallinago*. Coverts prominently tipped white. Neck and breast washed buffish-brown heavily streaked dark brown. Whitish lower breast, flanks, belly and vent strongly streaked with brown chevron shaped bars. Bill proportionately shorter than *gallinago*, slightly angled downwards along middle of upper mandible, dark brown tinged yellow towards base. Legs dull greenish or yellowish-grey. **Juvenile** Mantle and scapular 'V's slightly narrower. White tips to coverts narrower, less conspicuous.
Flight Slow, fairly straight and level, bill held more horizontally than *gallinago*, seeking cover rather quickly. White tips to median and blackish greater coverts form conspicuous 'speculum'. Narrow white trailing edge to secondaries and inner primaries. Outer tail feathers pure white (adults), barred dark brown (juveniles), especially obvious on birds landing.
CALL When flushed, a low gutteral croaking.
HABITAT AND BEHAVIOUR Breeds on marshy ground in woodland especially willow and birch. 'Lek' sites open, boggy ground with sphagnum moss and dwarf willow. No aerial display. Complex 'lekking' involves bill clapping, various twittering and whizzing sounds, whilst bird standing erect and 'flutter leaping', breast puffed out and tail fanned exposing white outer feathers. Outside breeding season occurs in small scattered groups favouring grass-covered marshy areas, high plateaux and dryish ground including stubble and crop fields.
MOVEMENTS Migratory, Russian and E European birds moving south-west across broad front during August–September, Fenno-Scandinavian birds migrate south with few records in Britain and W Europe. Winters in tropical Africa south to Namibia and Natal. Spring movement from late April, breeding-grounds reoccupied during May. Vagrant Spitzbergen, Canary Is, India, Burma, Cape Town.

Giant Snipe
Gallinago undulata L 41.90 cm
A huge, blackish snipe occupying tropical lowlands of S America from Colombia east to N Brazil and also SE Brazil south to Paraguay.
PLUMAGE Adult Bold dark brown lateral crown stripe, loral line and lower cheek patch extending onto rear ear coverts contrasts with broad creamy-buff supercilium, central crown stripe and throat patch. Mantle and scapulars very dark blackish-brown, with conspicuous broad cinnamon-chestnut 'V's to edges of outer mantle and lower borders of both upper and lower scapulars. Wing coverts dark brown broadly fringed warm creamy-buff. Tertials dark brown narrowly fringed yellowish-buff. Underparts whitish with entire neck heavily streaked very dark brown. Breast and flanks heavily barred dark brown, central belly patch unbarred. Bill blackish-brown, paler brownish-horn towards base. Legs dark grey. **Juvenile** Undescribed. **In flight** Very broad, rounded wings. Flight feathers dark brown, uniquely for snipe barred whitish-buff. Rump and uppertail coverts cinnamon-chestnut virtually unbarred, tail narrowly barred brown. Toes project well beyond tail tip. Underwing coverts and axillaries evenly barred brown and white.
CALL When flushed repeated 'kek'; also rasping trisyllabic display call.
RACES Two are recognized: *undulata* (Colombia east to N Brazil); *gigantea* (SE Brazil south to Paraguay) longer billed and longer winged with more boldly marked upperparts and more strongly barred underparts.
HABITAT AND BEHAVIOUR Occurs in swampy and marshy pastures with aquatic vegetation up to 1000 m, also drier, sandy savannah with short grass and dense herbage. Rarely observed except when flushed at very close range. Performs courtship display at night.
MOVEMENTS Sedentary, undergoing local seasonal movements in accordance with rains. Vagrant Tierra del Fuego.

Imperial Snipe
Gallinago imperalis L 29.85 cm
An extremely rare snipe, stocky and very dark brown with a characteristic aerial song display. Recently rediscovered in Peruvian Andes and more latterly Ecuador, having been thought extinct and only previously known from two specimens.
PLUMAGE Adult Dark chestnut-brown central crown stripe separates blackish lateral crown stripes. Entire upperparts including scapulars, wing coverts and tertials chestnut boldly barred black. Tertials cloak primary tips with short tail projection beyond folded wing. Sides of face, neck and breast chestnut heavily streaked blackish. Belly, vent and undertail coverts whitish heavily barred dark brown. Bill dark brownish-grey, swollen at base, drooping slightly towards tip. Legs greyish. **Juvenile** Undescribed. **In flight** Very broad, rounded wings, coupled with very short tail give distinctive silhouette. Chestnut mantle, coverts and tail and dark grey flight feathers produce overall dark appearance.
CALL 5–8 notes delivered on the ground resemble latter part of aerial song.
HABITAT AND BEHAVIOUR Recently found on E Andean slopes of Peru, 2700–3500 m at Piuva, Amazonas, La Libertad and Cuzco. Also now been observed in several sites in the Ecuadorian Andes including Cotopaxi and Podocarpus National Parks. Appears to favour timberline zone, with low elfin forest and tree ferns and marshy grassland matted with sphagnum mosses and peat. Crepuscular and nocturnal, almost exclusively located by characteristic aerial song display performed July–August. Rodes in large circles 50–150 m. above ridgetops, staccato song increasing then decreasing in volume, bird finally diving sharply with audible whirring from flight feathers.
MOVEMENTS Unknown.

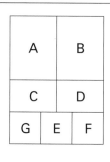

A Great Snipe adult breeding
B Great Snipe adult breeding
C Great Snipe adult breeding
D Great Snipe adult
E Great Snipe adult
F Great Snipe
G Giant Snipe adult

Short-billed Dowitcher
Limnodromus griseus L 26.65 cm
Shows racial variation in breeding plumage, nesting in sub-Arctic Canada from N Quebec, C and NW Canada and S Alaska.
PLUMAGE **Adult breeding** Crown cinnamon-brown streaked black, broad creamy supercilium and thin dark brown loral line narrowly extending behind eye. Face and hindneck pale cinnamon-brown and white finely streaked brown. Mantle, scapulars and tertials black centred broadly fringed chestnut, cinnamon-buff and white. Foreneck and breast pale cinnamon-red, variably shading to whitish belly and vent, variably spotted and barred dark brown. Bill length unreliable field character; typical snipe-like, blackish-brown, basal half tinged dull green. Legs dull greyish-green. **Adult non-breeding** Bold white supercilium contrasts with dark grey eye-stripe. Crown, face and neck finely streaked pale grey. Upperparts uniform greyish-brown broadly fringed pale buff. Underparts whitish, upper breast washed grey, lower breast, flanks and undertail coverts spotted grey. **Juvenile** Crown bright chestnut finely streaked black. Upperparts blackish-brown broadly fringed chestnut-buff. Tertials 'tiger striped' dark-brown and chestnut-buff bars diagnostic. Underparts warm salmon-buff, lightly spotted and barred on breast, flanks and undertail coverts. Legs yellowish-green. **In flight** Elongated white patch on back and pale trailing edge to secondaries and inner primaries contrast with rest of blackish-brown upperwing. Tail barred dark brown and white, white bars equal in width or wider than dark bars.
CALL Triple, mellow 'tu-tu-tu'.
RACES Three are recognized, varying breeding plumage only: *griseus* (E Canada) belly mostly white, breast densely spotted, flanks barred; *hendersoni* (C Canada) entire underparts reddish, lightly spotted; *caurinus* (S Alaska) variable underpart coloration.
HABITAT AND BEHAVIOUR Favours muskeg, boggy or marshy areas with low vegetation. Feeds with 'sewing-machine' action while standing in shallow water, frequently with head submerged. Occurs on various wetlands during migration. Winters on coastal mudflats, estuaries and saltmarsh.
MOVEMENTS Migratory, autumn passage commencing late June. *Griseus* moves along Atlantic coast to winter in Gulf States, Caribbean south to Brazil; *hendersoni* crosses Great Plains wintering on both coasts of C America south to Panama; *caurinus* migrates down Pacific coast, wintering N California south to Peru. Return passage from early March along similar routes. Vagrant Ireland, Norway, Spain.

Long-billed Dowitcher
Limnodromus scolopaceus L 28.55 cm
Easily separated from Short-billed Dowitcher in juvenile plumage, breeding in NE Siberia, coastal N and W Alaska and Mackenzie District, N Canada.
PLUMAGE **Adult breeding** Foreneck heavily spotted dark brown. Underparts entirely reddish, darker than Short-billed, with breast densely spotted or barred, flanks narrowly barred. Clean reddish belly. Bill length variable, overlapping with Short-billed but averaging longer, coloration similar. Legs dull greyish-green averaging longer than Short-billed. **Adult non-breeding** Extremely difficult to separate from Short-billed. Upperparts generally darker grey. Breast also darker grey, lower border lacking spots and contrasting more abruptly with white belly. **Juvenile** Duller than Short-billed. Head and neck greyish contrasting with buffish-brown breast. Upperparts dark brown finely fringed chestnut. Diagnostic patterned tertials plain dark grey narrowly edged buffish-brown, invariably lacking internal markings. Legs yellowish-green. **In flight** Differs from Short-billed in dark brown bars to tail considerably wider than white bars producing darker patterned tail.
CALL Shrill, high-pitched 'keek', sometimes rapidly repeated up to six times.
HABITAT AND BEHAVIOUR Nests in forest-tundra and moss-sedge tundra adjacent freshwater lakes and pools. Feeding habits similar to Short-billed, preferring to use longer bill in slightly deeper water. Outside breeding season shows preference for inland freshwater or brackish pools, largely avoiding intertidal habitat. Can occur alongside Short-billed both on migration and during winter.
MOVEMENTS Migratory, with markedly later passage than Short-billed. Adults commence moving south from late July, juveniles from mid-September. Siberian birds cross Bering Sea, moving with N American birds predominantly through western States to winter in California south to Guatemala. Passage also farther east reaching Atlantic States, wintering in S New Mexico to Florida. Spring passage from late March along more westerly route. Vagrant regularly to W Europe and Japan; also Bali, Brunei and Thailand.

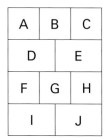

A	B	C
D		E
F	G	H
I		J

A Short-billed Dowitcher *hendersoni* adult breeding
B Short-billed Dowitcher *caurinus* adult breeding
C Short-billed Dowitcher adult non-breeding
D Short-billed Dowitcher juvenile
E Short-billed Dowitcher
F Long-billed Dowitcher adult breeding
G Long-billed Dowitcher adult breeding
H Long-billed Dowitcher first-winter non-breeding
I Long-billed Dowitcher
J Long-billed Dowitcher juvenile

Scolopacidae

Red Knot
Calidris canutus L 24.15 cm
A large, dumpy calidrid with racial populations nesting across the high Arctic tundra.
PLUMAGE **Adult breeding male** Face and underparts varying shades of chestnut-red, with variable amounts of white flecking on belly. Crown heavily streaked dark brown, with obscure brown smudging across lores and ear coverts. Mantle, scapulars and tertials blackish centred, edged rufous and warm buff, tipped grey, often becoming blacker with wear. Wing coverts plainer grey fringed pale. Bill short, almost straight and black. Legs dull olive-green. **Adult breeding female** Less evenly coloured underparts and more white on rear belly. **Adult non-breeding** Indistinct whitish supercilium with greyish lores and ear coverts. Upperparts brownish-grey with dark feather shafts and whitish fringes. Underparts white with breast suffused grey and lightly streaked. **Juvenile** Mantle, scapulars and coverts with darker submarginal line fringed warm buff, giving distinct 'scaly' appearance. Underparts white with pinkish-buff wash across breast finely streaked greyish-brown. **In flight** Narrow white wing bar and whitish lower rump and uppertail flecked brown, contrasting with dark greyish flight feathers and tail.
CALL Usually silent, but occasional low 'knut' from flocks **In flight**.
RACES Four are recognized: nominate *canutus* (central Siberia), long billed, extensive deep chestnut underparts; *rogersi* (E Siberia), shorter billed with paler underparts; *rufa* (W Canada and Alaska), palest underparts with extensive white belly; *islandica* (NE Canada and Greenland), paler underparts and yellowish fringed upperparts.
HABITAT AND BEHAVIOUR Nests on dry upland tundra, preferring barren and stony wastes with scattered vegetation. Winters on sandy beaches and mudflats, often forming dense feeding and roosting flocks.
MOVEMENTS Strongly migratory, mostly using coastal routes but also overland, with long flights involving staging posts. *Islandica* moves through Iceland arriving W Europe to winter from August onwards, often in vast flocks. *Canutus* migrates around the coast of NW Europe to winter in Africa, with *rogersi* largely wintering in Australia. *Rufa* winters on both coasts of USA and S America. Vagrant India, E Africa and Atlantic and southern Ocean Is.

Great Knot
Calidris tenuirostris L 26.65 cm
The largest calidrid, probably more closely related to the Nearctic Surfbird

than Red Knot, nesting in the sub-Arctic zone of NE Siberia.
PLUMAGE **Adult breeding** Face and neck heavily streaked dark grey-brown, with crown streaked blacker, and always darker than Red Knot. Supercilium virtually absent. Back blackish with greyish tips. Coverts and tertials greyish-brown fringed pale. Lower scapulars with chestnut oval patches edged black, tips gradually wearing to give bold chestnut area above the folded wing. Wings clearly extend beyond the tail tip. Underparts white with breast and flanks heavily spotted black, often forming solid black centre to breast. Bill longer than Red Knot, more pointed, and blackish with dull greenish tinge to base. **Adult non-breeding** Crown and hindneck streaked greyish-black. Upperparts greyish-brown with dark feather shafts and pale fringes. Underparts white with less bold spotting and more streaking, extending onto flanks. **Juvenile** Darker than non-breeding adult with blackish-brown mantle and scapulars fringed pale. Coverts and tertials paler brown with dark brown subterminal bars and whitish fringes. Underparts white with breast washed greyish-brown and spotted, extending onto flanks. **In flight** Thinner wing bar than Red Knot contrasts with blackish primary coverts. Lower rump and uppertail white, slightly streaked black, with dark grey tail.
CALL Usually silent, but occsionally a low 'nyut–nyut', not unlike Red Knot.
HABITAT AND BEHAVIOUR Breeds in the Alpine and Arctic zones, on upland slopes and ridges up to 1000 m, often on gravelly ground covered in lichens. Winters on tidal mudflats and sandbars.
MOVEMENTS Migratory, moving through SE Siberia and along the Chinese coast, arriving late August in Australia to winter in large numbers, probably in excess of 250,000. Smaller numbers winter from NE India to SE Asia. Spring passage through Hong Kong and China mainly late April/early May, with first-year birds remaining on the wintering grounds. Vagrant Oman, Israel, Spain, Norway, Scotland, Alaska.

A	B
C	D
E	F
G	H	I

A Red Knot *rufa* adult breeding
B Red Knot *rogersi* adult non-breeding
C Red Knot juvenile
D Red Knot
E Great Knot adult breeding
F Great Knot adult moult
G Great Knot adult moult
H Great Knot juvenile
I Great Knot with adult non-breeding Red Knot

Scolopacidae

Little Stint
Calidris minuta **L 14.50 cm**
A common 'peep' of the W Palearctic, Africa and India, breeding from NE Norway east across Siberia to River Yana delta. PLUMAGE **Adult breeding** Small-headed and round-bodied. Crown, face, neck and upperbreast rich orange-rufous streaked dark brown. Whitish 'split' supercilium thinly streaked and washed pale brown. Scapulars black centred fringed rufous, tipped grey and white when fresh. Prominent creamy mantle 'V's. Wing coverts and tertials brownish-grey also fringed chestnut-buff. Long primary projection. Chin, throat and rest of underparts white. Bill black, faintly downcurved, rather finely tipped. Legs blackish sometimes tinged brown. **Adult non-breeding** Upperparts brownish-grey with dark feather centres. Underparts white with grey wash across breast, finely streaked, often forming complete breast band. **Juvenile** Prominent whitish 'split' supercilium. Obvious white mantle and scapular 'V's. Both upper and lower scapulars blackish fringed bright chestnut and white. Greater coverts and tertials also black centred with chestnut fringes. Underparts white with sides of breast washed orange-buff streaked dark brown, often forming lateral patches. **In flight** Clear white wing bar and white sides to dark rump and uppertail. Grey sides to black centred tail.
CALL A short 'chit' or trilling 'tit-tit-tit'.
HABITAT AND BEHAVIOUR Breeds on the high Arctic coastal tundra, nesting on swampy or mossy ground. Winters on coastal mudflats, estuaries and inland lakes. During migration frequents inland wetlands. Gregarious, forming large flocks. Often tame and approachable.
MOVEMENTS Autumn passage commences with adults in July, and juveniles during August/September. Migration either south-south-west across a broad front, or east via the Caspian Sea, to winter largely in tropical and S Africa, Arabia and India. Return passage during May largely north-east so scarce on W European coasts in spring. Vagrancy widely recorded, e.g., USA and Canada, Aleutians, Japan and Australia.

Red-necked Stint
Calidris ruficollis **L 14.50 cm**
Overlapping in range and very similar to Little Stint, this eastern counterpart breeds in E Siberia between the Taimyr and Chukotski peninsulas, and also sporadically in W Alaska. PLUMAGE **Adult breeding** Short-legged and longish winged. Crown streaked dark

brown, with head, neck, throat and upperbreast brick-red, highly variable in colour and extent. Breast spotted brown, especially at sides. 'Split' supercilium lacking. Mantle and scapulars black centred fringed chestnut, tipped white when fresh. Wing coverts and tertials contrastingly greyish-brown fringed whitish or pale rufous, unlike Little Stint. Long primary projection. Rest of underparts white. Bill black, somewhat more blunt tipped than Little. Legs black. **Adult non-breeding** Paler grey-brown than Little Stint, with paler feather centres. Darkish lores sometimes form mask through eye. Underparts white with greyish streaking to breast sides. **Juvenile** Dullish supercilium not 'split'. Mantle and scapular 'V's faint or lacking. Mantle and upper scapulars blackish centred fringed rufous. Lower scapulars contrastingly dull grey fringed white. Wing coverts and tertials also plainish grey fringed buff or pale rufous, lacking rich chestnut coloration of Little Stint. Underparts white with greyish-buff wash to breast, often faintly streaked at sides. **In flight** Extremely similar to Little Stint.
CALL Similar to Little Stint but squeakier and coarser, with typically 'chit' or 'pit-pit-pit'.
HABITAT AND BEHAVIOUR Breeding habitat consists of Arctic tundra, nesting on higher ground including foothills of mountains. Winters on tidal mudflats, saltmarsh and pools, also at inland wetlands on migration.
MOVEMENTS Autumn passage commences early July with Alaskan birds joining those from Siberia to winter in S China west to Burma, and south through Indonesia to Australia. Routes are overland through Mongolia, along the E Asian coast, and over the W Pacific direct to Australia. Regular New Zealand, with vagrancy to Germany, Sweden, Britain (including the first W Palearctic record of a juvenile – September 1994, Shetland, Scotland), USA and Canada.

A	B
C	D	E
F	G	H
I	J

A Little Stint adult breeding
B Little Stint adult non-breeding
C Little Stint juvenile
D Little Stint adult
E Rufous-necked Stint adult non-breeding
F Rufous-necked Stint adult breeding
G Rufous-necked Stint adult breeding
H Rufous-necked Stint juvenile
I Rufous-necked Stint moult
J Rufous-necked Stint adult non-breeding

Scolopacidae

Semipalmated Sandpiper
Calidris pusilla **L 14.50 cm**
A dark legged 'peep' with webbed toes, similar to Western Sandpiper, breeding from the high Arctic coast of Alaska east across N Canada to coastal Labrador. PLUMAGE **Adult breeding** Crown rusty-brown streaked dark brown. Whitish supercilium faintly streaked with dusky lores and ear coverts. In fresh plumage upperparts blackish with buff fringes lacking strong orange or rufous coloration, but tips gradually wear off to reveal rusty tones. Short primary projection. White underparts with dark brown breast streaking extending onto upper flanks. Bill black, deep based and blunt tipped, sometimes overlapping in length with Western Sandpiper. Legs blackish, occasionally tinged brownish or green. Toes partially webbed. **Adult non-breeding** Uniform plain grey upperparts. Diffuse streaking on breast sides not joining across centre. **Juvenile** Crown streaked dark brown and grey. Supercilium streaked faintly grey accentuating pale eye-ring. Upperparts greyish-brown fringed buff or pale rufous giving 'scaly' effect. Mantle and scapular 'V's faint or lacking. Dark anchor-shaped subterminal marks to lower scapulars. Breast washed buff with extensive lateral streaking often extending across centre. **In flight** Narrow white wing bar and white sides to dark centred rump and upper tail.
CALL A low, harsh 'chrup' or 'krit'.
HABITAT AND BEHAVIOUR Breeds on coastal and inland tundra, favouring wet, grassy and hummocky terrain often adjacent pools. Winters on coastal mudflats but also frequents inland wetlands on migration. Tends to probe less deeply than Western Sandpiper. Highly gregarious.
MOVEMENTS Migratory, with populations using different routes south to winter in W Indies, Central and northern S America. Alaskan birds commence migrating during July across the Great Plains; central birds move via James Bay and Bay of Fundy, whereas E Canadian birds pass through the Gulf of St Lawrence and south possibly direct to E Caribbean. Many non-breeders remain in winter quarters. Vagrancy widely recorded, e.g., Azores, Britain, Europe, Argentina and Falklands Is.

Western Sandpiper
Calidris mauri **L 15.50 cm**
The western counterpart of Semipalmated Sandpiper, with breeding range overlapping but restricted to the Chukotski peninsula in E Siberia and W Alaska. PLUMAGE **Adult breeding** Distinctive. Sides of crown, nape and ear coverts chestnut.

Bases of lower scapulars rich chestnut with blackish subterminal crescents tipped grey. Coverts and tertials plainer grey fringed pale. Very short primary projection. Underparts white with dense black arrow-shaped markings across breast and flanks extending onto lateral undertail coverts. Bill blackish, slightly drooping with rather fine tip and averaging longer than Semipalmated Sandpiper. Legs black occasionally tinged green or brown. Toes partially webbed. **Adult non-breeding** Upperparts rather cold grey. Fine dark streaking across breast sides often extending across centre of breast. **Juvenile** Brighter than Semipalmated Sandpiper. Greyish crown often toned rusty. Clear white supercilium, with upper half of eye-ring less prominent. Upperparts generally fringed strongly rufous-chestnut, especially centre of mantle and upper scapulars. Contrasting greyish lower scapulars with dark anchor-shaped subterminal markings. Both mantle and scapular 'V's usually present but faint. Breast washed warm orange-buff with sharply defined streaking at sides. **In flight** Similar pattern to Semipalmated Sandpiper.
CALL Generally a thin, high-pitched 'jeet' or 'cheep'.
HABITAT AND BEHAVIOUR Nests on dryish heath-covered tundra especially in the presence of dwarf willow. Can appear inland on migration, but winters on coastal mudflats and beaches. Favours feeding at the tideline, typically in deeper water than Semipalmated. Highly gregarious forming large flocks. Often tame.
MOVEMENTS Migratory, with E Siberian birds joining Alaskan ones and moving SE from July to November. Abundant on Pacific coast with smaller numbers on Atlantic coast south of Massachusetts. Winters in S USA, W Indies, central and northern S America. Return passage through USA from early April. Vagrant Russia, Japan, Australia, Britain and Europe.

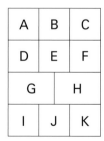

A	B	C
D	E	F
G		H
I	J	K

A Semipalmated Sandpiper adult breeding
B Semipalmated Sandpiper adult breeding
C Semipalmated Sandpiper adult non-breeding
D Semipalmated Sandpiper juvenile
E Semipalmated Sandpiper juvenile
F Semipalmated Sandpiper
G Western Sandpiper adult breeding
H Western Sandpiper adult breeding
I Western Sandpiper adult nonbreeding
J Western Sandpiper adult non-breeding
K Western Sandpiper juvenile

Scolopacidae

Long-toed Stint
Calidris subminuta **L 13.50 cm**
The smallest wader of the E Palearctic, breeding in the taiga zone of western C Siberia east to the Kamchatcka peninsula. PLUMAGE **Adult breeding** Longer legged and longer necked than Least Sandpiper. Rich chestnut crown streaked dark brown with clear, whitish supercilium not joining at base of forehead. Brownish ear coverts with dark area of generally pale lores confined to small spot just anterior to eye. Mantle and scapulars black centred, broadly fringed bright rufous-orange and white and tipped grey, whitish fringes often forming mantle 'V's. Tertials black broadly fringed bright rufous. Underparts white with greyish-buff wash to breast, streaked darker at sides. Bill blackish with dull yellowish-brown base to lower mandible, faintly drooped and quite finely tipped. Legs yellowish-green. Toes long, middle one longer than bill. **Adult non-breeding** Upperparts dull greyish-brown broadly fringed pale, with scapulars showing broad black feather centres. **Juvenile** Bright rufous cap streaked darker brown with 'split' supercilium often evident. Prominent white mantle 'V's. Scapulars and tertials black centred with broad rich rufous fringes, with greyer wing coverts fringed and tipped white, showing greater contrast than Least Sandpiper. **In flight** Weak wing bar with only outer primary showing white shaft. Toes project beyond tail.
CALL A fairly short, rippling 'chrrup'.
HABITAT AND BEHAVIOUR Nests in boggy and tundra-like openings where mosses, sedges and dwarf willow are present. Adopts 'alert' posture when alarmed and 'towers' when flushed. Toes probably adapted for feeding on floating vegetation. Winters mainly on inland wetlands with soft mud and clumps of vegetation.
MOVEMENTS Leaves breeding-grounds from mid-July, moving south both coastally and overland through Mongolia to China to winter from SE India, SE Asia and the Philippines, a few reaching Australia. Peak return passage through China April/May. Regular Aleutians. Vagrant Kenya, Ethiopia, Sweden and England.

Least Sandpiper
Calidris minutilla **L 11.50 cm**
The world's smallest wader, very similar to the Siberian Long-toed Stint, breeding from NW Alaska east across N Canada to Newfoundland.
PLUMAGE **Adult breeding** General outline typically hunched. Crown chestnut and brown streaked white with indistinct whitish supercilium meeting at base of

forehead. Dark lores with brownish ear covert patch separated from eye by pale diffuse area. Mantle and scapulars black centred fringed chestnut, grey and white, whitish fringes forming mantle 'V's. Tertials black narrowly fringed rufous. Underparts white with breast washed buff heavily streaked dark brown, often forming complete breast band. Bill blackish occasionally tinged brown at base, slightly drooped and very finely tipped. Legs yellow with greenish or brownish tinge. Middle toe, tarsus and bill about equal length. **Adult non-breeding** Upperparts uniform dull grey-brown narrowly fringed pale, with scapulars showing thin, dark feather centres. Underparts white with breast streaked and solidly washed grey. **Juvenile** Brighter than adult breeding. 'Split' supercilium usually lacking with mantle 'V's less obvious than Long-toed Stint. Wing coverts fringed rich buff showing little contrast to rufous fringed scapulars and tertials. Breast washed brighter buff. **In flight** Narrow white wing bar and white sides to dark rump and tail. White shaft to all primaries.
CALL Usual flight call a shrill 'kreeep' or 'prrrt'.
HABITAT AND BEHAVIOUR Nests on wet, well-vegetated and hummocky tundra, often around the edges of water near the treeline. Usually very tame. Winters on coastal mudflats and inland wetlands.
MOVEMENTS Autumn passage begins with adults moving south from mid-July to winter from the Gulf states south through C America and the W Indies to northern S America. Some birds migrate from SE Canada directly over the Atlantic to S America. Return spring passage through USA peaks late April/early May. Vagrant Japan, Alaska, Iceland, Britain and Europe.

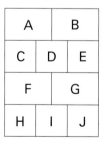

A	B
C	D	E
F	G
H	I	J

Scolopacidae

Temminck's Stint
Calidris temminckii L 14.00 cm
The plainest of the stints but with a distinctive tail pattern, breeding in the sub-Arctic zone of Eurasia from Scandinavia east to the Chokotski peninsula.
PLUMAGE **Adult breeding** Head brownish-grey streaked darker brown. Darkish lores with supercilium obscured by fine brown streaking. Mantle and scapulars mixture of new blackish centred rufous and grey-fringed summer feathers and new, grey winter-type feathers giving variegated appearance. Tail projects beyond folded wing tips. Pale chin and throat, with neck and breast mottled buff-brown streaked darker brown. Rest of underparts white. Bill brownish-black with paler brown tinge to lower mandible. Legs variable from yellow to greenish-grey. **Adult non-breeding** Upperparts generally even grey-brown. Breast washed dull grey-brown often forming lateral patches. **Juvenile** Similar to non-breeding adult but upperparts showing dark submarginal lines and warm buff fringes, giving 'scaly' effect. **In flight** Short, narrow wing bar with white sides to darker rump and centre of tail. Three outer tail feathers white, conspicuous, and unique amongst calidrids.
CALL Usual flight call a rapid, trilling 'tiririririr'.
HABITAT AND BEHAVIOUR Nests in sphagnum bogs close to pools of water. Also open, elevated positions with scrub willow and birch. Exhibits prolonged circular display flight. When flushed 'towers' rapidly with twisting flight, usually calling. Outside the breeding season favours all kinds of inland wetlands and freshwater sites, generally avoiding the coast.
MOVEMENTS Adults commence leaving breeding-grounds during July with juveniles one month later. Migration is largely overland, with small numbers wintering in Europe, but most move on to tropical Africa, Arabia, and east to SE China. Main return passage April/May. Breeds sparingly in N Scotland. Vagrant Azores, Seychelles, Philippines, Alaska and Canada.

White-rumped Sandpiper
Calidris fuscicollis L 16.50 cm
A small, long-winged calidrid, larger than stints, nesting on the Arctic tundra fron N Alaska east to Baffin Is.
PLUMAGE **Adult breeding** Dull chestnut cap and ear coverts streaked darker brown, with paler hindneck and dusky lores. Long, whitish supercilium curving over and behind eye. Mantle, scapulars and tertials blackish edged grey, chestnut and buff.

Coverts greyish-brown fringed white. Wing tips extend well beyond tail tip. Underparts white with thin black streaking on neck and breast, extending to 'V'-shaped markings on flanks. Bill shortish, slightly drooped at tip, black, with greenish-yellow base to lower mandible. **Adult non-breeding** Upperparts uniform brownish-grey with dark feather shafts and pale fringing. Underparts white with breast washed greyish-brown and lightly streaked. **Juvenile** Brighter chestnut cap, paler grey hindneck, with long white supercilium and dusky lores, cheeks and ear coverts. Mantle, upper scapulars and tertials mainly black fringed chestnut, with lower scapulars dark grey edged white. Edges of mantle and upper scapulars white forming characteristic 'V's. Coverts brownish-grey fringed white. Underparts white with breast washed grey lightly streaked darker and extending onto flanks. **In flight** Long winged, with narrow, short wing bar not extending onto primaries. Conspicuous white patch on uppertail contrasts with dark grey tail.
CALL A thin high-pitched 'jeet'. Aerial display song includes strange typewriter carriage and pig-like noises.
HABITAT AND BEHAVIOUR Nests on wet, hummocky, well-vegetated tundra, often adjacent lakes and pools, usually near the coast. On migration visits wetlands both inland and coastal, wintering predominantly on open mudflats.
MOVEMENTS Generally a late migrant, with main autumn passage during September, when birds largely pass down the Atlantic coast to winter in S America including the Falkland Is. Return passage late April/early May and mostly through the American interior. Frequent vagrant to W Europe; also S Africa, Australia and New Zealand.

Baird's Sandpiper
Calidris bairdii L 15.25 cm
A large, long-winged, short-legged 'stint', breeding in the high Arctic tundra from E Siberia to NW Greenland.
PLUMAGE **Adult breeding** Head generally buffish-brown streaked dark brown, with long downcurved buff supercilium extending behind eye. Mantle and scapulars black centred boldly fringed buff and white. Coverts and tertials greyer-brown fringed paler. Upperparts become very dark in worn plumage. Wing tips extend well beyond tail tip. Underparts white with foreneck and breast washed buff finely streaked grey, forming distinct breast band. Bill short, slightly drooped and finely tipped, black, sometimes tinged dull green. Legs short, greyish-black. **Adult non-breeding** Upperparts generally duller

grey-brown fringed pale. **Juvenile** Upperparts brown with dark brown submarginal line and buffish-white fringes, producing neat 'scaly' appearance. Underparts clean white, with neck and breast suffused buff and lightly streaked brown, occasionally forming lateral breast patches. **In flight** Long winged, with narrow inconspicuous wing bar to dark brown flight feathers. Whitish sides to dark centred rump and uppertail, with grey sides to tail.
CALL Usual note a trilling 'prreet' or 'kreep'.
HABITAT AND BEHAVIOUR Nests on dry elevated tundra, rocky slopes and even mountainsides, often overlooking the coastline or freshwater pools. Aerial display song includes frog-like trilling. On migration and in winter tends to avoid the coast, preferring margins of inland wetlands and short grassland. Relatively tame.
MOVEMENTS Migratory, with adults leaving the breeding-grounds late July, using the prairies of S Canada and N USA as important staging posts before overflying the E Pacific non-stop to the S American Andes to winter in Argentina. Spring passage mainly late April/early May, again bypassing central America and moving up the interior of the USA and Canada. Vagrancy widely recorded, e.g., Europe, Japan, S Africa, Australia and New Zealand.

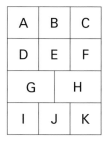

A	B	C
D	E	F
G		H
I	J	K

A Temminck's Stint adult breeding
B Temminck's Stint adult non-breeding
C Temminck's Stint juvenile
D Temminck's Stint juvenile
E White-rumped Sandpiper adult breeding
F White-rumped Sandpiper adult non-breeding
G White-rumped Sandpiper adult moult
H White-rumped Sandpiper juvenile
I White-rumped Sandpiper juvenile
J Baird's Sandpiper adult breeding
K Baird's Sandpiper juvenile

Scolopacidae

Pectoral Sandpiper
Calidris melanotos **L 20.95 cm**
A largish calidrid with distinctive underparts and yellowish legs, breeding along the tundra coasts of Siberia, Alaska, and Canada.
PLUMAGE Adult breeding female Dull chestnut cap streaked darker, and indistinct whitish supercilium with brownish lores and ear coverts. Mantle, scapulars and tertials blackish centred, heavily fringed pale brown and buff, often with poorly defined mantle 'V's. Wing coverts greyer-brown fringed buff. Neck and breast buff-brown strongly streaked darker brown forming distinctly demarcated pectoral band, the main differentiating feature from Sharp-tailed Sandpiper. Rest of underparts white with little flank streaking. Bill shortish, slightly decurved, and brownish-black with dull greenish-yellow base. Legs yellowish-green or yellowish-brown. **Adult breeding male** Larger than female with blackish-brown breast mottled white. **Adult non-breeding** Upperparts greyish with darker feather centres. Pectoral band greyish lightly streaked darker. **Juvenile** Richer cap, whiter supercilium, and upperparts blackish brightly fringed chestnut, buff and white, forming distinct mantle and scapular 'V's. Greyish-buff pectoral band streaked brown. **In flight** Generally dark above with indistinct wing bar and dark central rump and tail, with white sides to rump and uppertail coverts.
CALL Flight note a harsh 'krreet'.
HABITAT AND BEHAVIOUR Nests on well-drained grassy or sedgy tundra vegetation. Males extend chest into 'balloon' and utter remarkable hooting display call. Outside the breeding season frequents wet grassy habitats and freshwater margins, but also coastal. Relatively tame.
MOVEMENTS Adults commence autumn migration late June, with Siberian population mostly moving east to join with N American birds which predominantly move overland to winter in S America. Smaller numbers winter Australia and New Zealand. Autumn juveniles often caught in transatlantic depressions and hence commonest Nearctic wader to Europe. Spring passage from mid-March mainly through American interior. Vagrancy widely recorded, e.g., Hawaii, E and S Africa, Azores, and Europe east to Poland.

Sharp-tailed Sandpiper
Calidris acuminata **L 19.05 cm**
More angular and pot-bellied, this calidrid has a breeding distribution limited to the Siberian tundra, totally overlapped by its close congener, the Pectoral Sandpiper.
PLUMAGE Adult breeding Chestnut cap finely streaked brown, with dull supercilium broader behind eye. Prominent whitish eye-ring. Brownish lores and ear coverts streaked slightly darker. Mantle, scapulars and tertials blackish centred heavily fringed chestnut, buff and white. Wing coverts greyish-brown fringed brown. Rest of face, neck and upper breast buff, heavily streaked brown, with streaking becoming bold chevrons on whitish lower breast, belly and flanks. Bill shorter than Pectoral Sandpiper, blackish-brown, with dull yellowish-grey base to lower mandible. Legs also shorter, dull to greenish-grey.
Adult non-breeding Duller cap, with plainer grey upperparts and dark feather centres. Underparts white, with breast suffused grey lightly streaked brown.
Juvenile Bright chestnut cap and rufous lores and ear coverts contrast with prominent supercilium. Upperparts brightly fringed chestnut and white. Underparts white with bright orange-buff wash across foreneck and breast, with fine brown streaking across upper neck extending onto sides of breast. **In flight** Slightly stronger wing bar than Pectoral Sandpiper with black streaking to sides of uppertail. Diagnostic pointed central tail feathers invisible in the field.
CALL Flight call 'pleep', and a twittering 'pleep, trrt, trrt', recalling Barn Swallow.
HABITAT AND BEHAVIOUR Nesting area is wet, shrubby tundra interspersed with moss and sedge bogs. Male performs unique calidrid trilling display flight. Winters on coastal mudflats, lagoons and inland swamps. Gregarious, forming sizeable flocks. Tame and approachable.
MOVEMENTS Strongly migratory, with autumn passage commencing from July, mainly on a broad front east of Lake Baikal to coastal China, and south to winter in large numbers in Australia, but also New Guinea and New Zealand. Some move east to Alaska and migrate on with Pectorals. Return passage from mid-April along similar route. Vagrant widely to western Europe, India, SE Asia and Pacific coast USA.

A	B	C
D		E
F	G	H
I		J

A Pectoral Sandpiper breeding male
B Pectoral Sandpiper breeding female
C Pectoral Sandpiper
D Pectoral Sandpiper juvenile
E Sharp-tailed Sandpiper adult breeding
F Sharp-tailed Sandpiper adult breeding
G Sharp-tailed Sandpiper adult breeding
H Sharp-tailed Sandpiper adult non-breeding
I Sharp-tailed Sandpiper juvenile
J Sharp-tailed Sandpiper adult non-breeding

Scolopacidae

Curlew Sandpiper
Calidris ferruginea L 20.30 cm
A largish calidrid with a long decurved bill and distinctive breeding plumage, nesting in N Siberia and rarely W Alaska.
PLUMAGE **Adult breeding male** Face, neck and underparts rich chestnut-red, except for whitish vent and undertail coverts, with indistinct brown bars on flanks. Some pale flecking around base of bill. Crown and mantle brown fringed dark chestnut, with scapulars dark brown fringed chestnut and white. Coverts and tertials plainer greyish-brown fringed white. Bill longish, evenly decurved and black. Legs black. **Adult breeding female** Underparts paler chestnut, with more white feathering and brown barring. **Adult non-breeding** Long white supercilium, greyish lores and ear coverts, and evenly decurved bill readily separate this species from Dunlin. Uniform grey upperparts evenly fringed pale. Underparts white with sides of breast suffused grey, lightly streaked greyish-brown. **Juvenile** Buffish supercilium. Upperparts greyish-brown with dark submarginal line and neat buff fringing giving 'scaly' effect. Underparts white with foreneck and breast warmly suffused buff with fine brown streaking. **In flight** White wing bar and white patch across lower rump and uppertail, with grey flight feathers and tail. Rump patch sometimes obscured with brown bars.
CALL A soft rippling 'churrup'.
HABITAT AND BEHAVIOUR Breeds along the lowland coastal tundra, nesting on elevated areas of rough grass adjacent bogs and pools. Winters on intertidal mudflats and wetlands, both inland and coastal. Feeds by 'stitching', frequently wading in deep water. Gregarious, often forming large flocks.
MOVEMENTS Migratory, autumn passage commencing early July, with major routes along the coast of NW Europe to W Africa, overland E Europe and the Mediterranean to E and S Africa, and via the Black and Caspian Seas to India, SE Asia and Australia. Spring passage during April/May, mainly through Middle East and E Europe. First-year birds remain in winter quarters all year. Vagrancy widely recorded, e.g., Spitzbergen, Cape Verde Is, USA, Canada and S America.

Broad-billed Sandpiper
Limicola falcinellus L 17.15 cm
A somewhat scarce, stint-like wader with separate breeding populations in Scandinavia and eastern Siberia.
PLUMAGE **Adult breeding** Smaller than Dunlin with distinctive head pattern. Dark brown crown with double 'split'

supercilium, joining in front of eye. Main supercilium broader, and extending from base of bill to eye, contrasting with dark brown loral and ear coverts. Mantle, scapulars and tertials blackish-brown fringed pale chestnut and white, with white edges to mantle and upper scapulars forming characteristic 'V's. Coverts greyish-brown fringed buff. Underparts white with entire neck and breast heavily streaked, extending slightly onto flanks, forming pectoral band. Bill blackish-brown sometimes with paler base, long, and decurved towards tip. The flattened bill base is not a useful field characteristic. **Adult non-breeding** Main supercilium evident but upper one often obscure. Head and upperparts grey with dark feather shafts and and fringed white. Contrasting blackish lesser coverts forming dark carpal bar. Underparts white with soft grey streaking across breast. **Juvenile** Similar to adult breeding but upperparts fringed paler. Underparts lightly streaked brownish-grey. **In flight** Narrow wing bar and white sides to black-centred rump and uppertail.
CALL Usual flight call a buzzing or trilling 'churreet'.
RACES Two are recognized: nominate *falcinellus* (Scandinavia and Kola peninsula) and *sibirica* (Siberia east of Yenesei), with brighter fringes to upperparts and cinnamon tinge to breast.
HABITAT AND BEHAVIOUR Nests in small colonies in wet bogs and montane moorlands. Fairly tame. During migration favours inland wetlands, wintering chiefly on intertidal mudflats and estuaries.
MOVEMENTS Nominate race migrates largely south-east from early July across the E Mediterranean, Black and Caspian Seas to winter from the Persian Gulf to W India and E Africa. *Sibirica* routes unknown, mostly wintering in SE Asia and Australia. Return passage through Europe during May. Vagrancy widely recorded, e.g., most of Europe, N, W, and SE Africa, New Zealand and Aleutians.

A	B
C	D	E
F	G	H
I	J	K

A Curlew Sandpiper adult breeding
B Curlew Sandpiper adult breeding
C Curlew Sandpiper adult non-breeding
D Curlew Sandpiper adult breeding
E Curlew Sandpiper first-winter non-breeding
F Curlew Sandpiper juvenile
G Curlew Sandpiper adult non-breeding
H Broad-billed Sandpiper adult breeding
I Broad-billed Sandpiper first-winter non-breeding
J Broad-billed Sandpiper juvenile
K Broad-billed Sandpiper adult non-breeding

Scolopacidae

Purple Sandpiper
Calidris maritima L 20.95 cm
A dumpy calidrid of rocky foreshores, breeding on the north Atlantic and Arctic coasts, very similar and sometimes considered conspecific with the Pacific coast Rock Sandpiper.
PLUMAGE **Adult breeding** Larger than Dunlin, with chestnut crown streaked black, whitish supercilium with dark grey lores and dusky ear covert patch. Mantle and scapulars blackish centred fringed warm chestnut and buff. Coverts and tertials duller grey fringed white. Underparts whitish with heavy streaking and blotching down throat, neck and breast, extending onto flanks. Bill longish, slightly downcurved, blackish with yellow base, often tinged orange in spring. Legs yellow-green or yellow-brown, also tinged orange. **Adult non-breeding** Head, neck and upperparts dark slate-grey with faint purple gloss to mantle and scapulars. Coverts fringed whitish-grey. Small pale spot in front of eye. Whitish throat. Underparts slate-grey, mottled white on lower breast with grey-brown streaking on flanks. **Juvenile** Mantle and scapular feathers small, neatly fringed chestnut and buff. Coverts grey fringed whitish. Underparts whitish strongly streaked greyish across breast. **In flight** White wing bar contrasts with rest of upperwing, with white sides to rump and uppertail. Racial variants of Rock Sandpiper very similar, especially in non-breeding and juvenile plumage, differing by more definite spotting on underparts and bolder wing bar.
CALL Occasional flight call a soft 'whit' or 'wheet', recalling Barn Swallow.
HABITAT AND BEHAVIOUR Nests on lichen-covered tundra near the coast and rocky shores, but also mountain tundra and inland fells. Winters along rocky foreshores, often roosting on breakwaters, jetties and sea-defences. Exhibits 'winglift' display and 'rodent run' defence when disturbed at nest. Generally tame.
MOVEMENTS Partially migratory, with adults moving to the coast to moult from July, arriving at the wintering grounds later than most calidrids. Winters in S Greenland, Iceland and along Atlantic coasts of USA and Europe south to N Portugal. Non-breeders often summer just south of breeding-grounds. Return passage from April to early June. Vagrant inland N America, E Europe, Malta.

Rock Sandpiper
Calidris ptilocnemis L 21.60 cm
The Pacific counterpart of Purple Sandpiper, breeding on the coasts of E Siberia, W and S Alaska, Pribilof Is and Aleutians, Commander and Kuril Is.
PLUMAGE **Adult breeding** Virtually identical to *maritima*. Loral patch and ear coverts darker grey. Mantle and scapulars fringed darker chestnut. Streaking on lower breast often forming darkish grey patch. Bare parts as *maritima* with legs often appearing greenish black. *Ptilocnemis* readily separable by very pale, often whitish head, neck and breast and darker loral and ear covert patches. Mantle and scapulars fringed buffish-yellow. Underparts whiter with blackish patch to lower breast. **Adult non-breeding** Almost identical to *maritima*. Spotting to lower breast and flanks more defined. *Ptilocnemis* distinguishable by short, whitish supercilium, with crown, hindneck and upperparts ashy-grey. Coverts slightly darker grey. Underparts white with breast mottled soft grey. **Juvenile** Differing very slightly from *maritima* in warmer buff foreneck and upper breast. Lower breast and flanks showing slightly more defined spotting. *Ptilocnemis* separable by mantle and scapulars fringed pale buffish-chestnut. Foreneck and breast paler buff finely streaked brown. **In flight** Differs from *maritima* in noticeably broader wing bar across tips to greater coverts and whiter outer webs to inner primaries and secondaries. Both distinctly stronger in *ptilocnemis*.
CALL Very similar to *maritima*.
RACES Four are recognized: *ptilocnemis* (Pribilof Is) largest and readily separable; *couesi* (Aleutians, S Alaska) smallest; *quarta* (Commander and Kuril Is) and *tschuktschorum* (E Siberia, W Alaska) both intermediate.
HABITAT AND BEHAVIOUR Breeds on upland tundra up to 500 m above sea-level. Performs fluttering display flight while uttering trilling song. Forms sizeable flocks outside breeding season, wintering on rocky shores and stony beaches.
MOVEMENTS Partially migratory moving south late, similar to *maritima*, arriving N California from mid-November. Also regular south to Japan. Return passage from early April. Vagrant records south to Los Angeles probably *tschuktschorum*.

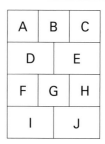

A	B	C
D		E
F	G	H
I		J

A Purple Sandpiper adult breeding
B Purple Sandpiper adult non-breeding
C Purple Sandpiper adult non-breeding
D Purple Sandpiper first-winter non-breeding
E Purple Sandpiper juvenile
F Rock Sandpiper *tschuktschorum* adult
G Rock Sandpiper *tschuktschorum* adult
H Rock Sandpiper adult
I Rock Sandpiper *quarta* adult
J Rock Sandpiper adult

Scolopacidae

Dunlin
Calidris alpina L 19.00 cm

The only wader with a black belly, showing marked racial variation in size, bill length and nuptial upperpart coloration, with an extensive circumpolar breeding range.

PLUMAGE **Adult breeding** Chestnut-brown crown finely streaked black. Whitish supercilium with dusky lores, cheeks and ear coverts finely streaked. Mantle and scapulars blackish centred fringed chestnut of varying shade dependent on race. Wing coverts and tertials greyer fringed whitish-buff. Foreneck and breast whitish streaked black. Diagnostic black belly patch with white vent and undertail coverts. Bill black, noticeably downcurved towards tip, length highly variable. Legs black. **Adult non-breeding** Clear white supercilium with plain greyish head, neck and upperparts, with wing coverts fringed white. Underparts white with sides of breast washed grey lightly streaked. **Juvenile** Mantle and scapulars black centred fringed chestnut and buff. Whitish mantle 'V's evident. Wing coverts and tertials greyer fringed warm buff. Foreneck and breast washed warm buff finely streaked black. Rest of underparts white with diagnostic black spotting on flanks and belly. **In flight** Clear white wing bar with white sides to dark centred rump and uppertail. Grey sides to dark tail.

CALL A short slurred 'treep'. Feeding flocks utter soft twittering call.

RACES Six are recognized: *arctica* (NE Greenland) and *schinzii* (SE Greenland, Iceland, Britain and S Scandinavia) together being the smallest, shortest billed with reddish-yellow fringes; *alpina* (N Scandinavia and NW Russia) and *sakhalina* (NE Russia and N Alaska) both intermediate in size with deeper, rusty-red fringes; *pacifica* (W Alaska) and *hudsonia* (C Canada) being largest and longest billed.

HABITAT AND BEHAVIOUR Nesting area varies from upland moorland to wet, boggy ground and low, grassy, sedge-covered tundra. Outside the breeding season frequents mudflats, estuaries and lagoons. Huge wintering flocks perform synchronized aerial manoeuvres.

MOVEMENTS Migratory, with adult birds from Eurasia moving south from early July to moult and then winter in W Europe, N and W Africa, and east to India, China and Japan. N American populations move to the coast significantly later to winter on Pacific coast and SE USA and Mexico. Return passage commences early March. Vagrancy widely recorded, e.g., S America, S Africa, Australia and New Zealand.

A	B	C
D	E	F
G	H	I
J	K	L

A Dunlin *schinzii* adult breeding
B Dunlin *alpina* adult breeding
C Dunlin *hudsonia* adult breeding
D Dunlin *pacifica* adult breeding
E Dunlin *sakhalina* adult breeding
F Dunlin *hudsonia* adult non-breeding
G Dunlin *schinzii* adult non-breeding
H Dunlin first-winter non-breeding
I Dunlin juvenile
J Dunlin juvenile
K Dunlin juvenile
L Dunlin

Scolopacidae

Sanderling
Calidris alba L 20.30 cm
Often seen dashing along the tideline, this largish calidrid nests in the high Arctic regions of N Canada, Greenland and N Siberia.
PLUMAGE **Adult breeding** Head, neck and breast variable dark chestnut finely streaked dark brown. Mantle, scapulars and tertials blackish fringed rufous, with grey tips gradually wearing to reveal increased chestnut colour. Lesser coverts blackish, with median and greater coverts grey fringed whitish-grey. Chin and rest of underparts white. Bill short, black and slightly drooped at tip. Legs black. **Adult non-breeding** Strikingly pale, with whitish supercilium and soft grey upperparts fringed white, with narrow, dark shaft streaks and contrasting blackish lesser coverts. Underparts white with breast washed grey. **Juvenile** Darker grey crown finely streaked white, with more distinct supercilium. Upperparts black, white and yellow-buff, giving distinct 'spangled' effect. Black carpal patch. Underparts white with breast lightly streaked at sides. **In flight** Bold white wing bar across blackish flight feathers, with black primary and lesser coverts contrasting with pale median coverts. In non-breeding plumage whitish sides to grey centred rump and uppertail, with pale grey sides to darker tail.
CALL Flight note a soft 'twick, twick', with feeding flocks uttering quiet, twittering calls.
HABITAT AND BEHAVIOUR Nests on barren, rocky tundra with scant vegetation, often inland from the coast, but usually not far from fresh water. Can occur at inland waters during migration, wintering primarily on sandy beaches. Runs at speed along the tideline catching prey. Often forms sizeable flocks. Relatively tame.
MOVEMENTS Migratory, moving largely offshore, with adults moving south from mid-July, juveniles a month later. Long flights are undertaken using favoured, regular staging posts. Greenland and some Siberian birds travel to Great Britain, Atlantic Europe, and Africa. Other Siberian birds winter on the coasts of India, Indo-China and Australia. Canadian birds winter on the coasts of central USA south to S America. Spring passage commences from late February, with non-breeders frequently remaining south all year.

Spoonbill Sandpiper
Eurynorhynchus pygmaeus
L 15.25 cm
One of the rarest and most enigmatic of all waders, with a unique spatulate bill, nesting in the north-eastern tip of Siberia.
PLUMAGE **Adult breeding** Slightly larger than very similar Red-necked Stint. Crown

brown streaked chestnut-buff, with creamy supercilium, paler behind eye. Rest of face, neck and upper breast chestnut-red faintly streaked brown. Upperparts blackish with rich chestnut-buff fringes, and white edges to mantle forming indistinct 'V's. Lower breast paler chestnut with dark brown streaking at sides, sometimes continuing as spots across breast. Rest of underparts white. Bill blackish, broad at the base, with characteristic spatulate tip. Legs black.
Non-breeding adult Crown, lores and ear coverts grey, with prominent white supercilium and forehead. Upperparts brownish-grey fringed white. Underparts brilliant white with sides of neck and breast lightly streaked grey. **Juvenile** Crown rich brown streaked darker brown. White supercilium and forehead contrast with dusky brown lores and ear coverts. Upperparts brownish-black fringed chestnut and warm buff, with white edges to mantle and upper scapulars forming characteristic 'V's. Underparts white with buff wash to sides of breast lightly streaked, often joining across centre of breast. **In flight** White wing bar and sides to black centred rump and tail.
CALL A high pitched 'prip' or 'whit'.
HABITAT AND BEHAVIOUR Nests on coastal tundra, preferring grassy banks adjacent freshwater pools and sandy banked lagoons. Song display flight includes a buzzing trill. Feeds with distinctive sideways sweeping of bill. Winters on mudflats and coastal lagoons, often associating with stints.
MOVEMENTS Migratory, wintering in tiny numbers around the coasts of SE India, east to Singapore, SE China and Hainan. Recently flock of 200 birds found wintering in Bangladesh. Uncommon but regular on spring passage Hong Kong and E China, chiefly April/May, and also autumn passage Korea and Japan, mainly September. Vagrant Alaska, Aleutians and Canada.

Stilt Sandpiper
Micropalama himantopus L 20.30 cm
A largish calidrid-type wader with long legs, drooping bill, and distinctive breeding plumage, nesting in Canada and Alaska north of the timberline.
PLUMAGE **Adult breeding** Crown brown streaked chestnut with long white supercilium strongly contrasting with chestnut lores, ear coverts and nape. Mantle and scapulars black, fringed chestnut and buff. Wing coverts and tertials greyish-brown fringed paler. Neck and upperbreast whitish heavily streaked brown, with rest of underparts strongly barred brown. Bill longish, black occasionally tinged greenish-brown at base, and drooping towards tip. Legs long, dull greenish-yellow, with toes partially

webbed. **Adult non-breeding** White supercilium contrasts with dark grey crown and eye-stripe. Upperparts uniform greyish-brown fringed pale. Underparts white with soft grey streaking on foreneck and breast, becoming more prominent on flanks. **Juvenile** Head pattern more diffuse. Mantle, scapulars and tertials dark brown fringed chestnut and whitish-buff. Coverts greyish-brown fringed buff. Underparts white with neck and upperbreast washed buff finely streaked brown. **In flight** Square white patch on lower rump and uppertail contrasts with uniform dark tail and upperwing lacking wing bar.
CALL Usual note a rattling 'kurrr', but also a whistled 'whu'.
HABITAT AND BEHAVIOUR Nests on open tundra with scattered vegetation, adjacent marshy or shallow pools. Often wades in deep water using dowitcher-like 'sewing machine' feeding action. Winters on inland and coastal pools, marshy fields and intertidal mudflats.
MOVEMENTS Migratory, with adults leaving breeding-grounds from mid-July, and juveniles a month later. The main migration route is through the Canadian prairies and interior USA, crossing the Gulf of Mexico and arriving on wintering grounds in central S America from September. Also moves east down Atlantic coast to northern S America. Main return spring passage is through the USA interior during April. A few birds winter in S USA. Vagrant Britain, W Europe, Japan and Australia.

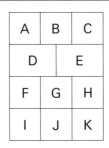

A	B	C
D		E
F	G	H
I	J	K

A Sanderling adult breeding
B Sanderling adult non-breeding
C Sanderling juvenile
D Sanderling
E Spoonbill Sandpiper adult breeding
F Spoonbill Sandpiper adult breeding
G Spoonbill Sandpiper juvenile
H Stilt Sandpiper adult breeding
I Stilt Sandpiper adult non-breeding
J Stilt Sandpiper first-winter non-breeding
K Stilt Sandpiper

Scolopacidae

Buff-breasted Sandpiper
Tryngites subruficollis **L 19.05 cm**
An unusually tame and distinctive wader of grasslands, nesting in the western Arctic from Alaska to W Canada, and also Wrangel Is, E Siberia.
PLUMAGE **Adult** Small head with streaked brown crown, steep forehead, and dark eye set in pale buff face help readily identify this species. Upperparts with blackish centres broadly fringed warm buff. Underparts rich buff, paler from belly to undertail coverts, with somewhat mottled breast, faintly streaked at sides. Bill short, straight and dark brown, with hint of dull yellow at base of lower mandible. Legs bright yellow-ochre. Males larger than females. **Juvenile** Upperparts very scaly, with dark brown submarginal lines and whitish fringes to mantle, scapulars and coverts. Underparts paler buff especially towards to rear. **In flight** Lack of wing bar gives virtually uniform dark upperparts. Gleaming white underwing with blackish trailing edge and tips to greater primary coverts.
CALL Usually silent, but occasional flight call a low 'prr-rr-eet'.
HABITAT AND BEHAVIOUR Nests on the grassy Arctic tundra, especially on well-drained, sandy soil, avoiding rocks. Males lack song flight, but perform at lekking display sites, not dissimilar from Ruff. On migration favours shortgrass plains, golf courses and airfields. Winters on open grassy plains. Extremely tame and confiding.
MOVEMENTS Adults commence leaving breeding-grounds in mid-July, with main passage in a narrow front passing through Canadian prairies and central USA, and across Gulf of Mexico to northern S America. Flight probably continuous since few records from C America and Greater Antilles. Onward passage to winter in S American grasslands. Also migrates via Hudson Bay and New England states to NE S America. Return passage begins late January returning across central N America, being exceptionally rare on the coast. Regular autumn transatlantic visitor to Britain, with vagrant records from most of Europe, Africa, Japan, New Guinea and Australia.

Ruff
Philomachus pugnax **L 29.20 cm (male); 22.20 cm (female)**
An odd-looking wader with small head and long neck, exhibiting both sexual dimorphism and male polymorphism, breeding from temperate to sub-Arctic zones in Britain, Europe and east through Russia and Siberia to Amadyrland.
PLUMAGE **Adult breeding male** Ear tufts and ruff highly variable, barred and unbarred, coloured white, buff, chestnut or glossy purplish-black. Face mostly bare except for small wattles. Upperparts admixed with similar colour variation. Underparts white often with extensive black or chestnut on lower breast and flanks. Bill shortish, slightly drooped, variable yellow to orange, sometimes tipped black. Legs long, yellow-orange. Facial wattles variable orangey-red, yellow or green. **Adult breeding female** Reeve distinctly smaller, lacking ear tufts, ruff and bare face. Upperparts dark greyish-brown fringed buff variably admixed with black. Underparts mottled and blotched blackish-brown. **Adult non-breeding** Similar to adult breeding female with upperparts greyish-brown with dark feather centres fringed white and buff. Underparts whitish mottled pale greyish-brown on breast. **Juvenile** Upperparts blackish neatly fringed creamy-buff producing scaly effect. Head, neck and underparts washed warm buff. Bill blackish-brown. Legs yellowish-brown to dull green. **In flight** Long wings dark brown with narrow wing bar formed by white tips to greater coverts. Rump dark brown. Long white uppertail coverts centred dark brown forming two large oval patches, almost reaching tip of mainly greyish tail.
CALL Invariably silent. Very occasionally low gruff 'kurr'.
HABITAT AND BEHAVIOUR Favours lowland grassy marshes, also river meadows, coastal saltmarsh and marginal vegetation surrounding freshwater lakes. Courtship occurs at leks when males display ear tufts and ruffs in ritualized aggression. Outside breeding season inhabits muddy lakeshores, coastal pools, estuaries and grassland, regularly forming vast flocks (1,000,000 in W Africa).
MOVEMENTS Migratory, vast majority of birds moving south-west to winter in Africa especially Sahel and N savannah zones, south to Cape Province, also smaller numbers in Britain, Mediterranean, Persian Gulf, India and Indo-China. Males commence leaving breeding-grounds late June, females and juveniles mid-July. Spring passage commences mid-February with more easterly bias. Regular farther east including S Australia. Vagrant Iceland, USA, northern S America, New Zealand.

A	B	C
D	E	F
G	H	I
J	K	L

A Buff-breasted Sandpiper adult
B Buff-breasted Sandpiper juvenile
C Buff-breasted Sandpiper juvenile
D Buff-breasted Sandpiper juvenile
E Ruff breeding male
F Ruff breeding male
G Ruff breeding male
H Ruff breeding female
I Ruff adult non-breeding
J Ruff juvenile
K Ruff breeding female
L Ruff breeding male

Thinocoridae

Rufous-bellied Seedsnipe
Attagis gayi L 29.35 cm
The largest of the seedsnipes, remaining in the high Andes throughout the year, locally common up to 5500 m from Ecuador south through Peru, Bolivia and NW Argentina to Chile and Patagonia.
PLUMAGE **Adult** On the ground very partridge-like. Upperparts variable tawny to blackish, fringed whitish, with several concentric dusky bars producing highly vermiculated pattern. Underparts variable pale cinnamon-pink to deep cinnamon-rufous, breast with pale brown to dark brown crescents giving barred effect, belly mottled whitish. Bill heavy, greyish-brown. Legs yellowish-brown, tibia thickly feathered. **Juvenile** Similar to adult with upperparts more finely vermiculated. **In flight** Wings pointed, broad-based lacking wing bar. Flight feathers brownish, secondaries, inner primaries and greater primary coverts fringed pale rufous, secondary coverts extensively fringed warm rufous. Uppertail coverts and tail pale olive-brown finely vermiculated. Underwing coverts and axillaries variable chestnut.
CALL In flight continuous 'glee-glee-glee'.
RACES Three are recognized: *gayi* (Chile, Patagonia) palest above and below; *simonsi* (Peru, Bolivia, NW Argentina) slighter darker; *latreillii* (Ecuador) darkest upperparts, less vermiculated, deep chestnut underparts with bold blackish crescents, underwing coverts and axillaries deep chestnut.
HABITAT AND BEHAVIOUR Confined to rocky slopes, scree, high Alpine terrain with sparse vegetation. When feeding often descends to nearest bog with cushion plant or similar vegetation. Usually occurs in pairs or small groups, forming larger flocks up to 80 during winter. Relatively tame and confiding. When flushed flies fast, low in zig-zag manner often for some distance.
MOVEMENTS Sedentary, remaining very close to snow line even in winter.

White-bellied Seedsnipe
Attagis malouinus L 27.95 cm
An uncommon seedsnipe, restricted to windswept terrain in S Chile and S Argentina south to Cape Horn.
PLUMAGE **Adult** Upperparts brownish-black scalloped and fringed cinnamon-rufous and buff producing cryptic, vermiculated pattern similar to *latreillii* race of Rufous-bellied Seedsnipe. Breast whitish-buff scalloped dark brown and black, sharply demarcated from rest of white underparts, with irregular dark brown chevrons to flanks and undertail coverts. Bill greyish,

paler towards base of lower mandible. Legs dull yellowish-grey to yellowish brown. **Juvenile** Very similar to adult, upperparts more neatly scalloped and fringed. Underpart ground coloration whiter. **In flight** Mantle and upperwing appear uniform dark greyish-brown. Uppertail coverts and tail dark brown vermiculated paler brown narrowly fringed white. Underwing coverts and axillaries strikingly pure white.
CALL In flight continuous 'too-ee, too-ee' or 'tu-whit, tu-whit'.
HABITAT AND BEHAVIOUR Nests above the tree line from 650 to 2000 m on bleak Alpine terrain, rocky slopes and exposed moorland, especially where *azorella* cushion plant present. Usually occurs in pairs, forming flocks outside breeding season when found also on stony areas of lower grassland including partly dried lakes and dry river beds. When flushed dashes off over next ridge in wild twisting flight.
MOVEMENTS Largely sedentary, usually descending to lower altitudes during winter.

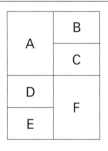

Thinocoridae

Grey-breasted Seedsnipe
Thinocorus orbignyianus **L 22.20 cm**
Differing from Least Seedsnipe in both size and flight pattern, breeding mainly at altitude from N Peru through the Andean Puna zone south to the tip of S America. PLUMAGE **Adult male** Plumbeous-grey face, neck and breast, latter narrowly, sometimes indistinctly, bordered black, with faintly streaked brownish lores and ear coverts. Chin and throat white bordered black. Crown buffish strongly streaked dark brown. Upperparts dark brown with tawny-brown submarginal bars, broadly fringed buff giving 'vermiculated' appearance. Rest of underparts white with dark brown chevron barring on flanks. Bill short, stout, yellowish-horn tipped dark brown. Prominent dark eye. Legs short, bright yellow. **Adult female** Plumbeous-grey coloration lacking. Throat patch indistinctly bordered dark brown. Head, neck and breast boldly streaked dark brown.
Juvenile Upperparts extremely 'vermiculated' with tawny-brown submarginal bar, dark brown subterminal band, fringed whitish. **Flight** Fast and zig-zagging. Greyish-brown mantle and upperwing with faint white tips to primary and greater coverts and indistinct thin white trailing edge to secondaries. Dark brownish rump narrowly edged white. Rounded tail dark brown with outer feathers edged and tipped white. Jet black axillaries, lesser and median underwing coverts contrast with white mid-wing panel and dark grey primaries and outer secondaries.
CALL When flushed usual flight note snipe-like 'cheu, cheu'.
RACES Two are recognized: *orbignyianus* (Tierra del Fuego to N Chile) and *ingae* (N Chile to Peru) both very similar in plumage.
HABITAT AND BEHAVIOUR Breeds up to 5000 m in Puna zone of Andes, favouring stony, rocky mountain slopes with dense bunchgrass, also cushion vegetation adjacent bogs. Farther south found at lower elevations down to sea-level on Tierra del Fuego. Usually in small family parties, male frequently keeping guard. Highly repetitive 'pu-coy' song delivered both in display flight and from ground song perch. When disturbed remains motionless using excellent camouflage.
MOVEMENTS Largely sedentary, descending to lower altitudes during winter.

Least Seedsnipe
Thinocorus rumicivorus **L 17.80 cm**
Unlike other seedsnipes, found at both sea-level and in the mountains, ranging from Ecuador, Peru, the Andean Puna zone and south to Chile. Patagonia and Tierra del Fuego.
PLUMAGE **Adult male** Forehead, face, foreneck, sides of neck and breast ashy-grey. Chin and throat white bordered by blackish line extending vertically down centre of breast to join blackish border to lower breast. Crown, nape and hindneck buffish strongly streaked dark brown. Upperparts dark brown with olive-brown submarginal lines broadly fringed buff. Rest of underparts white. Bill short, stubby, variable dull yellow to whitish-grey, dark brown towards tip. Eye prominent, dark. Legs very short, dull yellow. **Adult female** Lacks ashy-grey and black coloration. Head and breast pale greyish-brown streaked dark brown. Throat usually bordered dark brown, sometimes extending down centre of breast and border of lower breast. **Juvenile** Similar to adult female but dark brown border to throat and breast lines usually totally lacking or very indistinct. **In flight** Fast and erratic. Flight feathers greyish-brown with narrow inconspicuous wing bar across tips of primary and greater coverts. Thin white trailing edge to secondaries and inner primaries. Brownish rump narrowly bordered white. Wedge-shaped tail blackish-brown tipped white. Blackish axillaries, lesser and median underwing coverts with white mid-wing panel and greyish primaries and outer secondaries.
CALL Usual flight note snipe-like 'djuc'.
RACES Three are recognized: *rumicivorus* (Tierra del Fuego to N Chile) intermediate in size, darkest; *cuneicauda* (N Chile to N Ecuador) smallest and palest; *bolivianus* (Andean Puna zone) largest, suffused cinnamon-pink.
HABITAT AND BEHAVIOUR Breeds on arid plains, steppe and sandy areas with scattered, sparse vegetation. Often seen on dirt roads and gravelly lake shores. Also breeds over 2000 m in Andean altiplano. Monotonous 'pucui-pucui' song either delivered in aerial display flight on stiffly downcurved wings, or song perch. Common in flocks, usually very confiding. When approached runs with horizontal stance, often crouching close to the ground appearing very lark-like.
MOVEMENTS *Rumicivorus* partially migratory, with southern breeding birds moving north as far as coastal Uruguay. Vagrant Falkland Is.

A	B
C	D
E	G
F	

A Grey-breasted Seedsnipe breeeding male
B Grey-breasted Seedsnipe breeding male
C Grey-breasted Seedsnipe juvenile
D Grey-breasted Seedsnipe juvenile
E Least Seedsnipe adult
F Least Seedsnipe adult
G Least Seedsnipe juvenile

Pedionomidae and Chionididae

Plains Wanderer
Pedionomus torquatus L 15.00–17.00 cm
Formerly thought related to button-quails, recent studies confirm closer affinities of this rare 'wader' to seedsnipes, inhabiting native grasslands of SE Australia from south-east South Australia east to south central New South Wales and W Victoria. **PLUMAGE Adult female** Distinctly larger, showing brighter coloration. Forehead, crown and nape brown finely flecked black. Face whitish finely spotted black with chestnut-brown wash to cheeks and ear coverts. Upperparts dark brown finely vermiculated with black submarginal lines. Tertials cloak primary tips with very short tail projection. Chin white. Complete black collar boldly spotted white, bordered below by broad rufous-buff breast band. Rest of underparts whitish diffusely barred brown on lower breast, upper belly and flanks. Bill longish, pointed, straw-yellow. Large eye with prominent pale yellow iris. Legs straw-yellow. **Adult male** Distinctly smaller, duller, lacking black and white collar and rufous breast band. Chin, throat and entire underparts whitish with fine brownish crescents to foreneck, upper breast and flanks. **Juvenile** Similar to adult male. Darker crown, upperparts with bolder submarginal markings. Underparts diffusely spotted dark brown. **Flight** Weak, with characteristic fluttering action on rounded wings, legs trailing. Prominent outer wing bar to bases of primaries and tips of greater primary coverts. Whitish uppertail coverts to very short greyish-brown tail narrowly barred black. **CALL** Low-pitched, repeated 'oom'.
HABITAT AND BEHAVIOUR Favours grasslands, open plains, cereal stubble fields and sheep paddocks. Usually solitary. Partially nocturnal. Frequently stands erect with neck outstretched to survey surroundings. Also crouches motionless. Shy, reluctant to fly, running rodent-like through grass. Role of sexes reversed similar to hemipodes. Becoming increasingly rare as suitable habitat diminishes. DNA analysis confirms *Pedionomus* to be a charadriform related to Thicornidae.
MOVEMENTS Resident, undergoing local dispersal within range.

Snowy Sheathbill
Chionis alba L 40.00 cm
The only completely white wader of the Antarctic region, breeding on S Georgia, S Orkney, S Shetlands and the Antarctic peninsula.
PLUMAGE Adult Completely white, dumpy, somewhat pigeon-like. Bill stout, brownish-yellow shading to pinkish-yellow at base. Fleshy-pink wattle at base of bill and below eye. Large horny sheath covers nasal opening. Iris brown. Legs and feet sturdy, unwebbed, bluish-grey. **Juvenile** Horny sheath less developed. **Flight** Pigeon-like with legs frequently dangling during short flights overland, strong over open water.
CALL Undescribed.
HABITAT AND BEHAVIOUR Barren Antarctic and sub-Antarctic terrain, nesting in crevices amongst boulders. Scavenges voraciously among penguin and cormorant colonies and seal rookeries for poorly chicks, eggs and afterbirth. Regularly raids rubbish dumps and whaling stations. Prefers to avoid danger by running away fast rather than flying. Forms flocks of up to 300 during austral winter when scavenges along shoreline.
MOVEMENTS Migratory, moving north from early February to winter along shores of Tierra del Fuego, Patagonia and Falkland Is, juveniles dispersing more than adults. Breeding-grounds re-occupied from late October. Some non-breeding birds remain in winter quarters. Occasional Uruguay. Vagrant Britain (ship-assisted).

Black-faced Sheathbill
Chionis minor L 39.00 cm
The only white wader confined to the sub-Antarctic islands of the Indian Ocean.
PLUMAGE Adult Very similar to Snowy Sheathbill. Plumage wholly white. Bill completely black. Fleshy facial wattles variable pinkish-mauve. Horny sheath covers nasal opening. Iris brown. Legs and feet variable pinkish-white to black. **Flight** As Snowy Sheathbill.
RACES Four are recognized: *minor* (Kerguelen Is); *nasicornis* (Heard Is); *crozettensis* (Crozet Is); *marionensis* (Prince Edward and Marion Is). Differ largely in shape of sheath and colour of facial wattles, legs and feet.
CALL Undescribed.
HABITAT AND BEHAVIOUR Confined to the land masses of the sub-Antarctic islands, rarely venturing out to sea. Behaviour similar to Snowy Sheathbill.
MOVEMENTS Sedentary.

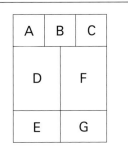

A	B	C
D		F
E		G

A Plains Wanderer adult male
B Plains Wanderer adult male
C Snowy Sheathbill adult
D Snowy Sheathbill adult
E Snowy Sheathbill
F Black-faced Sheathbill adult
G Black-faced Sheathbill adult

Species in systematic order

Lesser Jacana *Microparra capensis*
African Jacana *Actophilornis africana*
Madagascar Jacana *A. albinucha*
Comb-crested Jacana *Irediparra gallinacea*
Pheasant-tailed Jacana *Hydrophasianus chirurgus*
Bronze-winged Jacana *Metopidius indicus*
Northern Jacana *Jacana spinosa*
Wattled Jacana *J. jacana*
Painted-snipe *Rostratula benghalensis*
South American Painted-snipe *Nycticryphes semicollaris*
Crab-plover *Dromas ardeola*
Eurasian Oystercatcher *Haematopus ostralegus*
American Oystercatcher *H. palliatus*
American Black Oystercatcher *H. bachmani*
African Black Oystercatcher *H. moquini*
Variable Oystercatcher *H. unicolor*
Chatham Island Oystercatcher *H. chathamensis*
Magellanic Oystercatcher *H. leucopodus*
Pied Oystercatcher *H. longirostris*
Blackish Oystercatcher *H. ater*
Sooty Oystercatcher *H. fuliginosus*
Ibisbill *Ibidorhyncha struthersii*
Black-winged Stilt *Himantopus himantopus*
Black Stilt *H. novaezelandiae*
Banded Stilt *Cladorhynchus leucocephalus*
Pied Avocet *Recurvirostra avosetta*
American Avocet *R. americana*
Red-necked Avocet *R. novaehollandiae*
Andean Avocet *R. andina*
Stone-curlew *Burhinus oedicnemus*
Senegal Thick-knee *B. senegalensis*
Water Dikkop *B. vermiculatus*
Spotted Dikkop *B. capensis*
Double-striped Thick-knee *B. bistriatus*
Peruvian Thick-knee *B. superciliaris*
Bush Thick-knee *B. magnirostris*
Great Thick-knee *Esacus recurvirostris*
Beach Thick-knee *E. magnirostris*
Egyptian Courser *Pluvianus aegyptius*
Two-banded Courser *Rhinoptilus africanus*
Heuglin's Courser *R. cinctus*
Violet-tipped Courser *R. chalcopterus*
Jerdon's Courser *R. bitorquatus*
Cream-coloured Courser *Cursorius cursor*
Burchell's Courser *C. rufus*
Indian Courser *C. coromandelicus*
Temminck's Courser *C. temminckii*
Australian Pratincole *Stiltia isabella*
Collared Pratincole *Glareola pratincola*
Oriental Pratincole *G. maldivarum*
Black-winged Pratincole *G. nordmanni*
Madagascar Pratincole *G. ocularis*
Rock Pratincole *G. nuchalis*
Grey Pratincole *G. cinerea*
Little Pratincole *G. lactea*
Northern Lapwing *Vanellus vanellus*
Long-toed Lapwing *V. crassirostris*
Blacksmith Plover *V. armatus*
Spur-winged Lapwing *V. spinosus*
River Lapwing *V. duvaucelii*
Black-headed Lapwing *V. tectus*
Yellow-wattled Lapwing *V. malabaricus*
White-headed Lapwing *V. albiceps*
Senegal Plover *V. lugubris*
Black-winged Plover *V. melanopterus*
Crowned Lapwing *V. coronatus*
Senegal Wattled Plover *V. senegallus*
Spot-breasted Plover *V. melanocephalus*
Brown-chested Plover *V. superciliosus*
Sociable Lapwing *V. gregarius*
White-tailed Lapwing *V. leucurus*
Pied Plover *V. cayanus*
Southern Lapwing *V. chilensis*
Andean Lapwing *V. resplendens*
Grey-headed Lapwing *V. cinereus*
Red-wattled Lapwing *V. indicus*
Banded Lapwing *V. tricolor*
Masked Lapwing *V. miles*

European Golden Plover *Pluvialis apricaria*
Pacific Golden Plover *P. fulva*
American Golden Plover *P. dominica*
Grey Plover *P. squatarola*
New Zealand Dotterel *Charadrius obscurus*
Great Ringed Plover *C. hiaticula*
Semipalmated Plover *C. semipalmatus*
Long-billed Plover *C. placidus*
Little Ringed Plover *C. dubius*
Wilson's Plover *C. wilsonia*
Killdeer Plover *C. vociferus*
Piping Plover *C. melodus*
Black-banded Sand Plover *C. thoracicus*
Kittlitz's Plover *C. pecuarius*
St Helena Plover *C. sanctaehelenae*
Three-banded Plover *C. tricollaris*
Forbes's Plover *C. forbesi*
Kentish Plover *C. alexandrinus*
White-fronted Sand Plover *C. marginatus*
Red-capped Plover *C. ruficapillus*
Malaysian Plover *C. peronii*
Chestnut-banded Sand Plover *C. pallidus*
Collared Plover *C. collaris*
Puna Plover *C. alticola*
Double-banded Plover *C. bicinctus*
Two-banded Plover *C. falklandicus*
Lesser Sand Plover *C. mongolus*
Greater Sand Plover *C. leschenaultii*
Caspian Plover *C. asiaticus*
Oriental Plover *C. veredus*
Rufous-chested Dotterel *C. modestus*
Mountain Plover *C. montanus*
Black-fronted Plover *C. melanops*
Red-kneed Dotterel *C. cinctus*
Hooded Plover *C. rubricollis*
Shore Plover *Thinornis novaeseelandiae*
Wrybill *Anarhynchus frontalis*
Diademed Plover *Phegornis mitchellii*
Inland Dotterel *Peltohyas australis*
Eurasian Dotterel *Eudromias morinellus*
Tawny-throated Dotterel *Oreopholus ruficollis*
Magellanic Plover *Pluvianellus socialis*
Black-tailed Godwit *Limosa limosa*
Hudsonian Godwit *L. haemastica*
Bar-tailed Godwit *L. lapponica*
Marbled Godwit *L. fedoa*
Little Curlew *Numenius minutus*
Eskimo Curlew *N. borealis*
Whimbrel *N. phaeopus*
Bristle-thighed Curlew *N. tahitiensis*
Slender-billed Curlew *N. tenuirostris*
Eurasian Curlew *N. arquata*
Far Eastern Curlew *N. madagascariensis*
Long-billed Curlew *N. americanus*
Upland Sandpiper *Bartramia longicauda*
Spotted Redshank *Tringa erythropus*
Common Redshank *T. totanus*
Marsh Sandpiper *T. stagnatilis*
Common Greenshank *T. nebularia*
Spotted Greenshank *T. guttifer*
Greater Yellowlegs *T. melanoleuca*
Lesser Yellowlegs *T. flavipes*
Green Sandpiper *T. ochropus*
Solitary Sandpiper *T. solitaria*
Wood Sandpiper *T. glareola*
Willet *Catoptrophorus semipalmatus*
Terek Sandpiper *Xenus cinereus*
Common Sandpiper *Actitis hypoleucos*
Spotted Sandpiper *A. macularia*
Grey-tailed Tattler *Heteroscelus brevipes*
Wandering Tattler *H. incanus*
Tuamotu Sandpiper *Prosobonia cancellata*
Ruddy Turnstone *Arenaria interpres*
Black Turnstone *A. melanocephala*
Wilson's Phalarope *Phalaropus tricolor*
Red-necked Phalarope *P. lobatus*
Grey Phalarope *P. fulicarius*
Eurasian Woodcock *Scolopax rusticola*
Amami Woodcock *S. mira*
Dusky Woodcock *S. saturata*

Celebes Woodcock *S. celebensis*
American Woodcock *S. minor*
New Zealand Snipe *Coenocorypha aucklandica*
Chatham Islands Snipe *C. pusilla*
Solitary Snipe *Gallinago solitaria*
Japanese Snipe *G. hardwickii*
Wood Snipe *G. nemoricola*
Pintail Snipe *G. stenura*
Swinhoe's Snipe *G. megala*
African Snipe *G. nigripennis*
Madagascar Snipe *G. macrodactyla*
Great Snipe *G. media*
Common Snipe *G. gallinago*
Magellan Snipe *G. paraguaiae*
Noble Snipe *G. nobilis*
Giant Snipe *G. undulata*
Cordilleran Snipe *G. stricklandii*
Puna Snipe *G. andina*
Imperial Snipe *G. imperialis*
Jack Snipe *Lymnocryptes minimus*
Short-billed Dowitcher *Limnodromus griseus*
Long-billed Dowitcher *L. scolopaceus*
Asiatic Dowitcher *L. semipalmatus*
Surfbird *Aphriza virgata*
Red Knot *Calidris canutus*
Great Knot *C.s tenuirostris*
Sanderling *C. alba*
Semipalmated Sandpiper *C. pusilla*
Western Sandpiper *C. mauri*
Red-necked Stint *C. ruficollis*
Little Stint *C. minuta*
Temminck's Stint *C. temminckii*
Long-toed Stint *C. subminuta*
Least Sandpiper *C. minutilla*
White-rumped Sandpiper *C. fuscicollis*
Baird's Sandpiper *C. bairdii*
Pectoral Sandpiper *C. melanotos*
Sharp-tailed Sandpiper *C. acuminata*
Purple Sandpiper *C. maritima*
Rock Sandpiper *C. ptilocnemis*
Dunlin *C. alpina*
Curlew Sandpiper *C. ferruginea*
Spoonbill Sandpiper *Eurynorhynchus pygmaeus*
Broad-billed Sandpiper *Limicola falcinellus*
Stilt Sandpiper *Micropalama himantopus*
Buff-breasted Sandpiper *Tryngites subruficollis*
Ruff *Philomachus pugnax*
Rufous-bellied Seedsnipe *Attagis gayi*
White-bellied Seedsnipe *A. malouinus*
Grey-breasted Seedsnipe *Thinocorus orbignyianus*
Least Seedsnipe *T. rumicivorus*
Plains Wanderer *Pedionomus torquatus*
Snowy Sheathbill *Chionis alba*
Black-faced Sheathbill *C. minor*

Photographic Acknowledgements

An asterisk after a number indicates that the picture also appears on the dust cover.

Ardea/Hans & Judy Beste 65a, 71k, 87d; **Ardea/Graham Chapman** 71j; **Ardea/E. McNamara** 91a; **Chris Ba lchin** 139b, 139d; **Peter Basterfield** 11e, 11f, 21i, 27g*, 51a, 67e, 83c, 97f, 133b, 133c, 163d; **Nigel Bean** 59e, 97j, 97k; **Arnoud B. van den Berg** 105e, 105f, 105g; **David Bishop** 45d; **L.H. Brown** 9a; **Graham Catley** 143j; **Richard Chandler** 17c, 23i, 27e, 35h, 45e, 51b, 53b, 55e, 73g, 73h, 74j, 75d, 75e, 75f, 75h, 77f, 79a, 79e, 81c, 81d, 81g, 81h, 81i, 83d, 97d, 99c, 99j, 101f, 107c, 107g, 109e, 109f, 111i, 111j, 111k, 113b, 113g, 115b, 115c, 115e, 115i, 115k, 117b, 117e, 117f, 117i, 119e, 119i, 119j, 121e, 123c, 123i, 125c, 125g, 131c, 143b, 143g, 143h, 147a, 149i, 149j, 149k, 151h, 159c, 159d, 161c, 161d, 161f, 163c, 163i; **Richard Chandler/David Tomlinson** 153f; **Brian Chudleigh** 17e, 17g, 19a, 19b, 19c, 19d, 19e, 19g, 21h, 23j, 23k, 23l, 25b, 25d, 25e, 25f, 25i, 25j, 25k, 33a, 41g, 43f, 43g, 65d, 67j, 71e, 71f, 71g, 71h, 87a, 87b, 87e, 89a, 89b, 89c, 89d, 89e, 89f, 91c, 91d, 91f, 91g, 91h, 91i, 93c, 93f, 93k, 93l, 97i, 99f, 101k, 103d, 107j, 109a, 109d, 119b, 121a, 121b, 121c, 121d, 145b, 145i, 147e, 147j, 155c, 155g, 155h, 155i, 155j, 157a, 157b, 157k; **Nick Cobb** 141g; **Simon Cook** 11a, 39f, 39g, 59b, 85e, 159h, 167e; **Bill Coster** 17d, 27c, 31d, 47e, 63a, 63b, 85a, 993, 99g, 101d, 165l; **David Cottridge** 11j, 11k, 15h, 17a, 23a, 23b, 27b, 31a, 35a*, 35e, 35f*; 37c, 37d, 41a, 41d, 43a, 45h, 47a, 47d, 47j*, 49a, 49b, 49d, 49e, 53f, 55b, 55c, 55d, 59d, 67a, 67d, 69c, 69d, 71a*, 71b, 71c, 73c, 73d, 73i, 79c, 81a, 81b, 81e, 93g, 97a, 97b, 97c, 107a, 107b, 107d, 107f, 109h, 109j*, 111h, 113a, 113d, 113e, 113f, 117a, 117c, 117g, 117h, 117j, 117l, 119d, 119f, 123e, 125a, 125f, 125j, 125l, 131b, 139f, 139g, 147b, 149d, 149e, 151g, 153b, 153g, 153k, 157e, 159e, 161a, 161h, 161i, 161j, 161k, 161l, 163b, 163j, 165f*, 165g, 165i; **R.S. Daniell** 33f; **Jeff Delve** 151d; **Dept of Cons, New Zealand** 17f, 19f, 25a, 91b, 91e, 129d, 129e, 129f; **Paul Doherty** 15d, 15f, 21c, 35d, 43c, 55a, 69h, 113h, 117k, 121h, 125h, 147e, 157g, 165k; **Göran Ekström** 13c, 37a, 43e, 45i, 47k, 67h; **Tom Ennis** 115f, 123k, 145c; **Hanne & Jens Eriksen** 15a, 15b, 17b, 23d, 33b, 33c, 47l, 51d, 57e, 59c, 73k, 79g*, 93b, 93e, 103b, 103c, 111e, 113c, 119a, 119c, 139e, 125i, 145e*, 147f, 147g, 149g, 153a, 155b, 157c, 157i, 159g, 161e, 163a; **FLPA/G. Elison** 159j; **Dick Forsman** 29d, 73b, 99k, 123d; **Alan Greensmith** 9g, 11i, 11l, 63d, 77a, 77c, 95a, 95b, 95d, 101l, 125d; **Frank Hawkins** 81k, 81l; **Michael Hollins** 29h, 43h, 49g, 51c, 61a, 61c; **John Holmes** 113i; **Images of Japan** 127d, 127e; **Jo & Chris Knights** 29c; **Arie de Knijff** 27a, 47b, 67c, 69b, 69f, 69g, 69j, 73a, 99d, 99h, 101a, 101b*, 123a, 125e, 143a, 149a, 151e, 153e, 159a, 161b, 165e; **Peter de Knijff** 157j; **Marku H. Koivisto** 15i, 41b, 47g, 47i, 71d, 141d, 149f, 153d, 157f, 163k; **Gordon Langsbury** 9e, 21f, 23e, 23f*, 35g, 67b, 83g, 95h, 95j, 109g,

115a, 131a*, 135d; **Henry Lehto** 67l, 73l, 99j, 157h, 165b, 165h, 165j; **Ian Lewis** 37f, 53a, 61b; **Tim Loseby** 15j, 49f, 147i, 151a, 151b; **Mike McDonnell** 165a; **Arnold Meijer** 105b; **Arthur Morris** 145d; **Pete Morris** 45b, 71i, 137a, 137d, 137e, 137f, 171a, 171b; **Ian Nason** 45f, 57c, 79h, 79i; **Nature Photographers/Richard Chandler** 37b; **Nature Photographers/Peter Craig-Cooper** 29g*, 51e, 53d; **Nature Photographers/R.S. Daniell** 15c, 15e, 21d, 29i, 65c, 79f, 83a; **Nature Photographers/Michael Gore** 49c; **Nature Photographers/B. Hearns** 123b*; **Nature Photographers/E.A. Janes** 131e; **Nature Photographers/D. Osborn** 19h; **Nature Photographers/P.J. Newman** 159b; **Nature Photographers/J. Reynolds** 13b, 39c, 57d; **Nature Photographers/Paul Sterry** 9c, 17k, 21b, 31b, 45c, 53c, 101e, 123f, 123g, 123h, 159f; **Nature Photographers/Roger Tidman** 39e, 61e, 63c, 135c; **Urban Olsson** 41f, 79b, 81j, 97g, 121g, 123l, 133d, 133f, 137b, 137c, 141f, 145h, 147h, 163g; **D. Osborn** 135b; **Planet Earth/Nigel Tucker** 15g; **Peter Roberts** 13e, 69e, 167d, 167f, 169d; **Maurice Rumboll** 13g, 13h, 83h; **Paul Sagar** 129a, 129b, 129c; **Michel Salaberry** 95c, 139c; **Roland Seitre** 9b, 11d, 13d, 13f, 17h, 23g, 23h, 25c, 25g, 25h, 25l, 27i, 27j, 29a, 31c, 33e, 35c, 45g, 59a, 65b, 85b, 85c, 85f, 95f, 105a, 105c, 105d, 119h*, 121i, 121j, 121k, 121l, 131d, 133a, 135e, 135f, 143i, 167a, 167b, 169a, 169b, 169e, 169f, 169g, 171c, 171d, 171e, 171f, 171g; **Hadoram Shirihai** 41c, 43d, 47h, 77e; **Richard Smith** 97l, 109i; **Swan/John Buckingham** 23c, 57a, 115j, 143c; **Swan/T.G. Coleman** 41e; **Swan/Mike Weston** 111a, 111b, 111c; **Alan Tate** 13i, 19j, 313, 31f, 35b, 63e, 67g, 85d, 95e, 95i, 101j, 113l, 135a, 141e, 145f, 145g, 1553, 159i, 169c; **Don Taylor** 31g, 95g, 167c; **Nick Thorpe** 77g, 77h, 77i; **Roger Tidman** 9d, 29b, 39d, 47c, 61d, 67f, 83b, 83e, 111f, 127a, 127b, 127c, 147c; **David Tipling** 13a, 75b, 125b; **Ray Tipper** 11c, 97e; **Vireo/C. Speegle** 75a; **Vireo/Rod Curtis** 127f; **Vireo/Schillinger and Long** 139a; **Cyril Webster** 9h; **Margaret Welby** 9f, 45a, 77b; **Staffan Widstrand** 163e, 163f; **Mike Wilkes** 27f, 29e, 39a, 51f, 53e, 57b, 75c, 115d*, 157d; **Alan Williams** 2, 29f, 43b, 69a*, 69i, 79d, 99a, 99b, 107e, 125k, 149b, 53j, 155a, 161g, 163h; **Rob Wilson** 41h; **Windrush/Kevin Carlson** 77d; **Windrush/Paul Doherty** 107h, 117d, 119g; **Windrush/Göran Ekström** 33d, 109b, 109c, 111d, 111g, 115g, 119k, 133e, 141a, 141b, 141c, 143e, 151j, 153i; **Windrush/Brenda Holcombe** 39b; **Windrush/J. Lawton-Roberts** 153c; **Windrush/ D. Mason** 37e; **Windrush/Arthur Morris** 17i, 17j, 21a, 27d, 27h, 67k, 73f, 75g, 81f, 101c, 101h, 107i, 115l, 121f, 123j, 143d, 143f, 145a, 149c, 149h, 151f, 151i, 153h, 155d, 165c, 165d; **Windrush/Rene Pop** 19i, 21e, 67i; **Windrush/David Tipling** 11b, 11g, 11h, 41i, 73e, 87c, 103a, 115h; **Windrush/Ray Tipper** 93a, 93d, 113k, 151c, 155f; **Windrush/David Tomlinson** 9i*, 21g, 47f, 83f, 101g

Bibliography and References

Ali and Ripley, *Handbook of the Birds of India and Pakistan* vols 2 and 3, Oxford University Press, New Delhi, 1981

Alstrom and Olsson, 'The Identification of juvenile Red-necked and Long-toed Stints', *British Birds* 82 (1989), 360–372

Bacceti and Ven Ter Have, *Dutch Birding* 17 (1995) 40

Bent, *Life Histories of North American Shorebirds* part 2, Dover Publications Inc, New York, 1962

Bishop and Coates, *A Guide to the Birds of Wallacea* Dove Publications (in prep)

Bodsworth, *Last of the Curlews* Longman, London, 1966

Brazil, 'Birding Southern Japan', *Birding* XXV, 230–236

Brazil and Ikenaga, 'Amami Woodcock *Scolopax mira*: its identity and identification', *Forktail* 3 1987, 3–16

Campbell, *The Dictionary of Birds in Colour*, Michael Joseph, London, 1974

Carey, 'The Status and Field Identification of Snipe in Hong Kong', *Hong Kong Bird Report 1992* 139–152

Chandler, *North Atlantic Shorebirds*, Facts On File, New York, 1989

Colston and Burton, *A Field Guide to the Waders of Britain and Europe with North Africa and the Middle East*, Hodder and Stoughton, London, 1988

Cramp and Simmons, *Handbook of the Birds of Europe, Middle East and North Africa* vol. III, Oxford University Press, Oxford, 1983

Nethersole Thomson, D and M, *Waders. Their breeding, haunts and watchers* T & AD Poyser, Staffordshire, 1986

Delin and Svensson *Photographic Guide to the Birds of Britain and Europe*, Hamlyn, London, 1990

Dowding, Cumming, Jenkins and Hay 'Who will save the dotterels?' *Forest and Bird*, November 1992, 10–16

Dunn, 'The Identification of Semipalmated and Common Ringed Plovers in Alternate Plumage', *Birding* XXV, 238–243

Soothill, E and R, *Wading Birds of the World*, Blandford Press, Somerset, 1982

Fjeldsa and Krabbe, *Birds of the High Andes*, Zoological Museum, University of Copenhagen and Apollo Books, Svenborg, Denmark, 1990

Gollop, Barry and Iversen, *Eskimo Curlew. A vanishing species?*, Saskatchewan Natural History Society, Saskatchewan, Canada, 1986

Grant 'Four Problem Stints' *British Birds* 79 (1986) 609–621

Handel, *Population of Bristle-thighed Curlews*, unpublished data

Harrison, *An atlas of the Birds of the Western Palaearctic*, Collins, London, 1982

Harrison, *Seabirds*, Croom Helm, Kent, 1983

Hayman, Marchant and Prater, *Shorebirds*, Croom Helm, Kent, 1986

Hosking, *Eric Hosking's Waders*, Pelham Books Ltd, London, 1983

Johnsgard, *The Plovers, Sandpipers and Snipes of the World*, University of Nebraska Press, 1981

Jonsson, *Birds of Europe with North Africa and the Middle East*, A&C Black, London, 1992

Jonsson and Grant, 'Identification of stints and peeps', *British Birds* 77 (1984) 293–315

Kessel, *Birds of the Seward Peninsula, Alaska*, University of Alaska Press, 1989

Klosowscy, *The Birds of Biebrza's marshes* KSAT, Warsaw, 1991

Lane and Davies, *Shorebirds in Australia* Nelson Publishers, 1987

Lewington, Alstrom and Colston, *A Field Guide to the Rare Birds of Britain and Europe*, Harper Collins, London, 1991

Marchant and Higgins, *Handbook of Australia, New Zealand and Antarctic Birds* vol. 2, New Zealand, 1994

McCaffery and Gill, 'Antipredator Strategies in Breeding Bristle-thighed Curlews', *American Birds* 46 no 3 (fall 1992) 378–383

McCulloch, 'Status, habitat and conservation of the St Helena Wirebird *Charadrius sanctaehelenae*, *Bird Conservation International* 1 (1991) 361–392

Mullarney, 'Identification of Semipalmated Plover: A New Feature', *Birding World* vol. 4 no 7 254–258

Paulson, *Shorebirds of the North West Pacific*, University of Washington Press, Seattle, 1993

Pierce, *Field Identification of Black Stilts and Hybrids*, Department of Conservation, Christchurch, New Zealand, 1990

Pizzey, *A Field Guide to the Birds of Australia*, Collins Publishing, Sydney, 1980

Prater, Marchant and Vuorinen, *Guide to the Identification and Ageing of Holarctic Waders*, Maund and Irving Ltd, Hertfordshire, 1977

Pringle, *The Shorebirds of Australia*, Angus and Robertson, North Ryde, 1977

Rawlings, 'Lupins, Willows and River Recovery', *Forest and Bird*, November 1993, 10–13.

Reed and Murray, *Black Stilt Recovery Plan*, Department of Conservation, Wellington, New Zealand, 1993

Richards, *Birds of the Tideline*, Dragons World, Limpsfield and London, 1988

Roland and Julia Seitre, 'Causes of Land-bird extinctions in French Polynesia' *Oryx*

26 (1992) 215–222

Sharrock, *Frontiers of Bird Identification*, MacMillan Journals Ltd, London, 1980

Simpson and Day, *The Birds of Australia*, Lloyd O'Neil Pty, Victoria, 1984

Slater, *A Field Guide to Australian Birds, vol 1 non-passerines*, Rigby, Australia, 1970

Stout, *The Shorebirds of North America*, Viking Press, New York, 1968

'The *British Birds* List of English Names of the Western Palearctic Birds', *British Birds* 86 (1993) 1–9

Trevelyan, 'Shore Plover back on mainland', *Forest and Bird*, November 1992, 6

Tuck, *The Snipes*, Environment Canada Wildlife Service, 1972, Canada.

U.S. Department of Agriculture, *Final Environmental Impact Statement for Mountain Plover Management Strategy*, 1994

Urban, Fry and Keith, *The Birds of Africa*, vol 11, Academic Press, London, 1986

Vaughan, *Plovers*, Terence Dalton Limited, Suffolk, 1980

Index